CHEESE

This book is dedicated to Rose Gray, whose unique talent and strength of purpose shone through a love of produce and respect for the land, coupled with a generosity in sharing her knowledge.

CHEESE

THE WORLD'S BEST ARTISAN CHEESES

*A journey through taste,
tradition and terroir*

Patricia Michelson
OF LA FROMAGERIE

DAN & KRIS —!
RICHARD 2019

PHOTOGRAPHY BY LISA LINDER

First published in 2010 by Jacqui Small,
74-77 White Lion Street, London N1 9PF

Text copyright © 2010 Patricia Michelson
Photography, design and layout copyright
© Jacqui Small 2010

The author's moral rights have been asserted.

Publisher Jacqui Small
Editorial Manager Kerenza Swift
Art Director Lawrence Morton
Production Peter Colley
Main photography Lisa Linder/Wil Edwards
Illustrator Kate Michelson

ISBN 978 1 906417 33 8

2015
10 9 8 7 6 5 4

Printed and bound in China

CONTENTS

FOREWORD

By Jamie Oliver

If you've bought this book, or are thinking about buying it, chances are you're a person that already understands the joy that good food can bring to your life. My dear friend Patricia certainly is and in another life we'd probably be married with a hundred cheese-loving children by now! Her passion for sourcing, buying, maturing, selling and promoting quality cheese is unrelenting and I honestly believe her customers (of which I am one) are some of the luckiest in the world. Over the past 50 years a lot of the artisan love, care and attention that has traditionally gone into cheesemaking has started to flitter away as trends move more and more towards mass production. But thanks to people like Patricia, traditionally made British cheeses, as well as wonderful imported foreign varieties, have managed to keep their place in the food market and even raise their profile. Hopefully this beautiful book will help that to continue.

The world of cheese is so damn exciting and — without sounding too pretentious — life is too short to eat plasticky processed cheese week after week! If you feel a bit unsure or scared by the huge variety, this book is for you. Along with beautiful pictures that will help you next time you're faced with a well-stocked cheese counter, there's also loads of excellent and relevant information. Patricia tells you which animal each cheese comes from, as well as how and in which area of the country it is produced. She also profiles producers who are at the top of their game so you can look out for their cheeses. More importantly, she gives you an idea of what each tastes like, and what sort of things you can make or serve with it. It's really a sort of cheese encyclopedia and, hand on heart, I couldn't think of any better person to guide you through this wonderful world than Patricia.

When I flick through these pages I want to get straight in my car, drive to La Fromagerie and pick up some of the varieties she has featured here. But if you're outside London, or even the UK, the wonderful thing is that you can still have access to many of the types discussed here, thanks to mail order and the internet. I can guarantee that the guys producing them really want you to try their gear and you won't be sorry you did.

Like wine, each cheese has its own special personality. One person might walk the long way home to pick up a certain type of blue cheese, while his best friend might think it stinks and is repulsive. That's one of the things I love about cheese, and it is something Patricia really understands: it's so individual. I think when you read this book you'll end up with the ability to hunt down certain cheeses, whatever their character, and make them a part of your life.

What is cheese?

I came to love cheese not by a thoughtful evaluation over many years, but by way of a tumble down a mountain and a piece of cheese at the end of the day. It was more like what the French would term a *coup de foudre* or love at first sight. I often bless the fact that my skiing ability is less than athletic, and having lost track of my partner and consequently managing to traverse the mountain, I trudged through the village of Meribel in Savoie, exhausted and hungry. I was drawn to the golden glow of the cheese shop and bought a nugget of Beaufort to nibble on my way back to the chalet. That delicious piece of cheese changed my life and my livelihood. Today Beaufort Chalet d'Alpage is still the signature cheese at La Fromagerie.

The simple beginnings of just one cheese brought home after the skiing holiday slowly turned into a business, first by selling from my garden shed, then with a market stall in Camden Town, followed by a tiny shop in Highbury before moving to a larger premises opposite, and finally adding the beautiful shop and café in Marylebone. Of course, it has taken nearly 20 years to be where I am now, and along the way I have learnt and honed my trade, met many wonderful people and, above all, appreciated the fact that the land gives us so much. I am lucky to be able to do the work I love and to pass on my enthusiasm to others who share a similar desire to eat well and respect the land, our animals, and above all, our future. My shops are an extension of me. The Cheese Room is unique – a walk-in cooled and humidified room where cheeses can be seen and tasted at a temperature that enhances their ripening and keeping qualities. It has often been described as a library of cheese because you can walk around the room reading the tasting labels and then, instead of taking down a book and flicking through it, you can have a sliver taken from the cheese to taste, or chat with one of the enthusiastic assistants about what you would like to try next.

In this book the cheeses are arranged as on a journey of discovery, with maps to denote approximately where the cheeses are found. Use this book to inspire you on your own journey. There are many of my own photographs from my travels dotted throughout the book. When I set out on my foraging trips, I simply take a region and divide it into grids, then find the local towns and go from there. I look to see if there is a market, often calling the tourist information centre for addresses of the local artisans. It's amazing what you can glean, and before you know it you have several people to call and visit.

What is cheese? You would think the answer would be straightforward, wouldn't you – it's milk turned from its liquid state into curds, then formed into cheese. However, the steps a cheesemaker has to take in order to get to the end product are not so straightforward.

The milk must be heated in a careful progression, and an active yeasty-style starter must be added to the milk at just the right moment to bring the acidity levels up so that it will accept the rennet coagulant. The rennet (produced either from a calf stomach lining* or a vegetarian alternative and both high in acidity) helps to separate the watery whey from the solids. The solids are then cut into small pieces before being scooped into moulds or presses, salted or brine-bathed and then matured and ripened.

Along the way, cheeses can have moulds added to give white bloomy rinds, or sticky orange coats, blue veins, charcoal ash, or charcoal ash mixed with *Penicillium roqueforti*, or pinky-washed crusts. There is alchemy and science mixed with skill in cheesemaking, but none of this would be possible without that wonderful gift of nature, milk.

Patricia Michelson

---

* The reason why the baby calf 4th stomach lining is used for rennet is because the animal has to be suckling from its mother to obtain the right high acidity level in the 4th stomach. Calves are culled because if a dairy herd has a surfeit of male animals the farmer tries to sell them to beef herds, as well as keeping some for steers, but any others have to be slaughtered and the meat is sold and the 4th stomach is kept for rennet. The same goes for beef herds with their female animals. The historical connection probably lies in when milk was kept in animal stomach pouches for transporting from one place to another, and it was found that the liquid changed to a lumpy curd when the acidity within the lining mingled with the milk.

Moulds

Geotrichum candidum is a fungus that grows on surface-ripened cheeses during the early stages of ripening. On some cheeses such as St Marcellin, it is an evenly spread white and grey patchy mould. On soft cheeses such as Camembert and semi-hard cheeses such as St Nectaire, the fungus can prevent the *Penicillium candidum* moulds from overtaking and leading to bitterness. In washed-rind cheeses, it is used to de-acidify the surface of the cheese, creating a welcoming environment for the *B. linens* to grow.

Brevibacterium linens (*B. linens*) is a mixture of introductory bacteria cultivated on the surface of washed-rind cheeses, which create the orange or pinkish colour and the high aroma. *B. linens* requires a low-acid environment, moisture and oxygen to flourish.

Penicillium candidum (*P. candidum*) is a variant of the mould *P. camemberti* (a typical white bloomy mould that turns off-white to grey after several days). The *P. candidum* remains white and is the trademark of a bloomy rind cheese. This surface mould, given the right amount of salt and moisture, will develop a rind that breaks down from the outside in, creating an increasingly soft, buttery texture with time.

Penicillium roqueforti or *P. glaucum* is a mould that is added to the curds before the cheese is pressed and formed. This mould is a decomposing toxin that is activated by air. The air is introduced during the maturing process by piercing the cheese with needles to allow the spores within to grow and spread.

Styles of Cheese

Soft cheese has no discernible rind and high water content – Ricotta, Quark, Cottage Cheese, Curd cheese and Mascarpone are all good examples. Soft cheeses are very delicate and should be consumed soon after purchase.

Fresh cheese has no discernible rind, but may have a little more structure than a soft cheese. A high water content keeps it from drying out, and its shelf-life is limited. Good examples are the very light and frothy Primosale, fresh goat's cheese and non barrel-aged Feta.

Bloomy cheese has a white fluffy rind from *Penicillium candidum*. Cheeses such as Brie and Camembert have a little of the culture mixed into the curds, then more coated on top of the cheeses once they are in their moulds or forms, to help with the process of rind development. Brillat-Savarin is a triple-cream cheese from Normandy where the coat gently grows on the outside of the cheese and needs careful supervision to allow the moulds to adhere to the cheese and not become too furry. If the outside rind becomes too dry or too wet this triggers aromas and flavours that can be very unsavoury. Check the rind look 'perky' before buying these cheeses, and with some matured goat's cheeses the white rinds are flecked with golden moulds too.

Washed cheese is produced when a soft cheese has a *Lineum* smear, which is encouraged by washing the cheese in a saltwater solution, white wine or Marc de Bourgogne (a very fiery alcohol made from distilling vine pressings after winemaking). After about three weeks the reaction of the washing creates a surface colour change from white to orange. Some good examples of washed cheeses are Epoisses, Langres, Munster, Livarot and Taleggio.

Brevibacterium linens on a rind is the same bacterium found on human skin and associated with body odour.

Semi-hard (uncooked) cheese is made when the moisture is squeezed out before forming and includes such cheeses as Mimolette, Cheddar, Ossau, Cheshire and Pecorino. Cheeses such as Ossau ewe's milk from the Pyrénées are pierced with fine needles in the same way as Cheshire to encourage the whey to drain out.

Semi-hard & hard (cooked) cheeses are made when the milk is heated to a high temperature to encourage the draining process since the large size of the cheese requires this. When the curds are placed in their hoops or moulds a weight is pressed down to assist the process. These include the big cheeses such as Parmesan, Gruyère, Comté, Beaufort, Gouda and Fontina.

Pasta filata cheese is one that has spun or stretched curds such as Provolone, Mozzarella, Provola, Burrino and Scamorze. After draining, the fresh cheese rests for a while, then is placed in hot-water baths where pieces are pulled off, then stretched and kneaded until a soft, elastic, stringy texture is obtained.

Persille or blue cheese *Persille* means 'parsley' and in the old days cheeses were pierced so that the air-borne bacteria could penetrate the cheese and create the feathery blue moulds. In the case of Roquefort the outside of the cheeses were rubbed with a fine crumb of sourdough bread, which had become mouldy and dry and even today this process is used. However, the injection and piercing with *Penicillium roqueforti* in a more structured format is the way in which most blue cheeses are made.

Fat Matters

Determining the amount of fat in cheese is shown as a percentage of fat in the total 'dry matter' (defined as fats plus solids-that-aren't-fats). This percentage is constant throughout the life of the cheese after maturity, however the percentage of fat in the whole cheese increases as moisture evaporates with maturing and therefore detailing this would not give an accurate definition for the consumer.

A cheese that is 45 percent fat matter does not actually contain 45 percent. The fat is calculated on the whole cheese nutrients minus the water. This is specific to French cheeses, but in other countries the fat lipids are calculated on the total weight of the cheese, which will also include water. The following list of figures should be taken into account when assessing or calculating the nutritional value of cheese.

Cheese	% of actual fat
Fromage frais or any other fresh curd 0% fat	0
Fromage frais or any other fresh curd 20% fat	3
Fromage frais or any other fresh curd 30% fat	5
Fromage frais or any other fresh curd 40% fat	8
Fresh semi-salted cheese (ie Primosale fresh cheese)	13
Fermented cheeses such as Camembert	16–22
Fermented washed rind cheeses such as Livarot	20–23
Fermented pressed uncooked cheeses such as Cantal, Reblochon, Mimolette, Cheshire, Cheddar	20–26
Fermented pressed cooked cheeses such as Comté, Gruyère, Fontina, Parmesan	26–30
Fermented blue cheeses such as Roquefort	34–35
Cheese that is creamed like a fondue based on 45% fat	22
Goat's Cheese	15–25

Nutritional Value

Once a cheese is drained and pressed, then matured, the harder and more aged it becomes, and also the richer it becomes in nutrients. So if you want to calculate your nutrient intake from the following list, base it on about 30–40 g portions. If you are following a very strict low-cholesterol diet you may not be able to eat cheese, but for most of us it is important to obtain calcium from cheese. To have your quotient of calcium every day — even if you are on a diet — use the list opposite or stick to low-fat Fromage frais or goat's cheese.

Cheese	Protein %	Fats %	Calcium mg
White bloomy rind cheeses	15–20	16–22	180–200
Washed-rind soft cheeses	20–30	20–23	200–500
Pressed uncooked cheeses	25–30	20–26	650–800
Pressed cooked cheeses	30–35	26–30	900–1350
Blue cheeses	24	34–35	500–700
Creamed cheeses such as fondue	18	22	750
Goat	16–35	15–25	180–200

Gluten Intolerance

Hard and aged cheeses are gluten-free — the time taken to mature releases sugars and salts that are naturally part of milk, but retains proteins and caseins that are easy to digest. Cheddar, Parmesan and Pecorino are fine as are other cheeses in the same style.
Blue cheeses such as Roquefort are not gluten-free since bread that is allowed to go mouldy is used to help create the bacteria to give the blue veins.

Goat's and ewe's milk cheeses are easier to digest too, and can be eaten softer and creamier, but watch out for bloomy rinds since they may cause concern with their bacterial make-up.
Fresh cheeses such as Fromage Blanc and Fromage frais and Petit Suisses are fine as long as you read the label to make sure that no additives or preservatives such as gum have been used to thicken their consistency.

The British Isles & Ireland

What do Jervaulx monks and Wensleydale cheese have in common? In the 11th century the Norman Conquest had a major impact on life in Britain. It brought far-reaching changes, some would say order, wealth, landowning and agriculture, to an island that largely had been run in an unruly way. It was during this period that the religious order of Jervaulx monks came from Normandy and Flandres to Britain – in particular Yorkshire – with their desire to be self-sufficient as well as spread the word of their faith in a positive way. Their capabilities included sheep farming, cheesemaking and horse-breeding, and they are widely acknowledged as the original makers of Wensleydale cheese.

During the time of Henry VIII and the dissolution of the monastries, the Jervaulx abbey was destroyed, but the monk's legacy remains in influencing many of the traditional cheeses we know and love in Britain today.

This brief explanation encapsulates how this group of islands is partly defined by its history of farming and the skills and techniques that help to produce traditional foods, including cheese, many of which have been passed down through the generations and by communities despite centuries of war and conflict. This in turn reflects the history of cheesemaking throughout Europe and the New World, too.

There are literally hundreds of cheeses in the British Isles and Ireland, and there is now a thriving and exciting cheese movement that has not been seen since the start of the Industrial Revolution. Two World Wars almost finished the dairy industry in Britain, but like Philippe Olivier who revived cheesemaking in Normandy, which had been devastated by war, our own Randolph Hodgson of Neal's Yard Dairy has championed specialist cheesemakers and helped build their recognition and reputation all over the world.

I have very firm views about the cheeses of the British Isles. Nothing is more exciting than the crumbly, wet, grassy flavour of a traditionally made Wensleydale, the nutty intensity of Cheddar, the herby sharpness of Cheshire, and the mineral-rich, buttery texture of Stilton. These represent all that is fine and good about British cheese. I like to choose cheeses that represent their region, and I am fascinated by the way they evolve due to variations in soil, weather patterns and minerals. The amazing range of flavours experienced when tasting a Stilton (see page 28) or Stichelton (a new cheese

developed by Joe Schneider with Randolph Hodgson, see page 29) are magical. The flinty minerals are synonymous with Derbyshire; the creamy rich intensity of the cheese develops slowly and the crust, the crucial part of the maturing process that can make or break the taste, has a stone-like crumb made possible by the damp, cool ageing rooms. In Ireland, the microclimate and soft, sweet water in the south produce wonderfully rich, aromatic cheeses, both washed rind and hard. In the north of Ireland, one of my favourite goat's cheeses, Ryefield (see page 39), is light and airy with a salty freshness to be enjoyed first thing in the morning on toast.

Every region of the British Isles has something to offer, from Wales with Caerphilly (see page 30) to Scotland with its delicious Dunsyre Blue (see page 34). Ireland has so many different styles of cheese I am overwhelmed by the choice, but it is a relatively new cheese from the wild and dramatic coast of Kerry that has caught my heart. Called Dilliskus (see page 41), the cheese is made by Maja Binder and uses dillisk seaweed in the curd. It has all the makings of a fine territorial, utilizing traditional techniques such as the inclusion of dillisk seaweed to give the cheese its unique flavour. The farm is close to the sea and salty spray finds its way into the milk through the pastures, while the maturing caves are in old stone farm buildings with well-seasoned wooden shelving. All these factors contribute to the tastes and textures of this excellent cheese.

The British and Irish may be an island race, they may be small in comparison to other countries and continents, they may not have the extremes in temperature to produce different styles of cheese, but what they do have in bucketloads is a quality that is highly defined and, at last, recognized as being worthy of greatness.

The following selection features cheeses from all over the British Isles, that are representative of their regions. This may seem like a small selection, and I wish I could include more, but it is my way of starting the journey that gives a real view of life through cheese. Within every region of England there are plenty of weekend farmer's markets, and this is a great way of seeing and tasting at first hand the local produce. The markets are always the first place I visit on my travels, wherever I go, as it is an excellent way to meet the producers, chat and taste their wares. Sitting down in the market square, with a glass of locally made beer and a chunk of cheese is not a bad way to pass the time and soak up the atmosphere.

TOP Cows grazing on the Colston Bassett fields, Nottinghamshire BOTTOM Apple orchards in the Kent countryside

South West & Southern England

The south and south west of England enjoy good weather patterns throughout the year, enabling farm animals to graze outdoors. If asked what cheese is made in the south of England, most people would say Cheddar. The South West is the largest region in England: the area extends from Gloucestershire and Wiltshire to Cornwall and beyond to the Isles of Scilly. The majestic chalk cliffs of Dover over to the south east, indicate land that is well drained and gritty, and though this area is not as well known for its cheeses as the South West, there are plenty of individual stylish cheeses being produced by small-scale cheesemakers. As well as goat, cow and ewe's milk, there are also Buffalo milk cheeses being pioneered in Hampshire and other home counties. The landscape of the South West is romantic with rocky coastline, rugged moorland and verdant green rolling hills, whilst the South East is flatter, divided into arable and pastoral farming with the coastal marshes still maintaining grazing for sheep. The Sussex and Kent regions have vineyards with award-winning wine production, and Kentish hops to make beers that are perfect accompaniments for the regional cheeses.

Devon, Beenleigh and Harbourne Blue

TOTNES, DEVON

Robin Congdon's farm overlooks the Dart Valley in a very picturesque part of Devon. The three blue cheeses made on the farm are Devon Blue with cow's milk, Beenleigh Blue with ewe's milk and Harbourne Blue with goat's milk. All three cheeses weigh approximately 3 kg (6 ½ lb).

Devon Blue The unpasteurized Jersey milk is partly responsible for Devon Blue's fresh grassy, earthy, buttery flavour. It has a rich and creamy close texture, with tangy blue veins that gently bleed into the cheese.

Beenleigh Blue is made with unpasteurized ewe's milk and vegetarian rennet. The texture of the cheese is more chewy and dense than Roquefort, and the blue veins are well spread, with threads rather than the pockmarked craters often found in the former. The flavour has a flinty mineral sweetness, with a slightly aggressive briny hit. One would not imagine a British blue to taste like this, and it is much to Robin's credit that he has achieved such an individual style to his cheeses. Beenleigh is at its best between mid-summer and mid-winter.

Harbourne Blue is made with unpasteurized goat's milk and vegetarian rennet. The cheese's texture can be very crumbly, and the contrasting colours of pale almost alabaster curd and dark, inky blue veins give this cheese a delicate ethereal quality. However, its flavour dispels all of this. Strength and power are uppermost in the flavour ladder.

Many believe this to be Robin's best cheese, and it is at its optimum between early summer and late autumn. The sharp, tangy flavour that comes through with the early-summer cheese is stunning. Try serving Harbourne Blue alongside a chilled full-bodied white wine on a warm summer's evening — there could not be a more ideal way of enjoying this cheese.

At La Fromagerie, we also love serving quince 'cheese' paste with all of Robin's cheeses as they complement each other so well.

OPPOSITE, TOP CHEESE Devon Blue **MIDDLE CHEESE** Beenleigh Blue **BOTTOM CHEESE** Harbourne Blue

ABOVE LEFT The Kent countryside

ABOVE RIGHT The grazing pastures in Devon

Cornish Yarg 🐄 LISKEARD, CORNWALL

The original cheesemakers were Alan and Jenny Gray (the name Yarg is actually Gray back to front), and this was one of the first new speciality cheeses to come onto the market around 1980. The recipe is based on an ancient Caerphilly, which they brought with them from their home in Wales, with a nod to Cheddar. Instead of allowing a crust to form on the outside it is covered with nettles, found growing wild in the area. The cheese is made in open vats by hand, using pasteurized milk from local Holstein and Friesian cows and vegetable rennet. After pressing and brining (dipping the cheese in a salty water solution), it is wrapped in wild nettle leaves in a beautiful relief lacy pattern of blue and green, giving the finished cheese its unique appearance. The nettles impart a citrusy tang to the cheese, which mellows after maturing, and the aroma is gentle and subtle. A very popular cheese, especially with children who prefer a mild taste, Cornish Yarg also finds favour with pregnant ladies as it is very easy to digest.

Ticklemore 🐐 TOTNES, DEVON

This cheese was originally made by Robin Congdon, who has a true understanding of the variables in making handmade cheese in this part of the country. He has since passed the technique and recipe on to Debbie Mumford at Sharpham Creamery. This area of Devon is truly magnificent with the River Dart meandering through the farmland and the hills as a backdrop to the green fields rolling down to the water's edge. The semi-hard unpasteurized goat's milk cheese is made with a vegetarian rennet and is formed into an oval, which is actually achieved by placing the curds in kitchen colanders. The bloom on the crust grows during the maturing process and the flaky pate has tiny eyelet holes scattered through the cheese. This produces a young cheese with a slightly open texture, but during maturation the texture becomes closer and flakier. The taste is fresh, light and gentle with hints of fresh grassy woodland and only the faintest goaty aroma. These flavours make it perfect for cooking as well as part of a cheeseboard.

Alderwood 🐄 ASHMORE, DORSET

Cranborne Chase Cheese, the makers of Alderwood, is part of the Manor Farm estate in the hilltop village of Ashmore, north Dorset. The microclimate in this particular region is quite different to that of nearby areas with a warm breeze rippling over the land. The sweet and savoury minerals in the grass also influence the milk and finished cheese, making Alderwood very different to the

Cheddars from this part of England. It is based on a Bel Paese or St Paulin using unpasteurized cow's milk and a traditional rennet, resulting in a rather mild, sweetly nutty-tasting cheese. However, it has a brine-washed rind, which creates a warm apricot-coloured jacket and enhances the cheese's flavour.

The fine grazing pastures of this beautiful estate cross Cranborne Chase and Blackmore Vale, an area of outstanding natural beauty reserved as the hunting grounds for monarchs from the Norman Conquest until as recently as the 20th century. From the 18th century until 2007, the estate was owned by the same family but the new owner has since totally revamped the dairy, bringing it up to date. The flint, stone and brick buildings on the farm have been converted for cheesemaking and maturing, and the original recipe has been slightly re-worked but still retains all the relevant requirements for a handmade cheese using milk from their next door neighbour's herd of Holstein/Friesian cattle.

The cheese curds are placed in their moulds on day one, brined on day two and then the first washing occurs on day three. The cheese is then taken to the ripening room and kept at a low temperature with a high humidity to encourage the development of the rind. During the maturing period – about 12 weeks – natural moulds develop giving a mottled orange-brown appearance to the rind. The stone maturing buildings also impart their own mineral and flora from the air, which influences the flavour of the cheese.

Although Alderwood can be eaten young, I always like to give it a few extra weeks, with several washings in a local cider to further enhance the flavour.

Cardo 🐐 TIMSBURY, SOMERSET

This semi-hard, washed-rind goat's cheese uses cardoon thistles as a coagulant (rennet) to separate the curds from the whey. The washed, naturally bloomed rind is the result of a salt and water solution that is brushed on to the cheese, leaving a thin sticky 'film'. The aroma is not too strong but there is an earthy, mossy vegetal perfume that comes through, while the taste is fruity without being aggressive. There is also a lovely herbal mineral element, which comes from a combination of the milk and the brine washing. This is a brilliant relatively new cheese from cheesemaker Mary Holbrook whose very successful truncated pyramid Tymsboro has won many prizes at the British Cheese Awards and is made along the lines of the French goat's cheese Valençay. With Cardo she took inspiration from the Portuguese mountain cheeses that also use thistle as a coagulant but I think the cheese is also not dissimilar to the Corsican Casinca or a Tomme de Cléon from Vendée in France. The window of opportunity to sample Cardo is very limited, mainly due to the way Mary rears her animals, allowing them time for rest and play as well as kidding.

OPPOSITE TOP LEFT Ticklemore
OPPOSITE TOP RIGHT Alderwood
OPPOSITE BOTTOM LEFT Cardo
OPPOSITE BOTTOM RIGHT Cornish Yarg

ABOVE LEFT Jamie Montgomery
ABOVE RIGHT Cows at Moorhayes
OPPOSITE, TOP CHEESE Keens BOTTOM CHEESE Montgomery

Somerset Cheddars

The temperate climate and wetlands of the Somerset levels, together with the limestone of the Mendips, are the ideal conditions for growing lush pastures and producing Cheddars of outstanding flavour and texture.

Keen's Farmhouse Cheddar 🐄

WINCANTON, SOMERSET

The Keen's family have farmed at Moorhayes since 1899, which is both arable and dairy. The rather majestic 16th Century gabled farmhouse sits proudly on a hill overlooking the farmland, which in this part of Somerset is low-lying and prone to wet. The unpasteurized cow's milk cheese is made by hand using a traditional rennet, and what differentiates this Cheddar from, say Montgomery's, is its texture. Keen's has a heavier texture with a spicy, deep, almost tingling sensation on the tongue, and a nutty, fruity tang and rich, vigorous finish. The method of heating and pressing also differs to that of Jamie Montgomery's, but I think that in this little pocket of Somerset the *terroir* shows the way. I like Keen's Cheddar for its weighty chewiness, and the fact that it is a great cooking cheese.

Montgomery's Cheddar 🐄

NORTH CADBURY, SOMERSET

Jamie Montgomery makes a superb farmhouse Cheddar with immense skill, using unpasteurized cow's milk and traditional rennet, and every part of the cheesemaking process is overseen by him. What I love about this cheese is its fruity complexity and elegance – a combination that makes the perfect cheese sandwich! The grassy aroma of the cheese is offset by its mellow, rich taste that lingers gently on the tongue. The wines of Bordeaux are an obvious partner with their austere first impression, building up to a full-bodied flinty taste. Bordeaux and Somerset have comparable regional patterns.

Manor Farm, situated in North Cadbury, is in the heart of Camelot country and the epicentre of Cheddar. Jamie's family have been making cheese for three generations, utilizing milk originally from their pedigree Ayrshire herd, but latterly switching to Friesians as they have a higher milk yield. He has been careful to breed cows that retain as much of the Ayrshire characteristics as possible.

Montgomery's Cheddar is aged on wooden shelving in barns for a minimum of 12 months, but further ageing of 14–18 or even 24 months gives the cheese an even greater depth of flavour. The making of Cheddar is quite complex, requiring several stages of draining, cutting, milling and final pressing. Jamie uses an old peg-mill for the milling process to give a less even result; the cheese then develops a texture that breaks down with a crumble in the mouth. Jamie's cheeses have a texture and flavour that is somewhat different to other West Country Cheddars as he monitors the fat and protein levels carefully – too much leads to a much sharper taste – and he always aims for a drier, sweet-hay, earthy flavour. His smoked Cheddar is cut into sections and smoked over oak chips to give a really fruity, bosky taste. The cheese has a fine aroma that is both sharp and tangy.

Cheddar produced by members of the West Country Group, who make cheese using milk from local herds, if not their own, and who apply traditional methods to all aspects of production, now have a Protected Designation of Origin (PDO) to separate their cheeses from other Cheddars made elsewhere in the world. It was not possible to protect the name Cheddar, but at least the cheesemakers of the West Country Group have accreditation.

Waterloo and Wigmore 🐄 🐑 RISELEY, BERKSHIRE

I am often asked why handmade cheeses are so different from those made in larger dairies. I believe it comes down to a particular knowledge of how to treat the milk and turn it from its raw state into cheese. The intricate stages of production are fascinating and as much an art as a science. Wigmore and Waterloo are both washed-curd cheeses as opposed to washed rind.

The washed curd method involves replacing the whey with water and washing the curds, to reduce the number of starter bacteria and sugars (lactose). This in turn moderates lactic acid levels and helps to retain valuable moisture. The starter bacteria – a sort of yoghurty mixture that encourages the formation of curds – feed on the lactose and convert it to lactic acid, which all influence the final taste and texture of the cheese.

However, it's all a matter of balance. If not enough of the starter bacteria is washed away as the curds form then the cheese will be too dry and acidic, yet if too much is washed away, the result is a very soft, sloppy cheese with little flavour and a low acidity. Also, there is a risk that low acidity could allow the growth of harmful bacteria,

therefore, it is vital for Wigmore and Waterloo to contain a good level of acidity, but it does take much longer to reach this perfect balance before salting in order to retain the soft texture and the good flavour.

Once the curds are at the salting stage, a preparation of *Penicillium candidum* is used to produce the white bloomy rind (the same as for Brie and Camembert), but again it is essential to get the acidity or pH correct for the white mould to grow properly. As the mould relies on oxygen to grow, it is also very important to turn the cheese everyday during maturation to achieve an equal growth. This is where a 'refiner' or cheese 'maturer' takes over, and his or her skill can turn the rind into a lovely, soft satin-like finish.

Even though Anne and Andy Wigmore have been making Wigmore and Waterloo for over 18 years, they are still tweaking things here and there to improve their flavour and texture. Originally, they made the cheeses with unpasteurized milk but have turned to 'thermizing' to improve consistency. Thermizing milk for cheeses with rinds like Camembert, Livarot and Pont l'Évêque is more common now in France and other European countries.

The milk is heated before chilling, which kills off any harmful bacteria in the raw milk (if there is any) but leaves a significant number of good lactic acid and enzyme-producing bacteria (thermophiles) normally killed off by pasteurization.

Waterloo is made with Guernsey cow's milk and Wigmore with ewe's milk. Wigmore has a fruity iron flavour that develops with maturing to become a velvety and mellow-tasting cheese. Waterloo, however, has a buttery, slightly salty taste, which is balanced by a more acidic centre.

Tunworth 🐄 HERRIARD, HAMPSHIRE

The South Downs has long been associated with hop growing and agriculture, and vineyards are now bringing in another line of business. There are quite a few cheesemakers in the South East, producing a variety of styles, including goat's and ewe's milk cheeses, but Tunworth has attracted a vast amount of interest as it is a bloomy rind cow's milk cheese.

Julie Cheyney and Stacey Hodges are two friends who decided to go into business together, making cheese using milk from a neighbouring farm. From simple beginnings making cheese in the kitchen they have built a modern dairy in an old timbered

LEFT, RIGHT CHEESE Wigmore LEFT CHEESE Tunworth BOTTOM CHEESE Waterloo barn to create the right conditions to progress their cheesemaking. Their interpretation of a soft, mellow-tasting cheese with a thin bloomy rind has been achieved by adding a little *Penicillium candidum* (white mould) to the milk during heating, then quickly draining off the whey before forming the cheese by hand and placing it in the drying room for a few days. Almost magically the soft downy bloom starts to appear and then temperature and humidity levels have to be carefully maintained to continue the development. This process results in a cheese with an almost melting rind that clings to the fudgy centre within.

Tunworth is also a great leap forward for British cheesemaking, as it takes on a French style but with a distinctly English flavour. Perhaps not as nutty or earthy as a Camembert since Tunworth uses full-fat milk, giving it a slightly heavier texture, it is nevertheless a delightful addition to a cheeseboard to be enjoyed at around 5–6 weeks. You will see this cheese at farmer's markets in Hampshire as well as specialist cheese shops and served in restaurants.

Stinking Bishop 🐄 DYMOCK, GLOUCESTER

This cheese is in much demand, especially since such a limited amount is made. The farm is small and the commitment to rearing Gloucester cows means that the milk yield is not as high as say from Holstein cows.

Stinking Bishop has several similarities to French cheeses such as Epoisses (see page 60) or Vacherin (see page 90). The aroma is pungent, but that does not necessarily mean the flavour is equally strong. On the contrary, the prepared curds are not drained, milled and salted, but instead are washed in perry (pear cider) made from a variety of pear called Stinking Bishop, hence the cheese's name.

Like Vacherin, the curds are ladled directly into moulds to increase the moisture content and encourage bacterial activity. Salting takes place when the cheeses are turned out of the moulds and then wrapped in a bark collar, again like Vacherin.

The flavour of the cheese is not too strong when young, but given a little time in a high humidity and cool ageing room it develops to become more complex and rich.

Single Gloucester 🐄 CHURCHAM, GLOUCESTER

Diana Smart started making cheese in her sixties and wanted to keep to a very traditional recipe using milk from her Gloucester cows, although the paucity of female cows in her herd has meant that she has had to supplement milk from Holsteins for her cheeses other than the Single Gloucester. She first made the cheese in her kitchen, lining the moulds with cut down old sheets that she had boiled first to sterilize. The cheese has a deliciously light texture with a savoury, nutty flavour, which I prefer to eat on the young side.

ABOVE, TOP CHEESE Stinking Bishop BOTTOM CHEESE Single Gloucester

The recipe for Single Gloucester uses part skimmed milk, and Diana's cheeses are a true example of a traditionally made cheese of this type: the evening milk is skimmed of its cream and then combined with the full-fat morning milk. Very little starter is used and rennet is added 30 minutes later. Once the milk has set the curd is cut, heated again with continuous stirring and then allowed to settle before the whey is drained off. The curd is then cut into 16 squares, turned and then rested before being cut again into smaller squares, turned again, rested, and then further cuttings are made before the almost pea-sized curd is finally salted, milled, pressed and then matured for a minimum of three weeks; although further ageing of up to four months produces a denser, more crumbly cheese.

Traditionally, Single Gloucester was made solely for family consumption, and is therefore less well known than Double Gloucester, mainly because of its size, flavour and texture, which is somewhat different to the Double whose character is more in line with Cheddar and seemingly more popular.

In 1997, Single Gloucester received Protected Designation of Origin (PDO) status, which now means it can only be produced on farms in Gloucestershire with pedigree Gloucester cattle.

The flavour of Single Gloucester is very typically British, so I would say that English apples and pears are wonderful accompaniments to enjoy with this cheese.

The Midlands & Wales

The mineral-rich coal seams of the Midlands filter into the pastureland, to produce fine dairy and beef cattle and great regional cheeses. The Great North Road was the first main link into London and this brought fortune to the region, but the Industrial Revolution and the onslaught of manufacturing and mining reduced the pastureland and affected the sub-structure of the soil. However, land has been reclaimed and nurtured back to life and dairy and beef farming continues to flourish. Wales, located on a peninsula to the west of the Midlands, boasts 1,200 km (746 miles) of coastline and a varied landscape of mountains and outstanding natural parkland, dissected with rivers of clear, clean water. The wet and windy weather and often cold winters encourage cattle rather than arable farming. This climate produces the delicious Caerphilly cheese with its distinct mineral quality and soft crumble.

Berkswell 🐑 BERKSWELL, WEST MIDLANDS

Half-timbered stone houses, a medieval church and lush green pastures surround Ram Hall Farm in this delightfully picturesque corner of middle England, not too far from Shakespeare country.

Sheila, Stephen and Tessa Fletcher started making ewe's milk cheese in the mid-1980s experimenting with a Caerphilly recipe, and then tweaking it until they found a formula that was unique to them. The curds are heated, vegetarian rennet added and then left to rest. The milk soon starts setting, and looks similar to a wobbly blancmange when it is cut and then heated again before being placed into moulds in the shape of woven baskets, rather like a Pecorino or Manchego. The finishing touch, before placing in the maturing rooms, is to paint the outside of the cheese with whey to ensure that the rind stays firm but also thin.

The taste on first impression is fresh, becoming fruity and nutty as it warms in the mouth. We love the young cheeses for their sweetness, but it is only when we allow ourselves to hold back selling them and to mature for an extra five months that the texture becomes denser and the complexity of flavours more intense and rewarding.

LEFT Berkswell

ABOVE Tal-y-Llyn Lake, West Wales

Innes Button 🐐 TAMWORTH, STAFFORDSHIRE

Simplicity is key to this cheese: fresh, light and acidic are the only words necessary to describe the Innes Button goat's cheese. The dairy and farm are meticulously run by Stella Bennett with her son Joe, who is now at the helm. One of the highlights for me is when I arrive at the shop early enough to say hello to Joe, who delivers the cheeses sometimes. His shock of red curly hair and cheery demeanour are a welcome start to our day!

The recipe is simple as the process starts immediately after milking with the warm unpasteurized milk quickly transformed with vegetarian rennet to produce soft and fragile curds as well as preserving the flavour synonymous with Innes' cheeses. Since 1987, when they started with 100 goats, the herd has grown to 350, mostly crossed Saanen and Toggenburg. Around 220 nannies are milked morning and evening, each producing on average 3 litres (5¼ pints) of milk per day. In order to maintain production of the cheeses, kidding continues throughout most of the year, and the diet is carefully calculated in order to produce milk of the highest quality and also without any additives or pesticides. The delightful fresh, mousse-like tiny cheese is free of any rind, and as well as the plain version there are those with a coating of charcoal ash or fresh rosemary or a topping of pink peppercorns.

BELOW, TOP LEFT CHEESE Innes Button Pink Peppercorns
TOP RIGHT CHEESE Innes Bosworth Ash Log MIDDLE LEFT CHEESE
Innes Button Rosemary BOTTOM LEFT CHEESE Innes Button
French Salted Ash BOTTOM RIGHT CHEESE Innes Bosworth Leaf

Appleby's Cheshire 🐄
WESTON-UNDER-REDCASTLE, SHROPSHIRE

It is hard not to be bowled over by Shropshire, a region of great beauty with its lush pastures, thick hedgerows, undulating hills and great spreads of thickets and woodlands. The farm is on the edge of the river Dee and Mersey basin, where the top soil is sandy, changes to clay lower down then marl and sandstone, breaking down to form an underlying rock salt, which all help to explain the character of the cheese.

It is believed that Cheshire is Britain's oldest cheese, dating back to Roman times and mentioned in the Domesday Book. Records show it was transported to all the major cities in Britain from around the mid-17th century, either by road or canal. It was also the cheese of choice for ships' rations during times of war in the 18th century. (Records from Admiral Nelson's ship *the Victory* mention Suffolk cheese, which was a very basic, hard acidic Cheddar-style cheese, as well as Cheshire.) The cheese is very similar to that of Cantal (see page 70) from the Auvergne, France, which may mean that during the crusades of the 11th and 12th Centuries, the recipe for Cheshire could well have travelled to France and Spain.

The Cheshire from the Appleby's farm is handmade, cloth-wrapped, and made with unpasteurized milk using vegetable rennet. The addition of annatto (a natural red food colouring, see Shropshire Blue, below) gives a beautiful salmon pink colour to the cheese. The texture is crumbly and surprisingly light with a taste that is mild and mellow when young, becoming more savoury and herbal with maturing. It is also a surprising match for the lighter, sweet styles of single malt whisky.

Shropshire Blue 🐄 NOTTINGHAMSHIRE AND LEICESTERSHIRE

The name of this cheese does not actually identify its provenance. Originating in Scotland in the 1970s, production moved to Leicestershire then Nottinghamshire via Cheshire when the Scottish dairy closed. Its orange colour is due to the addition of annatto, a natural colouring from the pulp surrounding the seeds of the South American Achiote tree and it was probably originally added to differentiate the cheese from Stilton. The cheese is very similar in style to Stilton with a sharp, metallic edge coming from the blue veining. However, it is more mellow in flavour than Stilton, making it a good snacking cheese at any time of day, especially with a stick of crisp winter celery.

LEFT Appleby's Cheshire
OPPOSITE Shropshire Blue

Stilton and Stichelton

The mineral-rich soil in Nottinghamshire is said to encourage the blueing in Stilton, and the well-drained pastures encourage dense, creamy milk, which combine to produce the superb Stiltons of this region.

Colston Bassett Stilton 🐄 COLSTON BASSETT, NOTTINGHAMSHIRE

First served in local coaching inns for travellers, this famous cheese found its way to London in the 18th century as recorded by Paxton & Whitfield, the famous cheese shop in Jermyn Street, who organized deliveries.

The land around Colston Bassett is devoted to grazing and the soil is rich in minerals, which undoubtedly influences the flavour of the milk. The cheese is made using pasteurized cow's milk with either traditional or vegetarian rennet. I prefer the traditional (animal rennet) as I believe the slower method of maturing and ripening the cheese with this coagulant produces a more complex flavour and a richer texture.

The cheese made with traditional rennet is also treated a little differently to the vegetarian alternative. It is left undisturbed for longer, and piercing with thin stainless steel needles begins at around 12 weeks, rather than the usual 5–7 weeks. Once the air enters the holes, the added *Penicillium roqueforti*, which has so far been dormant,

ABOVE Grading Colston Bassett

ABOVE Salting Colston Bassett

starts to grow, forming as it does the typical blue veins associated with Stilton. This method also influences the texture of the cheese, which ideally should be crumbly and richly buttery rather than dense and claggy. The blue with its forthright metallic minerality is a good foil to the creaminess of the cheese.

Once the cheese is pierced the outside crust also starts to change as the calcium is released from within the cheese and starts to mingle with the moulds on the rind.

With careful brushing and controlling of the growth of the moulds, the crust starts to develop and resemble a craggy rockface. The aroma of the cheese at this point in the maturing process could be described as being similar to that of a damp cellar.

OPPOSITE Colston Bassett Stilton
BELOW Stichelton

By introducing the blue at a slightly later stage, the cheese has already begun the maturing process before the veins start to thread their way through. This encourages the development of a spicy tang to the rich flavour.

Weather patterns play a big part in how all blue cheeses develop, and for Stilton the perfect conditions are early-autumn when the grass is dry and sweet, the air is warm during the day and cools considerably in the evening. At this time of the year, the cattle are content since they can stay outside all the time and do not have to shelter from the elements. That is why we always look forward to Christmas when Stilton is one of the most sought after traditional treats.

Stilton is often served with a glass of Port, viewed as the perfect partner, but wines from south west France and some Spanish reds, like Priorat, with a bold structure work very well too.

Stichelton 🐄 WELBECK ESTATE, NOTTINGHAMSHIRE

Joe Schneider, an American who ventured first to Holland to make Greek cheese for a Turk, finally found his feet in Britain. With the help and friendship of cheese guru Randolph Hodgson they became partners, and together created a raw milk regional blue cheese. Their recipe uses a tiny amount of starter at the heating stage, and then a very small quantity of traditional rennet, meaning acidity is slow to progress and making the curd very fragile. Everything is done by hand, including the careful ladling of the curds, and the milling and salting take place the day after the milk is set. The cheese is not pressed, but left to sit in hoops in a warm room to settle over the next five days, when it is removed. The outside of the cheese is smoothed by hand using simple kitchen knives and a minimum of three months passes before piercing with a three-pronged fork implement takes place. Taste Stichelton alongside Stilton and note the difference: there is a definite richness to Stichelton with a dense and creamy paste, and the blue is spicier. The fragility of the various stages of making and maturing means that the flavour and texture can be markedly different, especially with seasonal variations too, but it is really exciting to see the progress made with each batch.

Gorwydd Caerphilly 🐄 TREGARON, CEREDIGION

Todd Trethowan, whose family moved to Wales from Sussex, first got the cheesemaking bug when he worked on Dougal Campbell's farm (see Lincolnshire Poacher, page 31) during his vacations from university. After graduating, he decided to learn more about cheese and spent time with Chris Duckett in Somerset, whose recipe for Caerphilly he has utilized, including the type of starter. It's not so strange that Caerphilly is made in Somerset: the cheese was first made near the mining communities of South Wales but due to its popularity over time it crossed over the Bristol Channel into Avon and Somerset. The generosity of cheesemakers!

As with other young cheesemakers, Randolph Hodgson of Neal's Yard Dairy was influential in giving Todd the encouragement he needed, and since the mid-1990s he has helped and advised in the development of the cheese.

Gorwydd Farm overlooks the Teifi Valley where the afternoon sun warms its pastures. Pastures located in temperate climates are at their best from mid-morning until mid-afternoon as the soil's goodness, warmed by the sun, is sucked up by the blades of grass making the grass sweetly fragrant and juicy. The farm is rather remote, and its grazing pastures have an underlying structure of lead, coal and lime. Todd buys in milk from neighbouring farms, and every stage of the cheesemaking process is done by hand and the moulds, which have been made for him by a local blacksmith, are a traditional cake-tin shape with a separate metal disc lid.

The Caerphilly takes about four hours to make: the fresh milk is first warmed before the starter is added and then heated again to a slightly higher temperature. It is left to ripen for two hours and reheated for the rennet to be added. The curd is left to set for about 45 minutes before being cut and scalded. It is then stirred for a further 45 minutes, until it forms a smooth, elastic texture that indicates that the acidity level is correct and the curds are ready for draining. Unlike Cheddar, which is piled into blocks and milled, this cheese is pushed into a heap, cut into 5 cm (2 in) cubes and then into 2.5 cm (1 in) cubes. Salting follows, then the cheese is placed into muslin-lined moulds and pressed for 30 minutes before another top-surface salting. The final stage is a 16-hour pressing and brining for 24 hours. The maturing time on the farm is around two months before being sold, although the cheese can be aged for longer.

The difference between a Duckett's Caerphilly and Todd's is the crust. The softer, velvety grey moulds are allowed to grow on Gorwydd, rather like those on the French Sainte Nectaire. These form in the high humidity, cold maturing rooms, and the lime, lead and coal minerality also play a part in the way the rind turns. The cheese has that familiar crumbly texture, yet tastes fresh and creamy with earthy mellow tones. A very versatile cheese, it can be used in baked dishes, crumbled over vegetables, or better still served as part of a cheeseboard with crunchy spring radishes dipped in a little sea salt.

There is a bright acidity to the cheese that marries well with white wines like Chablis or Riesling. I often pair this cheese with crumbly goat's cheeses, and also a Comté d'Estive (see page 84), and a Bavarian Blue with rich deep flavours. What is so likeable about Gorwydd is its versatility, allowing it to be placed on the cheeseboard with soft, washed and hard cheeses. Whereas the modern versions of Caerphilly lean towards a Cheddar style, this old-fashioned softer crumble embraces its origins.

LEFT Gorwydd Caerphilly
OPPOSITE Lincolnshire Poacher

Lincolnshire Poacher 🐄 ALFORD, LINCOLNSHIRE

The Fens are not an obvious choice for cheesemaking, since the land is mostly arable. Simon and Tim Jones' farm is situated at the southern-most part of the Lincolnshire Wolds where the land has a little more character other than the usual flat vista. The chalky, limey soil is a definite plus for the flavour of the cheese; this is counteracted by the fact that rainfall is low in this part of England, signifying that the quality of the grass in summer is not great. Consequently, cheesemaking takes place between mid-autumn and late spring when the rainfall is greater, and the smaller quantities of summer milk are sold to the main milk distributor.

The grazing pastures are not sprayed with nitrates, pesticides or fertilizers (which leave a tell-tale taste of bitterness in the milk and then the cheese), and are carpeted with clover, which is a natural way of fixing nitrogen into the soil and encouraging good grass growth and other nutrients in the soil, thereby benefiting the cattle. Their overall organic approach and land management encourages wildlife and flora, which again contributes to the quality of the soil on their land as well as the environment.

The cheeses made in spring have a sweeter milk taste, and if you compare the flavours of say the four- or five-month cheese with ones aged for 18 months or longer, you will taste how a cheese evolves from this sweet acidity, to a long lingering fruity flavour.

Simon Jones was taught cheesemaking by the late Dougal Campbell, whose famous Welsh cheese T'yn Grug is greatly missed. T'yn Grug was a cross between Cheddar and Swiss Gruyère, and this has influenced Simon's cheese. Poacher is made with unpasteurized cow's milk and traditional rennet, and whereas in appearance it looks rather like a Cheddar, when you cut into the cheese, the way it cracks and crumbles make it different. This is due to the fact that the milk is heated with a fast-reacting culture, unlike a West Country Cheddar, which uses a slower starter. Furthermore, the curds are cut in the vat and the flavour while meaty has a distinct savoury-sweet acidity, acquired through the chalky minerals that infiltrate the grazing pastures. There is a richness too from the milk of the Holstein cows, which is the same milk used for the Auvergne Cantal cheeses. I always insist on cheeses aged for 18 months plus for their structure and depth of flavour – they partner beer perfectly.

Northern England & Scotland

The stone mining tradition in the rugged Dales landscape has had a distinct effect on the soil and in turn on the structure and flavour of the cheeses produced in this area. Weather patterns also play a big part: the sudden change when spring appears shows directly in the cheeses. Scotland's cheese styles have associations with Suffolk due to the migration of cheesemakers, and also with Ireland. The landscape and weather determine the flavours and textures of the harder and blue cheeses. They have a bite and sting, and sometimes can appear aggressive on the tongue.

BOTTOM CHEESE
Doddington
LEFT CHEESE Sliced
Doddington
RIGHT CHEESE Richard III
Wensleydale

Richard III Wensleydale 🐄

BEDALE, NORTH YORKSHIRE

The Dales have a long history of cheesemaking. Suzanne Stirke, whose version of Wensleydale has a wonderful crumble and limestone mineral tang redolent of the local soil, was an academic lecturing in history before she tried her hand at cheesemaking. At first, she made the cheese with ewe's milk from her own farm, but it proved almost impossible to get a sufficient amount of milk, so she turned to cow's milk from a neighbouring farm.

Rather like a double-curd Lancashire, this is a semi-hard crumbly cheese with a nutty creamy texture and taste, and a salty tang. Serve the delicious young cheese with a slice of fruit cake for a lovely teatime treat.

In order to achieve the cheese's characteristic moist crumble, after heating and draining the curds are block-piled to drain further, followed by milling, salting and breaking up the curd by hand. The curds are then placed in moulds and left for a day before being turned and wrapped in cloth. They are left for another day before being turned again, brined and then closely wrapped in muslin to inhibit moulds growing. I receive the cheese after three weeks, as it is really delightful as a young cheese. However, if I want a more aged version, then Suzanne sets aside a cheese for us that has not been block-piled but milled directly after draining and then brined for two days to encourage the blooms on the rind. In this way, the cheese stays moist and crumbly. If you are wondering why the cheese is named Richard III, it is because Middleham Castle, the childhood home of the once king, is in the vicinity.

Doddington 🐄 WOOLER, NORTHUMBERLAND

The Maxwell family with their herd of Friesian and Normande cows have been making cheese on their farm for over 12 years: first very hesitantly at the kitchen sink before moving into production and changing the original recipe based on Leicester cheese to a Cheddar-type. The result is Doddington, which definitely suits the Normande cattle since their milk has a higher protein content than the Friesian, yet the proportion of fat in the Friesian milk helps to balance this out.

The semi-hard cheese made with unpasteurized milk and animal rennet follows a traditional recipe with a few tweaks, one being that the milk is scalded similar to that for a Leicester and then to 'cheddar' it the curds are cut and stacked resulting in an acidity quite similar to a Montgomery's Cheddar (see page 20). The cheese has a dense yet crumbly texture with a pleasing gentle aroma, while the taste is initially fresh and salty, then mellows to a rich, earthy fruitiness.

The salty, spicy tang is partly due to the farm's proximity to the coast, as the briny sea air permeates the pastureland. It is often thought that the taste and texture is similar to a Dutch Gouda but this may be due to the use of fresh whole milk from the morning milking. The sweetness of Doddington is apparent as it ages, rather like a mature Gouda, especially with cheese made from milk from spring, summer and the last flush of grass growth in September. The cheese is covered in a beetroot-coloured breathable wax bought in from the Netherlands, which also helps to prevent unwanted furry moulds appearing on the rind during the long maturing process.

Kirkham's Lancashire 🐄

GOOSNARGH, NEAR PRESTON, LANCASHIRE

The Kirkham family are third generation farmers, and the Goosnargh area, although in close proximity to the city of Preston and the motorway being only 3 km (2 miles) away from the farm, is in unspoilt green rolling countryside, and is deeply entrenched in agriculture.

The meadows have an abundance of wild flowers and herbs such as meadowsweet, which loves the damp conditions, and dandelion and clover, which all assist the acidity levels in the milk. They also encourage the development of the cheese's flavour and texture since very little starter is added to the first heating. These plant aromas can be detected in the finished cheese as well as a light lemony tang, which is nothing like the industrially made versions. The main reason for this is that the traditionally made cheese uses a blend of six milkings (from two days' production), which gives a unique flavour and texture – crumbly and savoury without any aggressive sharpness or acidity. The young cheese would be delicious made into a thick savoury cream, then spread onto the bottom of a pastry case and topped with apples to make a pie; or the apples could be sprinkled with shaved shards of cheese underneath a pastry lid. The more mature cheese is really delicious toasted under the grill until light golden and bubbling.

The cheesemaking process starts with heating of the morning and evening milk, and then when the curd has set, it is cut into cubes and left to stand before being drained off into a cloth-lined drainer where it is crumbled by hand three times over 1½ hours. The next day some of it is added to the previous day's curd before proceeding to milling, salting, moulding, then pressing and wrapping in muslin. Once the rind is dry, the cheese is lightly rubbed with melted butter to seal it and prevent any unwanted moulds from developing.

There is a rather a poignant story about the Kirkham's plan to increase the size of the dairy in 2008, due to demand for their cheese always exceeding supply. They spent a small fortune building a new, state of the art dairy, which replaced the old stone dairy-house they had used for years and years. However, they found that the cheese reacted badly to the new surroundings and developed a bitter flavour and an unpleasant grainy texture.

Interestingly, what they hadn't realized was that the cheese made from a traditional family recipe would take time to become familiar with the new building. The flora and bacteria had not had time to develop in the air, and the temperature inside the cheeseroom was too cold and killing what little cultures were present.

The new building needed time to 'bed-in' and drastic action was taken to warm up the area and introduce new flora and bacteria. By the end of the year things were more or less back to normal and the cheese is again tasting as it should with a buttery, grassy sweetness and citrus freshness to the flavour. It just goes to show how important it is to understand the vagaries of nature and go with them rather than against them.

Dunsyre Blue 🐄 CARNWATH, LANARKSHIRE

It is only since the 1960s that we have seen a real revival of Scottish cheeses, especially softer creamy styles that definitely have their own flavour profile quite unlike those south of the border. Humphrey Errington is one such cheesemaker who has adapted old recipes and for the last 25 years has worked tirelessly perfecting his methods. His 120-hectare (300-acre) farm overlooks the Pentland Hills with its austere, remote landscape, underlined in sandstone with peat, heather and abundant water, all of which give the soil and pastureland very particular qualities that are beneficial to dairy farming.

Humphrey is also noted for his work with EAT, the European Alliance for Artisan and Traditional Raw Milk Products, which offers help, advice and support to producers and creators of raw milk products. Milk from Ayrshire cows is used to make Dunsyre Blue, a cylinder-shaped rich and creamy-textured cheese. The flavour is neither too aggressive nor overly salty in taste. Made to a traditional recipe, the cheese was originally mentioned in *The Cook's and Housewife's Manual*, written by Meg Dods and published in 1826. It has a moist white rind with blue-green spicy-flavoured veins running through the cheese. During production, Dunsyre Blue is wrapped in foil and aged for 6–12 weeks. The cheese weighs about 3 kg (6 ½ lb).

ABOVE Dunsyre Blue
OPPOSITE Kirkham's Lancashire

All of Humphrey's cheeses are made with raw milk and animal rennet. Alongside Dunsyre Blue, Humphrey also makes his famous ewe's milk cheese, Lanark Blue, which is Scotland's answer to Roquefort (albeit more forceful in taste) and a crumbly cow's milk cheese, Maisie's Kebbuck, named after Humphrey's mother-in-law who does not eat blue cheese. This is an unpressed cheese in the style of traditional cheeses of Scotland. There is a sharp lactic edge reminiscent of a Wensleydale, and a 'peaty' taste and aroma: whisky is an ideal drinking partner.

In addition to his cheeses, Humphrey also produces Fallachan (Gaelic for 'lost treasure'), which is a rather interesting fermented alcoholic (13 percent) drink made from whey, a by-product of the cheesemaking process. Originally called 'Blaand', the revived recipe is made following traditional methods and is aged for a year in oak casks. The taste is not unlike a dry sherry, and it is actually rather good with his cheeses.

Caboc  TAIN, ROSS AND CROMARTY

This is Scotland's oldest cheese, dating from the 15th century. Originating in the Scottish Highlands, the cream cheese was first made by Mariota de Ile, the daughter of the chieftain of the Clan MacDonald of the Isles. At 12 years of age, Mariota was in danger of being abducted by the Clan Campbell who planned to marry her to one of their own and seize her lands. Mariota escaped to Ireland, reputedly taking refuge in a nunnery (in line with the clan's leanings towards Catholicism), where she learned how to make cheese. On her return, she married (within the family constraints) and passed the recipe to her daughter, who in turn passed it on to her daughter. The recipe is still secret and has been handed down from mother to daughter ever since; the current descendant of the clan and owner of the recipe is Susannah Stone.

Caboc has a deep, buttery colour and a mild, sour flavour. During production, the cheese is formed into logs and rolled in toasted oatmeal.

According to legend, the tradition of coating Caboc in oatmeal started by accident. A cattle herder stored the day's cheese in a box, which he had used to carry his oatcakes earlier in the day. When he opened the box to eat the cheese, he found that it had been covered in the oatmeal crumb, and he liked it so much that from then onwards Caboc has been made with an oaten coating.

To make your own version simply mash a full-fat soft cow's milk curd cheese or a triple cream Explorateur or a goat's curd cheese with a little crème fraîche to lighten and soften the mixture, add crumbled Maldon coarse sea salt to heighten the flavour, and then form into small balls before coating in toasted pinhead oatmeal.

Isle of Mull  TOBERMORY, ISLE OF MULL

Sgriob-ruadh Farm (Gaelic for 'red furrow' and pronounced ski-brooah) is on the Isle of Mull on the west coast of Scotland. Farm owners, the Reades, could not have found a more different way of farming from their origins in Somerset, than this wind, rain and sea-lashed landscape. The herd is mainly Friesians, with the odd Jersey and Ayrshire, and they have also recently introduced Brown Swiss cows, which creates a particularly interesting cheese.

Many lessons had to be learnt whilst building and restoring the farm, which had been abandoned for 16 years. During the rebuilding and renovation work, which they did themselves, they designed an innovative underground cheese room, the roof of which now looks like a grassy mound. It was incorporated to assist with controlling humidity levels and temperature since half of the year the island receives more than its share of extreme weather.

The cows spend seven months in a shed due to the weather conditions on the island. However, this is no ordinary shed, but rather a warm retreat with a thick rubber carpet flooring, which is then strewn with shredded recycled paper (collected from all over the island) rather than the usual straw.

The farm grows hay to make into silage for winter feed, and in

ABOVE Isle of Mull OPPOSITE Caboc

the spring the herd is able to graze outside until early autumn. The Reades had originally just sold their milk in Somerset, but Chris decided that with the move she wanted to make cheese and before leaving took lessons and made cheese with Cheddar-makers. I often look for Somerset Cheddars made in the warmer months for the more complex flavours, however, the Mull winter cheeses, which are paler in colour have a better flavour, since the controlled feeding of hay and mashed barley residue from the local whisky distillery allows the distinct spicy, herbal almost alcoholic tastes to come into play. The summer cheeses can have really aggressive herbaceous spiky notes, and sometimes it is hard to actually eat the cheese as part

of a mixed cheeseboard as the flavours are so dominant. I have often paired these summer cheeses with whisky served with a splash of water as they really work well together. The cheese is made with unpasteurized milk using a traditional rennet.

Although the Reades' expertise in cheesemaking started with Cheddar in Somerset, they do not consider Mull to be a Cheddar. The paler-coloured cheese has a lighter crumble with unique briny, tangy flavours, and the small amount of blue veining that sometimes runs through the edges of the rind into the cheese is a sign of its maturity and something to be enjoyed.

Ireland

Ireland has become a force to be reckoned with in the cheese world. There are links to Brittany and the west coast of France in the landscape and soil of the west and south coasts of Ireland, with the sandstone ridges and the high Carrantuohill in Co. Kerry together with the Upper Lake in Killarney helping with the movement of rain and drainage to fertilize the pastureland. There is granite and lime in the soil, with peat-covered uplands and rich clay, which combined with the Gulf Stream warming the west coast, create a landscape that is bright green and luscious. The rockier coastline of the south and south west encourage dairy farming rather than arable, and there is a concentration of cheesemaking in the south, taking in washed-rind styles as well as hard, soft and creamy cheeses. The air is clean and clear, the rain soft and the climate temperate. The peaty bogs give the whiskey a lighter flavour due to its three-phase distilling process (Scotland has two phases), and these sweeter styles are really delicious and easy drinking with the cheeses, especially the washed-rind semi-soft and the majestic Desmond and Gabriel (see page 41).

BELOW, BOTTOM CHEESE St Tola LEFT CHEESE Ryefield
RIGHT CHEESE Cashel Blue

Ryefield 🐐 BAILIEBORO, CO. CAVAN

Ryefield is a rindless goat's cheese made by the Fivemiletown Creamery Cooperative, owned and run by local dairy farmers. The co-op is situated in the rolling hills and lakes of Co. Cavan, and the cheesemaking facility is at the top of Stone Wall, which is 250 metres (820 ft) above sea level, and has spectacular views over almost half the county. Every day fresh batches of cheese are made after pasteurizing the milk slowly, giving the cheese a light, frothy texture and a really gentle milky, nutty taste. Ryefield is a perfect introduction to cheese for children, and can be used in salads, spooned on top of soups, as well as made into fillings for pasta and pancakes.

St Tola 🐐 INAGH, CO. CLARE

The weather in Ireland, especially in the south with its microclimate, gives the grass a vivid green quality that is unique. The clouds scud by at a rate of knots, and the rainfall is soft and silky, all contributing to the production of fine cheese.

Meg and Derrick Gordon were the original cheesemakers of St Tola, and in 1999 their neighbour, Siobhan Ni Ghairbhith, took over the farm and eventually brought it to full registered organic standards. The farm is not far from the west coast, about 16 km (10 miles), and the soil is peat and sand, producing lush meadowland. Meg is the sole cheesemaker, using milk from her herd of Saanen white goats with a few brown Toggenburgs. Her tiny cheesemaking unit is a haven of pristine cleanliness and good housekeeping practices. The milk is organic and unpasteurized and vegetarian rennet is used.

The best season for St Tola is mid-spring to mid-winter, although the early spring cheeses arrive in the shop without their bloomy rind, and we leave them for a few weeks in our cold room with high humidity to allow the wrinkled white rind to develop.

The cheese is light with a velvety texture that is fine and smooth. There is hardly a hint of goatiness in the taste, but there are subtle flavours of sweet peat and the sea. The goats love to roam and forage, and while there is all that lovely grass available, they prefer to chew on bracken, wild flora and leaves from the bushes. This is a very elegant, fine goat's cheese to be enjoyed with dry white wines, as well as light reds.

Cashel Blue 🐄 FETHARD, CO. TIPPERARY

Husband and wife team, Louis and Jane Grubb, have perfected their distinctive full-fat blue cheese by first heating the rich milk, provided by their pedigree Friesian cows, in a hundred-year-old copper vat. Once the milk is pasteurized then cooled, a starter with *Pencillium roqueforti* is added before heating again. Rennet (traditional or vegetarian) is then included and it is left to set for one hour. The curd is cut, left for another hour before being removed from the vat in linen cloths and left to drain. The curds are then dropped straight into the moulds and for the next two days left to drain further with occasional turnings. As soon as the cheese is dry enough, salting and piercing takes place.

At this point the cheese is creamy white, but after two weeks in a cold room moulds begin to appear on the outer surface showing that the blue is growing. The cheese is washed of this outer mould, dried, and wrapped in foil to inhibit further mould growth. It is then placed in a very cold room for at least 2-3 months, although at 4–5 months it reaches its full potential.

Cashel Blue has a rich and creamy texture. The cheese is well marbled with nutty blue moulds, which have a hint of sweet earthy saltiness. Maturing this cheese in the coolest part of the cellar with high humidity gives the texture an almost melting consistency and a very enjoyable and satisfying taste.

ABOVE Crozier Blue

ABOVE, BOTTOM CHEESE Gabriel LEFT CHEESE St Gall RIGHT CHEESE Coolea
TOP CHEESE Desmond

Crozier Blue 🐑 FETHARD, CO. TIPPERARY

This is a relatively new cheese, produced seasonally (it is
not available from mid-winter through to mid-spring)
from the milk of a flock of Friesland sheep recently
established on the limestone pasturelands. Throughout
the milking season, the ewes are allowed to freely graze the
fertile grasslands of Tipperary, producing the distinctively
flavoured milk that gives Crozier a smooth buttery texture,
countered by the salty grittiness of the blue veins.

Henry and Louis Clifton Browne are nephews of Louis
and Jane Grubb, makers of Cashel Blue, and the farm is
actually next door. Cheesemaking is interlinked with the
Grubbs overseeing the production of the cheese, while the
Clifton Brownes take care of the day-to-day running.

The story of Crozier Blue began in 1993 when Henry,
using the milk from six sheep, began experimenting with
blue cultures. Over the following five years he played with
the cheese recipe while also increasing the flock, including
importing the high-yielding Friesland ewes from Britain.
Making of the cheese has since been taken over by his
aunt and uncle.

The pasteurized vegetarian cheese has a similar flavour
and texture to Roquefort but is maybe a little sharper and
slightly drier. Crozier is slow to mature and can be eaten
young when it is crumbly and tangy (around two months)
although for a more strident flavour and a creamier
texture it is best matured for at least four months in a cold
refrigerated room.

St Gall 🐄 FERMOY, CO. CORK

Gudrun and Frank Shinnicks' cheesemaking skills are
rooted in Switzerland. Named after the monastery St
Gallen near Appenzell, this brine-washed, unpasteurized
cow's milk cheese has all the characteristics of a fine Swiss
cheese in its salty, caramel, fruity sweetness, but with a
rich, earthy creaminess of the Irish countryside. The
recipe includes traditional rennet and skimmed milk
giving a firmer texture. The cheese is pressed in
a traditional style.

Coolea 🐄 MACROOM, CO. CORK

Helene and Dick Willems, who originally came from
Linburg, Holland, started to make cheese on their farm
in the late 1970s. The herd of Meuse Rhine Issel (MRI)
cows are well known in Holland and Germany for being
sturdy, long-living and producing an abundance of milk,
and were first introduced to the UK in the 1970s. The
farm, which is quite remote, is situated a few miles along
very winding roads off the main Killarney highway, and has
a lovely aspect overlooking a valley. Helene and Dick on
retiring handed over the cheesemaking reins to their son
Dicky who then brought on board his wife Sinead to help
him run the business.

The cheesemaking process for Coolea uses
unpasteurized milk with traditional rennet, and in order
to speed up acidity the cut curds are washed twice to

remove some of the lactose. This creates a cheese with a sweeter and denser flavour. The curds are scalded twice during a two-hour period, continuously stirred by machine, and then moulded and pressed over six hours, followed by brining for around four days. As with all Gouda-type cheeses, their outer surface must be kept free of moulds, and in order to do this as well as promote ripening (cheeses ripen from the outside in, by the way), the cheese is sprayed with a food-grade melted paraffin wax coating that dries into a hard shiny skin.

The cheese is usually matured for a minimum of six months for the smaller wheels, and up to two years for larger cheese – in fact, the longer the better.

Gabriel & Desmond SCHULL, CO. CORK

Bill Hogan and Sean Ferry have together created two amazing cheeses. In the old days, I used to telephone the post office at Schull and speak to the postmistress who took our order for the cheeses. Nowadays, things are more structured, but the cheeses are still made to a traditional Swiss recipe (developed with Bill's mentors and Swiss cheese experts, Joseph Dubach and Josef Enz) in specialist imported copper vats and other equipment. Made with unpasteurized summer cow's milk and traditional rennet, the cheeses are aged for over a year.

The microclimate in the south west corner of Ireland, together with the lush pastures give the cheeses their unique flavour. Gabriel is like a Sbrinz or Parmesan with its hard, gritty texture, and deeply savoury, herbal flavour, while Desmond is also a dry, hard cheese but is less gritty with a hard fudgy texture. It is more fruity than Gabriel, which has a slight acidic edge, but really these cheeses are truly magical and quite unlike anything else in Ireland.

I remember meeting Bill Hogan in London many years ago, a rather larger than life character whose past employment as a teenager in the 1960s was as an office assistant to Martin Luther King. He was demonstrating cooking with his cheeses by making a fondue. The fondue included quite a lot of dry white wine, but it was really exceptional with a salty, spritzy tang coming through. I think Alsace wines work very well with these cheeses and also the rare Jura white wines, too.

Dilliskus & Kilcummin CASTLEGREGORY, CO. KERRY

Dilliskus and Kilcummin may not be the prettiest-looking cheeses, but they both pack a punch of flavours. Cheesemaker Maja Binder's farm overlooks the Dingle Peninsula where the roaring Atlantic sea spray finds its way onto the pastures close-by and gives the cheeses their wild and herbal flavours. Dilliskus has dillisk seaweed flecked through the curd, which is not for effect but rather an extension of the traditional use

of seaweed in Irish cuisine. I am reliably informed that smoked dillisk is still eaten in pubs throughout Ireland instead of crisps, and I have to say that I could think of nothing more delicious than a hand-pumped glass of Guinness from the tiny pub on Dingle Bay with Dilliskus cheese and soda bread!

First thing in the morning Maja collects the milk from a nearby farm still warm from the parlour, and by the end of the morning she has made her cheeses. She brings the milk up to 26°C to allow the starter culture to get the milk into its curdled state before adding the vegetable rennet. Within an hour or so she cuts the set curds into small pieces before stirring, reheating and then lifting the curds out of the copper vat with the help of a muslin cloth. She then drains the curds before placing into moulds and to rest overnight. The next day the cheeses are removed from their moulds, brined in a salt water solution for a several hours before going to the maturing room.

The cheese has a distinct fruitiness from milk heated in copper, and a wild complexity of style that is enhanced by the brushing and rubbing of the rinds with a brine mixture during the ageing period. The crusts take on a lovely dark pitted appearance and an aroma of the cellar mingled with earth and peat. The wrapping of the cheeses is just as carefully thought out as the making; the thick brown paper is folded around the cheeses and then tied with string. This allows the cheese to breathe and the crust not to get soggy and give off an ammonic aroma.

These cheeses are not delicate in taste or appearance, but they give you a true sense of place with the flavours, and one must admire cheesemaking of this calibre, which is not afraid to push the boundaries by bringing the land and the sea together in the cheesemaking process.

BELOW, LEFT CHEESE Dilliskus **RIGHT CHEESE** Kilcummin

Cheeses of Co. Cork

Co. Cork is considered an epicurean centre and produces a wealth of delicious cheeses. The area is dotted with restaurants, with the famous Ballymaloe hotel and cookery school at its heart.

TOP LEFT Fingal Ferguson of the Gubbeen Smokehouse TOP MIDDLE Giana Ferguson of Gubbeen TOP RIGHT Gubbeen washed-rind cheese BOTTOM LEFT Jeffa Gill at Durrus BOTTOM MIDDLE Grazing cows at Durrus BOTTOM RIGHT The Durrus farm

Ardrahan 🐄 KANTURK, CO. CORK

The original recipe for Ardrahan was developed by Eugene and Mary Burns, but the farm is now run by Mary with her son Gerald. They use milk from their pedigree Friesians, which is the oldest registered herd in Ireland. As with other cheeses from this part of Ireland, something magical happens during the cheesemaking process to produce an end product with great taste and appearance.

Ardrahan with its pinky-beige washed rind has a wealth of flavour and is crustier and more wrinkled than other washed-rind cheeses. The key is in the ripening process, but this can be tricky as the rind can become dry and bitter if allowed to go too far. In the south west of Ireland, the atmospheric conditions are perfect for encouraging the washed-rind flora or *B. linens* to grow. (This is a culture of yeast and bacteria mixed with water and then smeared onto the cheese either by brushing or rubbing with a cloth, to form a reddish sticky rind which develops through the stimulation of the lactic acidity in the cheese.) The milk is pasteurized and reheated with a vegetarian rennet. The curds are cut by hand, some of the whey is skimmed off and replaced with water, before it is scalded.

The curds are then ready for the moulds and the last stage involves brining in sea salt and washing twice over the following three days. These are classic procedures that are also used in the making of Munster (see page 47) and Livarot (see page 52), but being in South West Ireland with all the flora and cultures alive in the air, progress is quick and in no time Ardrahan turns into an earthy, tangy cheese, with the character of the region very evident.

Gubbeen 🐄 SCHULL, CO. CORK

Tom and Giana Ferguson's farm is very close to the sea, and surrounded by the sort of luxuriant foliage seen in parts of Cornwall, or even the South of France. The Ferguson family have been farmers for five generations, and Giana, who is part Hungarian and brought up in Spain, has an interesting background in food, even making fresh cheese curds as a child. Her cheesemaking technique is quite different from other producers in this region and this results in a distinctive, complex-tasting cheese. The milk is from a mixed herd of Jersey, Friesian, Simmenthal and the local rare black Kerry breeds. It is unpasteurized and uses a vegetarian rennet.

The difference between Gubbeen and other washed rinds is that the whey is diluted to slow down the growth of bacteria, rather than washing the curd, which would mean draining off some of the whey. The maturing process is also very carefully monitored with humidity and temperature closely observed, and frequent rind washing to avoid any unwanted moulds growing other than *B. linens* cultures. The resulting cheese has a slightly firm texture pitted with crevices, rather like the French Bethmale, with a more wrinkled, crusty rind, and a rather darker beige-pink hue. The taste is definitely more intense and earthy, with herbal flora and grassy notes.

Durrus 🐄 COOMKEEN, DURRUS, CO. CORK

Jeffa Gill makes this washed-rind cheese along Swiss lines. She uses copper vats rather than stainless steel, and a 'harp' (a fork-like tool) with vertical blades to cut through the curd. Vegetarian rennet is then added to the unpasteurized milk from a neighbouring farm. Although Jeffa washes the curd in the same way as Ardrahan, she sprays on the *B.linens* cultures rather than relying on air-borne flora. This may explain why her cheese is a little more subtle and delicate than the more robust Ardrahan. The rind is smoother and the texture more supple and springy, with a taste that is mellow and fruity with a hint of apple. Durrus is delightful when young, but with maturing it livens up to become rather strong. I think a red wine or a Trappist-style beer work well with this cheese.

France

The French, I believe, have a great respect for the identity and diversity of their regions, but all the regions share a common approach to food – that you will eat and drink well, and that what you consume will be local, seasonal and traditional.

This is especially true when it comes to cheese, such as those made with goat's or ewe's milk, which will not be seen all year round, when made by the small artisan cheesemakers who would never dream of freezing or drying milk during periods of greater supply to be used in the 'dry' months. The enjoyment of cheese, particularly very fresh styles, is so much more satisfying at the perfect time of year when the animals are grazing and foraging freely, rather than trying to reproduce the flavours all through the year using stored or dried milk.

France is blessed with a wide range of climates and weather patterns, which greatly influences the types of cheese produced throughout its regions. The north produces chewy, dense-textured cheeses laden with the milk from cattle grazed year-round on lush meadowland. The eastern regions make cheeses ranging from washed creamy types to Alpine hard cheeses, while goat's cheeses are prevalent in the west. As you travel southwards down the Atlantic coast, you find hard crumbly cow's and ewe's milk cheeses as well as blue varieties. In the warmer south there is an array of small goat's and ewe's milk cheeses, and a few cutting cheeses with flavours that vary from spicy and crumbly to creamy and herbal.

Alongside the climate, the landscape and the soil also influence the many hundreds of cheeses produced in France. Limestone is the underlying mineral throughout the country, and whether on the lush northern pastureland, the rocky south west, or the heavy clays of the central region, the soil is conducive to agriculture and in particular to milk production and wine-growing in varying forms.

The hills, valleys, mountains and climate variations account for hundreds and hundreds of cheese varieties throughout the country. This infinite variety of *terroir* – that magical combination of local terrain, altitude, soil and climate – accounts for the great diversity of cheese found in France; some of these cheeses only make their way as far as a local market, while others are shipped all around the world. This is a major industry made possible by a deep-rooted belief in agriculture and a respect for the land and what it offers.

By travelling around France through the regions and tasting some of the cheeses, it is possible to gain a little understanding of the culture, the people and the lie of the land. There are winding back roads leading to hilltop villages, or hidden hamlets to be found by following the rivers and streams rushing beside narrow paths. Market days are at the centre of life, and the produce and cheeses, should one happen to be there on market day, will always be worth a try.

Some French cheeses are only sold locally, and many have their own distinctive characteristics – for instance, some are wrapped in leaves, while others are thickly coated in herbs, or washed in brine and alcohol. The names of many cheeses tie them to and can indicate the village or particular hill or mountain where they are made, and some of these delightful place names are linked to artistic and literary works.

We all look to France as a country with a great wealth of taste when it comes to food, and there are still plenty of tiny, special places to be found where people are working and living off the land in a time-honoured way.

The following chapter gives you a taste of France, taking you through the regions and highlighting local cheeses. Enjoy this journey through a country steeped in rich culinary history and regional influences.

ABOVE **Sheep at Roquefort Carles**

OPPOSITE TOP LEFT Cheeses maturing in south west France

OPPOSITE TOP RIGHT Cows during transhumance in the Pyrénées

OPPOSITE MIDDLE LEFT Sheltering sheep, southern France

OPPOSITE MIDDLE RIGHT Vineyards in the Pyrénées

OPPOSITE BOTTOM LEFT Urns at Bonnaserre Farm, Pyrénées

OPPOSITE BOTTOM RIGHT A small cellar maturing room, west France

Northern France

A glance across the map of northern France reveals a vast and varied landscape of sweeping farmland, orchards and a long expanse of coastline. For centuries this northern region has produced an abundance of seafood, apples (this is Calvados and cider country), and most significantly, dairy products from the lush pastures that abound here. These days, the dairy industry is dominated by mass production, and the small farms that once made their own cheeses to sell at markets, now supply big co-operatives with milk.

The regions of the north produce a wide selection of cheeses in great quantity, which can mean that style and flavour are sometimes sacrificed. This makes it increasingly important to protect the small independent farms and cheesemakers. Cheeses synonymous with this area include Camembert, Livarot and Pont l'Évêque from Normandy (Basse); and Neufchâtel, Brillat-Savarin, Petit-Suisse and Fromage Blanc from Normandy (Haute). Île de France, the region that surrounds Paris, is famous for its Brie de Meaux and Brie de Melun.

Further east, the regions of Picardy and Flandres produce washed-rind, strong-scented, chewy-textured cheeses much like those of their Belgian neighbours, while Mimolette (see page 50), from Lille, is the French version of a Dutch Gouda. The Artois region just below inland Flandres is known for its beer, and the cheeses made there have a peculiar affinity with that drink, probably because they are washed in the stuff! Cheeses produced in the Avesnois/Thiérache area beside Ardennes Forest pick up flavours and styles that are Alsace/German.

The centre of this vast region is Paris – as well as being the capital of France it is also a city with a great food culture. It is a fact that the importance and popularity of Camembert since its inception in the early 18th century was due in no short measure to Normandy's close proximity to the capital.

Munster 🐄 ALSACE

The Alsace region is French, but has Germanic leanings. Munster cheese from Alsace has a more strident taste than those across the border, partly due to French skill at ripening but also in order to distinguish their cheese from German ones. The flavours are nutty and the texture smooth, with summer cow's milk giving a more earthy flavour and the winter milk a more buttery one. The orange-yellow rind is pungent from brine washings, which are brushed over the cheese rather than rubbed in. This gives the texture a little roughness that can dry out if not cared for properly. If your cheese has become dry, rub over a little salty water (boiled and cooled water mixed with a pinch of sea salt) with your fingertips. Wrap in waxed paper and store in the refrigerator. Munster is delightful with dry, fruity white wines or Pilsner-style beers.

Rollot 🐄 PICARDY

This cheese, from unpasturized cow's milk, was originally made in the 17th century by the monks of Maroilles Abbey, close to the river Somme. The cheese became famous when Louis XIV stopped in the village of Orvillers for refreshment, sampled it and gave Rollot his seal of approval. By the 1970s Rollot had all but disappeared due to the popularity of Maroilles (see page 48), but with the influence of hugely respected and knowledgeable cheese expert Philippe Olivier, Didier and Sylvie Potel from Marchelepot decided to make Rollot. Its pungent soft-washed rind and earthy mushroom taste is fast gaining it the reputation and respect it richly deserves. Rollot is matured for about four weeks and it develops quite a distinctive, salty flavour. Enjoy this delicious, semi-soft cheese with a glass of dry white wine.

Maroilles 🐄 THIÉRACHE

The difference between a mass-produced cheese and a farmhouse one is in the flavour. The flavour of Maroilles does need time to develop, but because it also has a high aroma, commercial producers favour a quicker ripening process to get the cheese on the shelves before it becomes too 'aromatic'.

This cheese requires a long, slow ripening and repeated brine washing in cold, damp, airy caves. The cultures in the air of the maturing rooms are alive with good bacteria that help give the cheese its unique taste. The thick square cheese acquires ridged sides from the wire racks they sit on, and takes on a high pungent aroma (it is advised not to take this cheese on public transport), which usually indicates a strong cheese to most people. However, Maroilles has a surprisingly mellow, nutty, earthy taste with a chewy texture and no hint of bitterness.

Eating it on the young side is fine, but a fully aged cheese has quite a different taste, and the robust full-bodied flavour requires either a beer or red wine with fruit and tannins – a Beaune, Châteauneuf-du-Pape or Côte

ABOVE LEFT Maroilles
ABOVE RIGHT Boulette d'Avesnes
LEFT Vieux Boulogne
OPPOSITE Crayeux de Roncq

Rôtie sit well alongside these flavours. A white dessert wine from the Loire, Coteaux du Layon, provides a sweet finish to the strong flavours.

Like many cheeses of the region, Maroilles was first made by monks; in this case by Benedictines who had an abbey in the village of Maroilles from around the 12th century. Village life revolved around the abbey and the community was encouraged to donate milk (and their own cheeses) to the monks for cheesemaking.

Vieux Boulogne  PAS-DE-CALAIS

This is a relatively new Boulonnais cow's milk cheese, created by the cheesemaker Antoine Bernard, with the help of Philippe Olivier whose influence in reviving northern French cheeses is legendary. In early July 1982 at an informal dinner at the Château-Musée in the centre of Boulogne town, Bernard and Philippe presented the cheese as part of the cheese course. The cheese was obviously well received as it was suggested the name be 'Vieux Boulogne' in honour of its place of origin.

Production is limited to three producers at present, and this is purely to keep it within the Boulogne area thereby ensuring its uniqueness. The cattle graze on pastures not far from the coast, so there is evidence of iodine and salty herbaceous notes in the milk. The bright orange rind is washed regularly in a local beer from Saint-Leonard, and ripened for about 7–9 weeks. As the cheese matures, the flavours become more pronounced and earthy, and the rind has an almost wild-mushroom aroma, which some find overly pungent. However, in reality this rich and dense cheese is more buttery and mellow than powerful, and a white dessert wine from the Loire, such as Coteaux du Layon with its honeyed sweetness, seems a perfect accompaniment to cheeses such as this.

Boulette d'Avesnes THIÉRACHE

A soft conical-shaped cow's milk cheese, Boulette d'Avesnes is coated in paprika to give it a reddish-gold colour and distinctive flavour. It is hand-moulded and made with the same curd as Maroilles (see opposite), then enriched with tarragon, parsley, crushed cloves, salt and pepper to give a rather strong, definitive taste. This cheese requires a good beer, or even gin as an accompaniment.

The cheese is also made in the shape of a dolphin, which some say symbolizes the Dauphin in the Court of Louis XIV, although the animal has strong biblical connections too. There is a story that the monks of Maroilles Abbey were banished from their monastery and as they fled taking what they could, some cheeses were dropped in the herb garden. When they returned the cheeses were found nestled in amongst the herbs, and on tasting the cheeses the monks discovered that the herbs had imbued the cheeses with a herby, savoury quality. The monks decided to dedicate the herb-infused cheeses to the Dauphin by making them in the shape of a dolphin.

Crayeux de Roncq HAUT ARTOIS/FERRAIN WEPPES

This is a modern style washed-rind cheese from a small family-run farm not far from Lille. Cheesemakers Thérèse-Marie and Michel Couvreur of Ferme du Vinage devised this cheese with the help of Philippe Olivier, who has made it his mission to revive cheesemaking in this part of France.

The marshy land in this area has many canals and tributaries rather like parts of Belgium and Holland, and there are even windmills dotting the landscape of patchwork fields.

The brick-shaped cheese is made with rich, buttery cow's milk, and could be quite bland, but the *affinage* or ripening process gives this cheese its full flavour. The cheeses are matured for up to eight weeks in cold, damp, airy cellars with frequent washing in a mixture of water, salt and local beer. As the weeks progress, the rind turns orange and the aroma becomes more fruity.

This cheese is delicious when partnered by Chimay, which is a strong beer with a fragrance of fresh yeast. It has a light, flowery touch that accompanies the full flavours of Crayeux de Roncq perfectly.

Crayeux is always a surprise because it sometimes arrives at La Fromagerie with its rind a supple, pale pink with an earthy mushroom taste, and at other times the rind is dark, the texture drier and the flavours deliciously big and powerful.

Mimolette of Flandres

The lush, green fields of Flandres produce this delicious cheese. Mimolette is a cheese with an interesting history, which has had an influence on the development of its flavour.

Mimolette 🐄 FLANDRES

This French version of a classic Dutch cheese grew in popularity when General Charles de Gaulle mentioned that Mimolette was his favourite cheese, a fact that was subsequently quoted in the formal government publication *Journal Officiel* in 1966. Following this statement both the French and the Dutch claimed that it was their version of the cheese he was referring to!

It is an interesting cheese due to the fact that it has a kind of double life – when young its softer texture makes it a perfect breakfast cheese. But the more aged or super-aged versions are often chosen by wine and cheese experts as a good match for fine wines, since its waxy yet crisp texture lends itself to wines with age and dry tannins, and even to dry sherry. Tasting the matured cheese with a wine, giving a mouth-puckering dry edge and an austere taste, quite magically opens up the fruit flavours in the wine.

Mimolette emerged during the reign of Louis XIV, who wanted a French version of the Dutch cheese Edam (this was swiftly counter-swiped by the Dutch who brought out their own version). To make Mimolette distinct from Edam, the French cheesemakers infused carrot juice in the cheese curds turning it orange – probably a snub at the Dutch royal house of Orange – and latterly using annatto natural colouring derived from the soft pulp around the seed of the South American Achiote tree. At the time, Dutch cheeses were very popular with French consumers, which irked the king and prompted a ban on their importation. Its original name was Boule de Nord or Boule de Lille, or Vieux Hollande, and these are sometimes still used in northern France, but Mimolette is the modern name. The name is a reconstruction of the word *mollet*, which means soft or supple in French; the cheese curd is soft when first formed into balls, and only after the maturing process does the crust develop and the cheese within become harder and harder.

However, Mimolette has certain characteristics that set it apart from the Dutch cheese: the size of the cheese is 20 cm (8 in) diameter; and unlike the Dutch version, which is essentially an orange Edam recipe not restricted to a particular region of the country, the French cheese is made to a traditional recipe in the Flandres and Weppes pockets of the region with La Meuse being a particularly good area to find the cheeses. Look for the Maison Losfeld label as its Mimolette is very impressive.

The crust of this cheese is fascinating since microscopic cheese mite are brushed onto the rind to encourage the burrowing of tiny holes that allows the cheese to 'breathe' and develop. As the cheese ages its crust becomes pitted and dry, and needs constant attention, brushing and tapping to get rid of as much of the ever-growing cheese dust as possible. Neglecting the crust means that it becomes very thick and dusty as the mites burrow further into the cheese. Very aged cheese has the appearance of a cannonball, which is the nickname it has been given, and it is this very aged version that is most prized, not only for its flavour but also its ability to complement beer, wine or even Madeira or Port. It is truly a refined-tasting cheese.

BELOW Cows grazing in Flandres
OPPOSITE Mimolette

LEFT Coeur de Neufchâtel
OPPOSITE TOP LEFT Camembert Fermier Durand
OPPOSITE TOP RIGHT Brillat-Savarin
OPPOSITE BOTTOM LEFT Livarot
OPPOSITE BOTTOM RIGHT Pont l'Évêque

Coeur de Neufchâtel NORMANDY

Produced in the shape of a heart or tile, this cow's milk cheese has a rind with a downy, velvety bloom, while the interior is close-textured with a soft crumble and a gentle salty tang. Made to a very old recipe, the curds are slowly drained and a small amount of the previous day's curds are added to the following day's. Coeur de Neufchâtel is best eaten quite young as the fresh mushroom aroma and light nutty flavours can become rather sharp and aggressive if allowed to ripen for too long.

The gentle rolling countryside around Forges-les-Eaux is the best area to find this cheese. In the past, women were the cheesemakers, while men tended the herds. As a gesture of love and devotion, the women made the cheeses in a heart shape, especially when the men went to war; a cheese was carefully wrapped and placed in a parting soldier's breast pocket.

Camembert Fermier Durand NORMANDY

This is a traditional cheese, handmade with unpasteurized cow's milk from the village of Camembert in the territory of Orme. The maker, François Durand with his wife and son, is the last remaining independent producer of Camembert in the village of Camembert, as the other farms that produce this cheese are now part of co-operatives or much bigger productions taking milk from numerous farms in the area. The cheese comes to us at La Fromagerie quite young, but after two weeks maturing in our temperature- and humidity-controlled rooms it acquires a beautiful soft and pliable texture with a surprisingly lighter and nuttier aroma.

Cider and Calvados producers abound in this area of France, and a glass of dry cider is lovely with this cheese, but also a light red Gamay-style wine, or indeed a local blonde beer is equally good. Camembert is sometimes soaked in Calvados and then covered in crumbs, which makes a delicious finale to a meal (see page 231).

Brillat-Savarin NORMANDY

This cow's milk cheese was named by Henri Androuët, a hugely famous *maître fromager*. Brillat-Savarin replaces a cheese called Magnum, which ceased to be made in the early 1970s, by a small family producer Dubuc located near Forges-les-Eaux, a beautiful spot in the heart of Normandy. Brillat-Savarin is made in Normandy as well as the Île de France, using a similar recipe to Magnum of full-fat milk with cream added and *Penicillium candidum*, which gives it a white bloomy rind and a flaky, buttery interior. This cheese is rich and silky eaten fresh, when there is a lactic earthiness to its taste. If allowed to mature, the texture becomes more dense and nuttier in flavour. It is particularly good with a vintage Champagne, but even a blonde beer works well with the creaminess of this cheese.

Livarot NORMANDY

This is a semi-soft cow's milk cheese with an orange washed rind that is gently ridged from the wire racks, and bound with five strips of raffia. The raffia is more decorative than practical, but in the past the cheese was bound in this way to prevent it breaking apart.

It has a springy texture with scattered pinholes, a pungent aroma and a spicy taste. The flavour is achieved by allowing the milk to 'ripen' naturally in large 'baths' for 24 hours before being heated, after which the rennet is added. Curds are large for easy drainage, and once in the mould, the salting and brining process follows before ripening for 3–4 weeks. Livarot comes from the Pays d'Auge area, and this pocket of Normandy also produces Calvados, which marries well with the cheese, although it is particularly good with robust wine from Burgundy.

Pont l'Évêque NORMANDY

Reputedly the oldest Norman cheese still being made, modern versions of Pont l'Évêque are often pale in comparison and tend to be rather bland. The supple-textured cow's milk cheese has a ridged crust with a delicate bloom, which is a pinky-beige. It has a chewy texture that is quite tender, and an almost earthy aroma.

The best-tasting cheeses are those made by smaller dairies. Look for cheeses made by the Ferme du Bours, since it only uses milk from its own herd. Production is kept small and the cheese is totally handmade from start to finish, with the salting adjusted according to the time of year and the creaminess of the milk.

Pont l'Évêque remains a favourite due to the fact that it works well on a cheeseboard and matches both wine and beer, especially the lighter styles.

Abbaye de Trois Vaux 🐄 HAUT ARTOIS

This is a handmade unpasteurized cow's milk cheese
created by the nuns at the Abbey, who work alongside
the Trappist monks at the neighbouring monastery at
Mont des Cats. The history books and tapestries show
that cheesemaking was the main source of income for the
monasteries, which may have been because the religious
orders encouraged the farming community not only
to grow crops, but also to make cheese from the milk
rather than just sell the milk. The Trois Vaux cheese is
one of the 'boutique' cheeses to evolve from the ancient
Mont des Cat recipe – which is a rather interesting way
for a religious community to further its expertise in
self-sufficiency. The dark red-brown rind is washed in
local beer, and the tender, supple texture of the cheese is
not overwhelming or bitter, although a definite 'hoppy'
flavour comes through. The taste is nutty and savoury,
and the cheese is delightful as a light meal or snack, served
with crusty bread.

It is important that the cheeses don't hang around too
long to mature, as the revenue is vital. The monastery
cheeses have a big, almost 'meaty' taste because they are
often washed in brine, spirits, cider or beer to give them a
powerful taste as well as causing them to mature at a faster
pace. As well as the cheeses being sold commercially, they
are also served at the Abbey where they are surely much
appreciated, since the normal meals in religious orders
are very simple and the cheese course is the highlight of
the meal. A wine may be lost against the flavours coming
through from this cheese, and my preference would be for
a full-bodied beer from the locality.

Explorateur 🐄 ÎLE DE FRANCE

This cow's milk cheese is very rich and creamy with a
light, soft fudgy texture and a downy-white bloomy rind.
Explorateur was invented in the 1960s to honour the
explorer Bertrand Flornoy, who was mayor of the town
of Coulommiers and a lover of good cheese. He also

LEFT Abbaye de Trois Vaux
ABOVE Explorateur

helped to create the annual Foire aux Fromages in La Capelle. This is a magnet for cheese-lovers, and there is a competition for ladies with a prize of 30 bottles of Champagne for the one who eats the most Fromage Blanc!

Its earthy, gentle mushroom taste is enhanced by the addition of cream to the milk, which also increases the fat content to 75 percent. It is a good accompaniment to hard fruity-tasting cheeses, and it is also especially good partnered with a chilled glass of Champagne.

Fougeru 🐄 ÎLE DE FRANCE

Although shaped the same as Coulommiers, the Fougeru is thicker, with a texture and flavour that is flaky and rich. The thickness of the cheese and its size mean that it requires careful ripening as the tender bloomy rind can become too soft, with the cheese too runny around the edges closest to the rind, yet too solid to the centre. The unpasteurized cow's milk Fougeru is better in flavour, less pronounced than a Camembert, and at its best with the edges only just melting and the soft texture almost to the centre, which should be just flaky. This is the perfect way to enjoy the cheese. Topped with a frond of bracken or *fougère* (where it gets its name), this is a good cheese as a party centrepiece.

Olivet 🐄 NORTH ORLEANNAIS

These small (half the size of a Camembert) soft creamy cow's milk cheeses with a bloomy white rind, are either plain or have coatings of cinders, hay wisps or black peppercorns. They are simple in taste and style but when served with a Beaujolais, I think they are a lovely lunchtime snack, especially those with a gritty crunch of cinders before one reaches the cheese within. Although made all through the year, it is the spring cheeses that are particularly noteworthy, when the fresh grass gives the flavours a lovely lightness, rather than the more dense and earthy Brie (see pages 56–57) or Coulommiers (see page 57) cheeses.

ABOVE Fougeru
RIGHT Olivet with hay wisps, peppercorns and cinders

Brie de Meaux ÎLE DE FRANCE

Brie is a big wheel of dense curds made from cow's milk, and originally the preferred way was to eat it fresh with only a hint of the bloomy rind appearing; as it became more known and admired the cheesemakers further developed their skills. A little of the *Penicillium candidum* is mixed into the curds before placing the cheese in its mould, and after draining and salting some more is brushed on top. It takes several weeks maturing in varying degrees of cold in high-humidity cellars before the bloom starts to cover the outside of the cheese. These delicate moulds need careful attention, and the humidity levels are adjusted in order to avoid those nasty black spots developing if the rind is too wet. The outside bloomy rind is a vital part of the cheese and if it is too wet it imparts a

bitter taste, and if too dry lends no pleasure to the taste. Some people like to cut away the rind, but as cheese ripens from the outside to the centre, you are effectively taking away all the flavour profile, which is a pity. However, if the rind is not in perfect condition it should be removed.

If you cut through a Brie to create two wheels you can see how the curds have been loosely cut to form fat chunks, which gradually meld with ripening. While Camembert curds are simply scooped out of the pan, ladled into moulds and drained, the Brie curd is drained and then cut before being layered into the moulds. By comparing the two you see the difference in the style of the pate, which also tells in the taste of the two cheeses too. Camembert has a distinct mushroom-earthy flavour with a somewhat mellow cream texture, while Brie has a sharper, almost fruity tang from the fermentation process of the milk (as well as the final draining on the straw (reed) mats before going to the maturing room), which is often mistaken for ammonia on the nose. There is a difference – the light fermented acidic aroma will not make your eyes water unlike a full-on ammonia hit.

Brie de Melun 🐄 ÎLE DE FRANCE

Brie de Melun, alongside Brie de Meaux, obtained Appellation d'Origine Contrôlée (AOC) status in August 1980, and this controls how and where the cheese is made. However, because of the strict rules, the more esoteric cheesemakers in the region have disappeared as they cannot call their cheese 'Brie' unless it is made exactly to the guidelines. This is a little sad, since cheesemakers like to imprint their own quirks and style when making cheese.

The Brie de Melun can often be too salty because of the AOC recipe. At certain times of year, especially at the changeover from winter to spring feed, the milk can create problems for cheesemakers, and the salting has to be controlled. If it isn't controlled, then the result is a Melun with a very soft texture and salty flavour. You have essentially two problems: one being the bloomy rind and the other the curd. The rind should not dry out too quickly, but the cheese being a shallow disc of soft curds will ripen or even dry to a solid mass. I have found that winter cheeses are often more successful than spring cheeses because the feed has more hay and legumes in it. Spring feed has very fresh grass, which produces milk of varying quality and cheese which is difficult to ripen. It is somewhat easier to control with the 3 kg (6½ lb) Meaux, but trying to get that soft velvety texture inside and out in a 1.5 kg (3⅓ lb) Melun is often a problem.

OPPOSITE Brie de Meux
BELOW LEFT Brie de Melun
BELOW RIGHT Coulommiers

I always prefer to eat this cheese slightly immature with the 'heart' of the cheese still flaky unless having tested the cheese first by 'ironing'. I can determine how far to take the ripening process by inserting an elongated metal instrument into the cheese to release a small cylindrical section for tasting before replugging into the cheese. The flavours of Melun are more nutty and assertive than the Meaux, and especially good with a Beaujolais wine.

Coulommiers 🐄 ÎLE DE FRANCE

There is no comparison between a *fermier* Coulommiers handmade with unpasteurized cow's milk and those made by co-operatives and large-scale producers. The soft bloomy rind should cling onto the fat, juicy interior, where the flavour is rich and buttery, yet not quite as fruity as a Meaux or Melun (see opposite). It is a great size for a party as it sits well on a cheeseboard with six or seven other cheeses, or for a dinner party of eight to ten people it could be the single cheese served with thin slices of walnut bread.

A bloomy rind cheese does need a little attention because if it becomes too dry and cracked around the edges, the inside will not be pleasant. Conversely, if the rind is wet with patchy black or brown moulds, this will impact on the cheese. Always check the rind or crust (*croûte*) to make sure it is velvety and the aroma is pleasantly earthy and mushroomy. A slightly acidic ammonia aroma is not bad as it means the cheese is at the height of its ripening, but if it is too strong, then the cheese is past its best.

When you get the cheese home don't be tempted to wrap it in plastic clingfilm; wrap it in double-wax or thick greaseproof paper and then newspaper, and pop into the bottom of the fridge or in the salad drawer. The newspaper is a good way of incubating the cheese and as it is pulped paper, will retain moisture and keep the cheese in good condition.

ABOVE, BACK CHEESE Chaource RIGHT CHEESE Charolais

The tributaries, canals and waterways are an interesting way of journeying through this central area of France, and they are still very much a part of life, whether for transporting livestock, grain or produce. This is a useful and less stressful way of working with animals, and interesting too from a cheesemaking point of view. When cattle are moved from one field to another by canal, and even within the same farmland, there will be variations in the milk and the way the cheeses turn out, as each pasture or meadow has different elements giving the milk its contrasting character.

We are zig-zagging across this terrain following the rivers as one did in the past, because the river system holds the key to how the regions survived and developed, and also how the cheeses evolved. In the Burgundy and Berry regions in the heart of France the soft, creamy-textured cheeses were made to be consumed quickly, and sold within weeks or even days. In Orleannais, for instance, the coatings of ash, hay or leaves were used to protect the delicate creaminess of the cheeses. The region's cheesemakers looked to Camembert as a guide since that was such a popular cheese and developed their own Orleannais versions.

However, once you enter regions such as Franche-Comté and Savoie/Dauphiné, you see the importance of large wheels of hard cheeses so necessary to feed the people throughout the long harsh winters. Cheese was both food and currency in the past, and even now the aged cheeses are savoured not only for their taste, but also for the good return they provide for the hard-working cheesemakers.

France's rich and chequered history is written in the influences found in French cheeses of other countries' cheesemaking styles. There are Swiss and Northern Italian styles in Savoie and Franche-Comté, for instance, and Southern Italian and Spanish styles in the Pyrénées.

Chaource 🐄 CHAMPAGNE

This drum-shaped, solid, cow's milk cheese with a flaky texture and a white bloomy rind is produced very close to the border with Burgundy. Chaource has a bitter nutshell-like flavour, with an earthiness reminiscent of the style of the wine here and you would think that it would be a perfect match for the cheese. However, because the cheese is also on the salty side, great care should be taken to find the perfect flavour partner. The solid shape often means that the cheese does not ripen all the way through, and trying to push this on can make the rind bitter, causing the centre, which is still intact, to become overpowered by these flavours. This is no fault of the cheese since the milk is allowed to ripen at the first stages at its own pace before the rennet is added to separate the curds. When you do have the chance to taste the real thing with a glass of dry, crisp Champagne, it is a wonderful marriage.

Charolais 🐐 BURGUNDY

This goat's milk cheese is a tubby drum-shaped cylinder, with a close-textured crumbly pate. The rind is natural and slightly dry in texture with patchy grey, blue and white moulds, and the taste is rich and sophisticated with a fine clean mineral nuttiness. There is a slight taste of salt and a mildness that develops on the palate. Charolais is quite unlike goat's cheeses of the west coast with their salty, herbal freshness; the beauty of this cheese is that the more ripened and dry crumbly textures are perfect with fine white full-bodied wines, some of the region's red wines such as Santenay, as well as a vintage Champagne. The designated zone for making these cheeses is not littered with cheesemakers, but several sell from their farms. One farm called Earl de Guillaumin in Neury-Granchamp, run by Sylvie and Gilles Aurousseau, concentrates on just the Charolais and maybe one other small cheese.

Fromagerie Gaugry

The Gaugry family have been cheesemakers since 1946. They produce their raw cow's milk cheeses using a fusion of traditional and modern techniques.

Epoisses BURGUNDY

Fromagerie Gaugry is one of two certified larger producers of Epoisses and Ami du Chambertin, and they also make their own version of Soumaintrain and a Petit Creux with its crater-like top in the Langres style. These washed-rind cheeses from the heart of Burgundy are as much a part of the region as the beef breed Charolles, Dijon mustard and the fine wines. This is a soft, tender cow's milk cheese with a brine-and-Marc-washed rind that turns deep apricot with a wrinkled finish.

There are two schools of thought as to how to enjoy this cheese: either ripened all the way through until almost running away; or almost melting with the centre of the cheese still intact. Smaller than a Camembert (see page 52) but not as stout as an Ami du Chambertin cheese (see opposite) this cheese is easier to ripen and the almost

Soumaintrain 🐄 BURGUNDY

A pattern emerges with cheeses from this region
– they tend to be rich and buttery, with a little
mineral acidity coming through in the flavour.
They are also perfect for the fine wines of the
region, and a close partnership like this makes
the learning process of food matching not only
enjoyable but also enduring. Consider why you
like that cheese with that wine, and why it didn't
work with another one.

This cow's milk cheese is the same size as an
Epoisses, but the natural bloom on Soumaintrain
has patches of annatto or rocóu (an orange
vegetable extract from the South American
Achiote tree). This natural extract is used in other
cheeses to add colour both inside and outside, and
its flavour is slightly peppery with a sweet warmth.
Once sprayed on the outside of the cheese, a soft
bloom forms giving the cheese a pretty colour,
and the flavour within is rich, mellow and fruity,
almost like a clotted crème fraîche.

Ami du Chambertin 🐄 BURGUNDY

A distinctive glistening, wrinkled orange rind,
more stout in appearance than Epoisses, this cow's
milk cheese has almost melting edges through
to a fudgy centre. The cheese was perfected by
Raymond Gaugry in 1950, as a more crumbly-textured
cheese in the Epoisses style was deemed to be better for
tasting the fine, rare wines of Burgundy. The aroma is
pungent due to the Marc de Bourgogne spirit wash on the
outside, but inside the cheese is buttery and rich, with a
little saltiness to sharpen the senses. Fine red wines are the
obvious choice of accompaniment. The orange colour is
the result of a happy accident when the Marc spirits meet
the milk enzyme in the high humidity of a cold cellar.

Langres 🐄 CHAMPAGNE

A small drum-shaped, fudgy-textured cheese, purchased
from Fromagerie Gaugry. Langres has a soft, bright
orange natural rind that needs to be kept cool but not
so cold that it hardens. The texture and taste of this
cow's milk cheese is rich and crumbly, with a spiciness
that is more earthy resin than hot. There is a crater-like
depression in the top of the cheese, which can be filled
with a Marc or dry white wine that soaks slowly into the
cheese. An excellent match for Langres is the speciality
of the region – Champagne, with the younger cheeses
beautifully partnering a rosé Champagne, while the more
ripened versions complement the dry style.

juicy, rich flavours are a rare treat. The brine-and-spirit
washing on the rind imparts the characteristic pungent
aroma of this cheese. The milk is hand-ladled and drained
like Camembert and the ripening period in the cellar is
four weeks before selling.

If you are travelling with this cheese, or wish to prevent
the aroma from escaping, the trick is to wrap it first in
waxed paper before then wrapping in a thick layer of
newspaper. This way the cheese aromas are contained
within the 'pulpy' paper.

Epoisses is a perfect cheese on a board of mixed
flavours and styles, and especially good with a dry red
wine such as Savigny le Beaune.

Given the delicate balance between transforming the
milk to cheese, and the numerous washings to produce the
shiny, moist rind, a lot can happen to the milk's bacterial
growth. In the past there were problems with rinds being
almost 'alive' with bacteria, which led to the cheese nearly
being banned completely. However, there is now a very
strong association to which the Gaugry family belongs,
and the rigorous checking and monitoring at every stage
of production ensures that all cheeses are in perfect
condition before sale.

ABOVE LEFT Pouligny-Sainte-Pierre
ABOVE RIGHT Valençay

ABOVE, LEFT CHEESE Sainte-Maure
RIGHT CHEESE Selles sur Cher

Pouligny-Saint-Pierre 🐐 BERRY

Its proximity to the Poitou border with its scrubby heathland and flinty minerality in the water gives the flavour of this cheese a true goaty identity that is enhanced with ripening (the famous Sancerre white wine also comes from this region). A tall tapered pyramid with a small squared-off top (think of the Eiffel Tower), this cheese's natural rind becomes more blue with ageing. Its texture is close and crumbly and a little dry, with a herbal nuttiness to the flavour. Pouligny-Saint-Pierre is perfect served with dry white wines.

Valençay 🐐 BERRY/INDRE

A pyramid with a flat, square top, this cheese is supposedly made this way because an angry Napoleon sliced the top off the cheese in a fit of fury. Valençay follows the flavour profile of the region with its nutty, slightly earthy and acidic taste. The natural rind is dusted with charcoal and white bloom appears as the cheese dries and matures. The texture is slight and fudgy when young, and becomes closer and denser with ripening. Although Valençay is available all through the year, the spring through to the summer cheeses showcase the flavours best. The white and rosé wines of the region are the perfect accompaniments for this delicious cheese.

Selles sur Cher 🐐 LOIRE/CHER

A perfect shape for a cheeseboard, this small cylinder of 8 cm (3¼ in) is coated in charcoal with scatterings of white bloomy moulds. The cheese within is bright white with a fine crumbly texture, and the taste is fresh and lemony. As with all goat's cheeses from this region, they link to each other; some such as Sainte-Maure (see below) have more earthy notes, while others have a salty, nutty flavour. However, the wines of the regions have a true affinity with the cheeses and show just how *terroir* can work in harmony.

Sainte-Maure 🐐 TOURAINE

This famous log-shaped cheese is from a region known for its white wines, and is right next door to Anjou, which is renowned for its rosé. The soil is mineral-rich, with slate and stone containing chalk, sand and lime that contribute to the goat's diet. A straw is placed through the centre of the cheese to aid handling in the first stages when the log is at its most delicate and soft. To avoid too many moulds appearing, charcoal ash is dusted on, and as the cheeses dry out patchy white moulds appear. It is important not to let these get too thick as they can detach themselves from the inner cheese; gentle patting down of the outside moulds achieves a thin rind closely adhering to the cheese. The handmade versions are not as salty as the more industrial cheeses where the charcoal is mixed with salt. The flavours are nutty and rich and perfect for dry white Sauvignon wines.

Crottin de Chavignol 🐐 SANCERRE

This is a small, flattened ball of crumbly-textured goat's cheese with a rich smooth taste. The region has Berry as its neighbour, and provides a nice link for the west of Burgundy to the centre of France — and the white wines of the Loire with their flinty, chalky, stony flavours have a true affinity with goat's cheeses. The landscape of the region is irresistibly romantic, dotted with fairy-tale chateaux as ornate as wedding cakes. However, looking at a matured Crottin, whose appearance is more like goat's droppings, suggests something less romantic, save for the lovely nutty flavours once tasted. Crumbly with a tart lemon acidity and nutty edge, this very versatile cheese is often grilled for a salad.

BELOW, LEFT TO RIGHT Fresh Crottin de Chavignol, Medium Matured, Matured

Poitou-Charentes

The Vendée waterways thread through this region and became famous for goat's cheese through the Saracen invasion of the south west and west France. In the Middle Ages armies came equipped with everything from soldiers to cattle and livestock to literally take over countries and implant themselves lock, stock and barrel. When the Saracen army was in retreat they simply left everything behind as they fled, and the result was that their goats found a new home, and thrived on the herbal well-watered pastures of Poitou-Charentes. There are many shapes and styles of cheese in this region, taking names from the villages or even the shape of the castle turrets, but with the ideal temperate weather patterns, the goats can keep producing delicious fresh-tasting milk for cheese throughout the year.

ABOVE LEFT Goats in Poitou ABOVE RIGHT A Charentes village

Fleur de Chèvre 🐐 POITOU

The producers make the most of their cheeses by giving us different shapes and textures to enjoy the flavours. This soft drum-shaped cheese with its tender natural rind is wrapped with a chestnut leaf to ease the handling process. It is salted with the delicate fine grains of Fleur de Sel from the famous salt-pans on the Île de Re, giving the taste a gentleness quite unlike the usual goat's cheeses.

Cendré de Niort 🐐 POITOU

A small, round ash-coated rind with a contrasting white goat's cheese within, it is flaky textured, tasting fresh and herby with a hint of salt.

Mothais 🐐 POITOU

A thick disc with a natural wrinkled rind and a chestnut leaf to help with handling. The flavours of this cheese are nutty and earthy, and with ripening become denser as the blue and white moulds grow on the outside. The more mature cheeses are good with red wines.

Bonde de Gâtine 🐐 POITOU

This goat's cheese takes the shape of a small tubby drum coated in charcoal. The natural rind with scatterings of white mould and charcoal are classic features of cheeses in this region. This cheese with its close, crumbly texture but surprisingly smooth dense bite has a light fruity tang and a depth of mineral richness to accompany fine wines.

Chabichou 🐐 POITOU

This natural-rinded semi-soft, yet quite close-textured cheese has a gently tapered cylinder shape. Chabichou is possibly the most well known of the goat's cheeses, due to its fresh taste and lovely aromatic rind. When allowed to ripen under proper conditions the earthy sweetness goes all the way to the heart of the cheese — the crumbly texture becoming denser as it is allowed to dry out.

TOP LEFT Fleur de Chèvre
TOP MIDDLE Cendré de Niort
TOP RIGHT Mothais
BOTTOM LEFT Bonde de Gâtine
BOTTOM RIGHT Chabichou

Persillé du Marais 🐐 VENDÉE AND POITOU

The Marais canals meander through the region to the Atlantic coast, and parts are extremely picturesque. You can see cattle being transported on barges from one meadow to another, and goats, more temperamental and adventurous than sheep or cows, have to be fenced in otherwise they fall into the water as they forage for food by the riverbank. This cheese is an intensely tasting blue cheese, with that bittersweet accent often found in very dark chocolate. A perfect complement to the sharp white wines of the region, but also the sweeter versions too.

ABOVE Persillé du Marais
BELOW Tomme de Cléon

Tomme de Cléon 🐄 PAYS NANTAIS, PAYS DE LA LOIRE

This is a semi-hard cheese with its smooth hard rind washed in Muscadet wine to give an aromatic, floral perfume to the cheese, as well as permeating the pate. The smooth, white-textured pate tastes full and fruity and is perfect as a dessert cheese, especially after seafood.

AUVERGNE

The Massif plateau stretches across this region, with minerals of iron, bronze, silver and gold beneath the surface – the dairy farming enjoys an excellent reputation here as does the famous beef produced in the region. Burgundy has Charolais beef and Auvergne has Salers. The cheeses are grand, majestic and full of flavour – from the Cantal Laguiole to the garlic- and pepper-infused soft Gaperon. This region has a true identity, and with the Bordeaux and south west wines you have huge flavours that are meaty and robust.

ABOVE The grazing pastures in the Auvergne

Sainte-Nectaire 🐄 AUVERGNE

This cheese has a coat of many colours. On first sight it looks like a flattened boulder covered with moulds of grey, brown, patches of white and even a little blue or green shadow. The touch is soft and velvety. The aroma is like a damp cellar, with earthy farmyard underfoot, and within is a rich, dense texture and a nutty mineral taste. It is curious, but also delicious especially in spring and autumn, which are the best seasons to eat this cheese. Always look for a farmhouse version of this cheese, which you can identify by rubbing the crust to reveal an oval dark-green plaque providing the taste sensation, whereas the industrial versions will be more bland.

Gaperon á l'ail 🐄 AUVERGNE

If you place this cow's cheese in the palm of your hand, cup your fingers around the cheese and very gently squeeze, the texture should be supple, tender and not solid. That is how a farmhouse handmade cheese should be. The cheese is made with partly skimmed milk with the addition of smoky garlic and pepper. The bloomy white moulds should be patted down gently and not allowed to get too thick, since they may peel away from the main body of the cheese and allow off-flavours to develop in air pockets. A younger cheese has a 'Boursin' style, while the ripened versions are closer-textured and fruitier.

Tomme Fraîche 🐄 AUVERGNE/AUBRAC

This cheese can usually be found in 300 g (10½ oz) vacuum packed blocks, or cut from 1 kg (2 lb 4 oz) slabs. It is made with the freshly washed and pressed curds that go to make Cantal Laguiole (see page 70). The supple almost rubbery texture with no rind and light flavour is the vital ingredient for the famous regional recipes of Truffade (sautee'd potatoes and lardons with cheese, see page 278) and Aligot (a 'stretched' mashed potato, see page 284).

BELOW, LEFT CHEESE Sainte-Nectaire MIDDLE CHEESE Gaperon á l'ail RIGHT CHEESE Tomme Fraîche

ABOVE, LEFT CHEESE Fourme d'Ambert TOP CHEESE Bleu d'Auvergne
BOTTOM CHEESE Bleu des Causses

Fourme d'Ambert 🐄 AUVERGNE

This cheese is capsule-shaped and often referred to as the
'connoisseur's blue cheese' as the flavours work well with
other cheeses and it isn't an aggressive-tasting blue.

The crust is a thin dry rind patched grey/white, and
if it does get a little wet the flavours will become sharper.
The overall texture is rich and buttery with a mellow, nutty
subtle flavour. A great addition to a cheeseboard and a
lovely accompaniment for fine dry red wines.

Bleu d'Auvergne 🐄 AUVERGNE

This creamy, rich blue cheese takes its style from
Roquefort, but the heavier texture from the cow's milk
gives it a more fatty element, which is great for cooking.
It is often seen as a good addition to the cheeseboard as
there is strength but not bitterness. If partnered with the
Cheddar-style hard cheeses or even the Gruyère styles
it doesn't overpower, but rather adds a minerality to cut
through the heavier weightiness of the cheeses.

Bleu des Causses 🐄 AVEYRON/AUVERGNE

The defined area for production of this cheese is covered
by Aveyron and some of Lozère south of Lot. Look for
the label Peyrelade as it is from the village of that name,
which nestles in a valley surrounded by the limestone cliffs
of the Gorge du Tarn. The cheese is ripened in humid
caves where *fleurines*, natural currents of air, filter into
the atmosphere through the minerals via cracks in the
limestone. This process further contributes to the flavours
of the cheese. The milk from Laguiole cows is heated,
renneted, cut into large cubes and stirred before draining,
and the *Penicillium roquefortii* added. The curds are placed
into moulds and stacked in the draining room for 3–4
days with several turnings before being rubbed with dry
salt and left for another three days. Before entering the
caves, the cheeses are scrubbed of their thick salt coat and
pierced to encourage the oxygen to thread the blue veins
through the cheese. The ripening process takes place in
the caves on oak shelves with regular turnings, for 3–6
months. Prior to sale the cheeses weighing between
2.5–3 kg (5½–6½ lb) are wrapped in foil and marked
with the AOC standard.

If you are presented with a cut cheese, look for an
ivory-coloured pate (although more white in winter),
with well-distributed blue moulds rather like those of
Roquefort. The texture is soft and almost melting on the
palate with flavours that are rich but not assertive, creamy
and without too much saltiness, which is often the case
with some Roquefort. Cheeses from this part of France are
beautifully structured and work well on a cheeseboard.

THE DAUPHINÉ & CÉVENNES

The Dauphiné, of which the Rhône-Alpes and Drôme are part, is the southern area of this large region. Here the wines are spicier and their dry heat complements the cheeses – mostly goat, with some soft cow's milk. In the markets you will also see some ewe's milk and blue cheeses. The famous little Picodon of the region can be eaten fresh, or left to dry out to taste very gamey. They are available all through the year, but it is with the early summer cheeses, when the goats forage on scented leaves, bushy herbs and flora, that you get a real sense of this part of France. Try to get to the annual Fête du Picodon held in late July at Saou, between Crest and Bordeaux, to taste cheeses from all the local farms as well as quaffing the deliciously strong and fruity local wines such as Tricastin.

Saint Marcellin and Saint Félicien
DAUPHINÉ/ISÈRE

Nowadays it is very rare to find the goat's cheese versions of these cheeses, and more's the pity, since they are little mouthfuls of pure luxury. But goat's milk in this part of France is very seasonal, and in order to make a living cheesemakers are producing the cheeses with cow's milk. However, if you get one that is properly ripened and almost melting as you break through the rind, its richness will reward you, especially with a lovely Côtes du Rhône wine. It is important with both of these cheeses to allow the moulds to grow as they form a little protective barrier to the cheese, as air-borne bacteria can infiltrate these tender cheeses. The flavour of Saint Marcellin is rich, with a little nuttiness, and the larger Saint Félicien has a slight blackcurrant earthiness to the flavours. When soft and yielding they are delicious, but at certain times of the year when weather conditions alter the flavour of the milk, it is sometimes harder to ripen and they are firmer.

Picodon DRÔME

The name Picodon is derived from Occitan meaning 'small bite'. The Drôme region suffered a severe decline in farming over the years; however, the dairy co-operative has encouraged small producers to work again, and today there is a good supply of these delightful cheeses. The subtle nutty flavours become more intense with further ripening, and you can enjoy the cheeses with the white natural bloom, or at the more robust stage, called *dieulefit*. With further washing and refining in high humidity the rind turns a more golden-beige and the texture is drier and fruiter, partnering the southern Rhône wines perfectly. The best season to enjoy these cheeses is high summer.

Pelardon CÉVENNES

This small, thick medallion-shaped soft cheese with natural scraped (slightly rough) white crust is much better after a little maturing when its rind is dotted with blue moulds. Pelardon is a traditional farmhouse cheese with a gentle goaty, nutty taste and fudgy texture in the centre. The best season to enjoy this cheese is late summer, with really rich and buttery cheeses appearing in the early autumn. It partners perfectly with a light and gentle white wine.

BELOW, FRONT LEFT CHEESE Saint Marcellin
FRONT RIGHT CHEESE Pelardon BACK LEFT CHEESE Saint
Félicien BACK RIGHT CHEESE Picodon

Cheeses of the Aubrac

These semi-hard cheeses are produced on the plateau of Aubrac, an area with mineral-rich pastures and volcanic soil, environmental features that impart flavour to the cheeses.

Salers d'Estive & Cantal Laguiole ✍ AUBRAC

What makes Salers d'Estive and Cantal Laguiole cheeses special is not only the cow's milk from Laguiole and Salers breeds, but also the terrain – the plateau of Aubrac. The breed of cow for the Laguiole is the ancient Laguiole-Aubrac, a small, sturdy cow with a pale golden/fawn coat and long upwardly curved horns. This old-established breed may not give huge quantities of milk but the quality is ideal for cheese, and being native to the region they naturally thrive on the wild flora and rich pastures.

The Salers cow is another ancient breed whose rich, luscious milk is used both for the cheese of the same name and the simplified Cantal.

The climate of the grazing areas on the high, vast, rough pastureland is hot and stormy in summer and cold with biting winds and snow in winter. The grass is never cut at the higher altitudes as it is reserved for the transhumance (summer grazing) between May and the end of October. Volcanic soils, with underlying granite are rich in phosphates, potassium and magnesium and a profusion of flora contribute to the flavours in the cheeses; remember this when choosing wines to accompany the cheeses as the southern Rhône wines have a particular affinity. The cheeses made on the high pastures during the summer months are labelled Salers, and the cheeses made during the rest of the year in the lower valleys are marked Cantal. However, Cantal is a very popular family-style cheese and made in both large commercial dairies and also smaller, artisan ones too. It is easy to dismiss Cantal as a basic cheese, but if you find a true artisan-made version that has been well matured, it is delicious. It has a smooth texture and a fruity, nutty taste that is not too aggressive. Salers has a firmer texture and an edge to the flavour when the cheese has been aged.

ABOVE LEFT AND RIGHT Grazing cows on the plateau of Aubrac **OPPOSITE, LEFT CHEESE** Salers d'Estive **RIGHT CHEESE** Cantal Laguiole

South & South West France

This massive region, encompassing Provence, the Languedoc (east to west), and the Pyrénées, has the beauty and heat of the Mediterranean, and the mountains and valleys towards the Spanish border and the Atlantic Ocean.

In Provence we find many different styles of goat's cheese, because goats can easily find food, and can withstand the heat of the summer. Some cheeses are wrapped in leaves to preserve their rinds, and others dry out to spicy-flavoured morsels.

We know the Côte d'Azur as a summer playground, but driving inland there is a stark simplicity to the land broken up with brilliant colours of lavender and sunflowers against the sky. It is heavenly but also harsh, and given the spicy, dry and fruity wines of the region, the cheeses are a perfect match.

Travelling to the western Languedoc, we skirt the southern parts of Aquitaine and Gascony, venturing to Béarn and Pyrénées Atlantiques, and get a completely different view of

France. Here you can sense the Spanish influences, not only in the people, but also in the cheeses.

In some areas you can see the cheese caves etched into the mountainside, where the farmers would bring their cheeses to be stored and ripened. In the summer months the farmers and their cattle travel from the lower valleys, which become extremely hot, to the higher lush mountain pastures to graze. This ancient tradition, known as transhumance, has been practised in mountain regions all over Europe in the summer months. The lead cows wear heavy bells around their necks and dogs make sure there are no strays. It is wonderful to see traditions still in place and the ways of the land respected.

The wines of this part of France are probably the best accompaniment to enjoy with the cheeses, and the gastronomy of this region is so rich and varied you will never be bored. We taste strong, spicy and earthy flavours that have links with British cheese styles such as Gloucester and Cheshire from the time of Henry II's marriage to Eleanor of Aquitaine. The wines of the south west include Madiran and Irouléguy, both bold enough to match the hard ewe's milk cheeses, and also the fine charcuterie, roast chicken and duck rillettes.

Banon Feuille ✄ PROVENCE

This plump goat's cheese is dipped in eau de vie and sprinkled lightly with pepper before being wrapped in chestnut leaves and tied with raffia string. The flavour becomes more pronounced and stronger with age, and the natural rind more golden with patches of blue.

Monsieur Ripert collects nearly all the 1,500 litres (330 gallons) of milk himself for making Banon cheeses. His farm is not far from the small town of Banon, announced with a sign stating: 'Fromage de Chèvre'. Banon Feuille was originally made with ewe's milk, but as the cheese became popular it was clear the milk supply could not cope, so cow's milk was used for many years and sold to tourists. However, the goat's milk cheeses are the most sought-after, and since the 1960s, according to M. Ripert, small farms and 'Chèvriers' have gradually increased in the area, and the tradition continues.

The cheesemakers have to endure the long hot summers with the Mistral winds blowing through the region, drying out the little medallion cheeses much quicker than at other times of the year. As the cheeses dry out, wrapping them in chestnut leaves provides an effective and natural form of protection, without interferring with the ripening process. They are ready to sell in 3–4 weeks and the flavours are bosky and herbal with a sharp acidity of the goat's milk. I have these cheeses for a couple of months during the summer at my shop; just opening this cheese reminds me of Provence.

OPPOSITE Banon Feuille
RIGHT Buchette de Banon

Buchette de Banon ✄ PROVENCE

This small, log-shaped goat's cheese is stacked on a flat wooden base, like cigarillos in a packet. Its natural thin wrinkled rind is topped with a sprig of fresh *sarriette* (summer savoury), and the taste is creamy and slightly flaky with a light fruity tang. The best time to eat these little cheeses is between mid-spring and early autumn.

LEFT, FROM TOP CHEESE Le Gabiétout, Napoleon Montréjeau, Bethmale cow's milk, Bethmale goat's milk, Haut Barry

ABOVE, LEFT CHEESE Zelu Koloria RIGHT CHEESE Val de Loubières FRONT CHEESE Anneau du Vic Bilh

Bethmale ARIÈGE

This rustic farmhouse cow's milk cheese has earthy mushroom aromas that have a farmyard resonance. The supple texture to the crust is washed, giving it a rosy glow, and the pate is semi-hard with tiny pinholes. The taste is unique with a zingy tingle on the tongue, yet mellow and nutty as an overall sensation. These cheeses are rarely seen outside their immediate region, but with the wines of the Pays d'Oc are a perfect example of identifying a place.

Bethmale ARIÈGE

This is the goat's milk version of Bethmale. A rubbed, brushed and lightly washed rind houses a chewy-textured cheese pitted with tiny pinholes. It has lovely earthy, floral flavours with nutty rustic additions to the taste. This seasonal cheese starts from early summer to autumn. It is perfect when partnered with a red wine with body, fruit and well-defined tannins.

Haut Barry LARZAC

This is a raw ewe's milk cheese with a lovely natural crust that has been brushed allowing the natural moulds to evolve on the rind. The texture is semi-hard with tiny eyelet holes through the cheese, and the taste has a gently earthy sweetness redolent of the milk with a fresh hazelnut bite. It makes a delicious end-of-meal cheese.

Le Gabiétout PYRÉNÉES

This supple-textured mixed cow's and ewe's milk cheese has a fruity, nutty bite and a smooth chewy texture. The rind is lightly brine-washed and rubbed to give a pale ochre glow, and the aroma is gentle and earthy. It is best eaten when quite young, although matured cheeses have a more strident taste.

Napoleon Montréjeau HAUTES-PYRÉNÉES

The name is derived from the mountain facing the farm, and is called 'Le Nez de Napoleon' as the top of the mountain bears an uncanny resemblance to Napoleon's profile. Only a small amount of this ewe's cheese is made and matured by Dominique Bouchait, who gives it a certain style that is quite unique – in the Ossau style (see opposite) but with a softer texture and a nutty tang.

Zelu Koloria 🐑 PAYS BASQUE

An unusual ewe's milk cheese from the mountain region of Pays Basque, it is semi-hard with blue veins through the dense, mellow-flavoured pate. The natural brushed crust is quite dry when young, but as the cheese ages it becomes a little moist thereby giving it an extra tangy richness. It is a rare treat as blue cheeses are not normally made in this area. The spring cheeses have a lightness in taste and texture, and as the season progresses, the flavours become more intense and the texture heavier. The season ends in the autumn, although a few cheeses do appear after the autumn, which are fully matured and rather too strong.

Val de Loubières 🐐 ARIÈGE

With a washed and brushed crust encircled by a bark collar from local pine trees, this is a rich handmade creamy goat's cheese with a sweetly sappy taste rather like a Vacherin du Mont d'Or (see page 90). It has a very limited production, but is well worth waiting for as its flavours are quite unique.

Anneau du Vic Bilh 🐐 PYRÉNÉES

This is rather like the Rouelle (see page 78) in shape but much more tender and prone to almost collapsing with softness. However, the flavours of the goat's milk are so sweet and fragrant, with an earthy nuttiness, it is impossible not to just scoop it up with a piece of bread. It is a very seasonal cheese as it is made high up in the hills and really only comes to market to be enjoyed in the late spring and summer months.

Tomme d'Aydius 🐐 BÉARN

This is a relatively new cheese from the Vallée d'Aspe close to the snowline of the Béarn Mountains. A wild and rocky terrain allows the goats to graze freely. The resulting cheese is smooth and semi-hard with a lovely, pale rosy hue to the brine-rubbed crust. The taste is sweetly earthy and nutty with delicious tones of wild flowers and herbs. The main cheesemaking period is between early spring to late autumn, although the cheese is available throughout the year at varying stages of maturity.

Tomme de Cabrioulet 🐐 ARIÈGE

The washed pinky-peach downy crust of this goat's cheese is simply beautiful. The cheese is semi-soft and gently billows making it look very attractive. The pate is white with small eyelets and tastes fresh, almost like a rich Fromage Blanc with a gentle creamy nuttiness. It is mostly sold locally, although a few cheeses do venture to larger towns and cities but are extremely expensive.

Ossau 🐑 PYRÉNÉES

A handmade mountain ewe's milk cheese made by small isolated communities high up in the hills, it is a semi-hard cheese with a brine-rubbed crust. A firm yet supple cheese, in that the hard crust holds within a cheese that crumbles and breaks down on impact, and with a complexity of tastes that tingle on the tongue. With a little age the pate becomes flakier and the taste more pronounced and nutty. The cheesemaking process is somewhat similar to that of Cheshire.

BELOW LEFT, RIGHT CHEESE Tomme de Cabrioulet **LEFT CHEESE** Tomme d'Aydius   **BELOW** Ossau

Roquefort

This is a land where neither vineyard nor corn will grow, but thankfully the 'king of blue cheeses' soaks up the limestone minerals from the Cambalou maturing caves to enhance its unique flavours.

BELOW, TOP CHEESE Roquefort Carles BOTTOM CHEESE Papillon

Roquefort Carles 🐑 ROUERGUE

Jacques Carles, who joined his father's small cheese business in 1958, now runs it with his daughter. He stores thousands of wheels of cheese in damp four-level cellars cut out of the Cambalou rockface. The freshly made cheeses sit on heavy oak planks of wood, which get saturated with the water seeping out of the rocks. The oak planks are ideal for holding the cheeses and also imparting their woody aromas and flavours into the cheeses. Intense, powerful flavours and gritty texture make this a truly individual cheese.

There are numerous stories surrounding the conception of Roquefort, one being that a shepherd, sheltering from the midday sun in the entrance to one of the Cambalou caves in Roquefort, saw a lovely young girl and hurriedly put down his soft cheese sandwich to pursue her. His passion obliterated everything else that afternoon, and it was a while before he came back to the same shelter; there hidden in a crevice were the remains of his lunch! The bread had turned grey and mouldy and the soft cheese had developed a speckled blue, with a strong mineral odour. Nevertheless, he decided to taste it and was amazed at how delicious the cheese and blue mould combination tasted. And so Roquefort was born when dried and mouldy bread was used as a base for introducing bacteria into a white cheese.

Of course, the mineral-rich cool, damp Cambalou caves also contribute to the unique flavours and textures of this cheese. Jacques Carles or his daughter Delphine can arrange a special visit in the caves and then to the production site in the village of Martrin, 50 km (31 miles) from Roquefort. Largely a wholesaler, he does not offer commercial tours, but he will explain (in French) to visitors how he makes his own *penicillin* mould from a secret recipe based on sourdough bread. He then burrows with a 'cheese iron' (an implement used to test the ripeness of cheese) deep into a round of cheese to determine the progress of the blue mould from the edge to the centre, which should be evenly distributed to indicate its perfect state. In my view (and also the view of others more expert than me) his cheese is regarded as the finest Roquefort in Roquefort.

Papillon 🐑 ROUERGUE

M. Albert Alric created the Papillon (butterfly) brand in 1906, and set high standards by working closely with the farms supplying the milk. He wouldn't allow the sheep to be fed industrial fodder as supplements, only cereals such as hay and legumes, grown organically and only in very small quantities in relation to fresh grass. Although up-to-the-minute machinery is used to milk the sheep, there is still no newer way of introducing the spores to the cheeses than M. Alric's invention of a machine that brushed the mould into the curd at a rate of 4 grams to the kilo (about 100,000 million spores!). What gives Papillon its particular style is the softer, more open blue moulds, and a really rich buttery texture to the white paste. The Papillon brand is now big business, but I am sure that M. Alric is looking down from above making sure the ivory pate is richly unctuous and suitably 'sheepy'-tasting alongside the dusty blue moulds – just as he likes it! The perfect wine to serve with this cheese is a Sauternes; in particular look out for the names Yquem, Raymond-Lafon and Rieussec, which are probably the best dessert wines in the world. The noble rot (a milky white film that covers the grapes) assists in the sweetly savoury taste of the wine. Serve it with freshly cracked walnuts and the Papillon cheese.

Brique du Larzac 🐑 TARN

This is a rectangular, shallow pavé (brick-shape) ewe's milk cheese with a natural rind and a soft creamy, smooth texture. The younger cheeses have a light tangy taste that is rich and sweet, and with age they develop to become drier in texture and the flavours become fuller with a more earthy taste.

Lou Bren 🐑 AVEYRON

This ewe's milk cheese has a natural washed golden-brown crust, and a flaky almost melting texture within. The taste of Lou Bren is fruity and rich with delicious earthy aromas and a sharp burnt caramel aftertaste.

The cheese is produced in very small quantities by artisan cheesemakers using very traditional methods, hence its rather rustic appearance and limited availability. Lou Bren is delicious when partnered with a fruity red wine like a Vin de Pays.

Rove des Garrigues 🐐 LOT, MIDI-PYRÉNÉES

This is a beautiful, arid area with scrubby grasslands of wild thyme and gorse, and dense woodland of chestnut trees. The goats roam free and eat herbs and chestnuts, which give the milk its definitive herbal bosky flavours.

The early spring cheeses are fresh and tangy and as the season progresses the flavours become more full. They are best eaten between early spring and early autumn. Try a gentle white wine in a simple style with this cheese.

Pérail 🐑 LANGUEDOC

This cheese is a fresh shallow, creamy disc with a natural thin rind and rich melting pate. The flavour of the cheese is pronounced and delicious with the familiar sweet earthiness of fresh ewe's milk.

A light white wine with a zesty structure is perfect with this cheese.

Lingot Saint Nicolas de la Monastère 🐐 LA DALMERIE, HÉRAULT

An ingot of pure goat's milk with a flaky, fudgy texture and a wrinkled rind. The goats graze on meadows studded with thyme and this is clearly evident in the taste of the cheese, which is light, gently earthy with the richness of the milk and a herbal essence at the end. A perfect handmade cheese from the monastery at La Dalmerie under the supervision of Father Marcel, in the heart of Hérault. The season runs from spring to autumn.

Rouelle 🐐 TARN

A fragile cheese when fresh and young, with a creamy floral tang becoming richer with ripening. In the shape of a wheel, the top of the goat's cheese is lightly dusted with charcoal or left plain white. The best time to eat it is March to October.

Cabécou du Rocamadour 🐐 LOT

A small medallion-sized cheese with a thin natural rind, this goat's cheese makes a velvety, melting mouthful with a rich full taste. A perfect pre-meal appetizer, it suits a red wine with some spice to its dry flavours. Available all through the year but the best season is late summer and autumn to capture the nutty earthiness.

LEFT, TOP LEFT CHEESE Pérail, TOP RIGHT CHEESE Brique du Larzac, BOTTOM LEFT CHEESES Rove des Garrigues, BOTTOM RIGHT CHEESE Lou Bren

ABOVE TOP LEFT Lingot Saint Nicolas TOP RIGHT Rouelle BOTTOM LEFT Louvie BOTTOM RIGHT Cathare ABOVE RIGHT Cabécou du Rocamadour

Cathare 🐐 LAUREGAIS, CARCASSONNE

This cheese is approximately the size of a coffee saucer, with an ash-coated top emblazoned with the cross of the Cathars (a medieval religious group living in and around Carcassonne that was persecuted in the Middle Ages). The taste is mild and gently nutty, and should be enjoyed fresh and creamy rather than allowed to over-ripen when its flavours become too 'goaty'. This cheese is delicious partnered with a light and gentle white wine – try serving it with a white from the Manseng grape in the south-west of France.

Louvie 🐐 PYRÉNÉES

A natural thin rind with bloomy patched moulds gives this cheese a crumbly fruity, nutty taste with the edges just melting. The richness of goat's milk is evident but not overwhelming. These tubby drum-shaped cylinders of flaky textured goat's cheese are available during summer and into autumn. This area was famous for mining iron-ore, as well as being known for white marble, and the mineral flavours in the cheese give a quite unique imprint on the taste buds, quite unlike those of the Loire, Provence or the Ardèche.

Bouton d'Oc 🐐 TARN

These are tiny little pyramid 'cocktail' cheeses with a stick at the top for ease of handling. The fresh curds are simply drained and dropped into their moulds, and the thin natural rind forms to hug the cheese perfectly.

This is an ideal aperitif cheese, as it has a smooth yet firm texture and a thin natural rind. If allowed to mature and dry a little further the flavours become nutty and slightly tart. This cheese works very well when served with crisp, dry white wines or even Champagne.

Pechegos 🐐 TARN

The farm is situated in the fine grazing areas of Le Causse, where goats forage in a natural meadow habitat. The cheeses have a lovely lightness, with sweet hints of flowers and herbs coming through the nutty sharpness.

There is a band of spruce encircling the cheese to keep the soft, almost melting texture intact. The rind is brine-washed to give an extra depth of flavour and aroma to the cheese, which is seasonal — late spring is a good time to taste it.

Serve Pechegos with an aromatic dry white wine, with a citrus zest and grassy aromas to really bring out the flavours of the cheese.

ABOVE TOP Bouton d'Oc
ABOVE Brin d'Amour
RIGHT Tomme Corse
OPPOSITE Pechegos

CORSICA

This island has been overrun by several Mediterranean cultures, including France, and these multiple influences are evident in Corsican cooking and food production. The Orezza mineral waters from Rapaggio, south of Bastia on the east coast are prized for their medicinal properties. In fact this east coast is where some of the best cheeses appear, and the flavours reflect the minerality and the *maquis* – the shrubby bushland of bay, thyme, rosemary and savoury where the animals graze. In early spring, Brocciu, a light and airy ewe's milk ricotta, requires only a dribbling of dark honey for dessert. Explore the island's narrow mountain roads and be rewarded at the end of the day with platters of roasted wild boar and charcuterie, chunks of chewy bread and cheese washed down with local crisp white.

Brin d'Amour 🐑 CORSICA

This is a relatively new ewe's milk cheese, reflecting the maquis with its thick coating of herbs. The cheese is simple, almost like a young Pecorino, soft, flaky and pale in colour. The herbs are augmented with chilli and black peppercorns, and if you allow the ripening process to include a few bloomy moulds while the cheese dries out a little, the flavour is sweeter, earthier and bosky. Produced in all the more mountainous areas, the best season to eat this cheese is early spring until summer when the pastures are not too parched.

Tomme Corse 🐑 CORSICA

From the area called Orientale, this cheese is not dissimilar to a Sardinian Pecorino, or a Pyrénées Ossau. The best time to eat these cheeses is winter through to late spring when the pastureland is studded with flowers and herbs from the early winter rain. The cheeses are matured for three months minimum but are often ripened longer to produce semi-hard medium strength to full-bodied cheeses good for grating. The flavours are rather robust and tangy, and the real artisan-made cheeses partner strong Madiran or a local robust red wine.

Alpine

Alpine meadows and pastures are alive with the sound of cow bells. This reassuring ringing means that a long-standing tradition is alive and will continue for the foreseeable future. Summer is a perfect time to explore these vast regions of mountain pasture with their superb grazing conditions and hiking trails.

It is fitting to begin our odyssey in Franche-Comté, since the Jura Massif straddles this region from the edge of Alsace, down to the Rhône-Alpes via Savoie, through to Switzerland and into Bavaria in Germany. This amazing range of mountains, the national parks and the passes are a magnet for skiers in the winter months, but only when the land returns to the farmer do we see how they are linked by agriculture.

The Italian Alpine regions start as soon as one crosses from Grenoble in France to the magnificent Gran Paradiso National Park within Piedmont and Aosta. It threads across Lombardy, to Stelvio – Italy's largest national park – which stretches into Trentino-Alto Adige/Südtirol, which in turn borders Switzerland, southern Germany and Austria.

There is a common thread in the cheesemaking too, using copper vats, and producing the large Gruyère-style cheeses, but there are also very individual cheeses from the tiny isolated communities, which you have to reach by foot rather than by car. The lower slopes and Alp hillsides are often family-owned, or in some cases in Switzerland,

owned by bank trusts and rented out to farmers and cheesemakers. This ensures the protection of the areas and continued usage by farmers as in the past.

The bucolic picture of happy cows grazing on flower-studded Alpine pastures is alluring, but in reality, especially in times past, the work was harsh and unforgiving in the colder, bleak months. Farmers barely made a living, and idled away lonely cold nights or summer evenings by carving objects to sell at local markets or to tourists and hikers. In the early 18th century, this was a serious hobby and the fine pieces of carvings and intricate shavings of tiny flowers and animals were greatly admired.

Ironically this whittling led to watchmaking and a new 'industry' developed using the abundance of readily available minerals and quartz crystals in the vicinity. This meant that many young members of farming families would go to work in watch businesses, thereby putting even more strain on the agricultural businesses. However, local government officials finally saw sense and with the new-found wealth helped farmers regain strength, and with tourism becoming a booming business, the dairies were able to grow and develop their cheese production.

BELOW The Pillar family's high Alpine cheesemaking facility
OPPOSITE TOP AND BOTTOM The pastures at Käserei Boschenhof

French Alpine

The route to Comté and Haut-Doubs is a network of farms, vineyards and cheese cellars well worth exploring. The landscape is deeply rooted in agriculture and driving along the winding roads in late autumn, you are totally absorbed in the autumnal golds, rust burgundy and ochres. In the commune of Les Fins, close to Morteau (famous for their delicious sausages and charcuterie), I have forged wonderful friendships and working relationships, through regular visits to choose the cheeses. I like the hot, spicy flavours of Comté from the late summer months, but some of the late spring and late autumn cheeses have wonderful complex qualities. Once the selection is made the cheeses are put in the maturing rooms to await shipment. Storing cheeses in their familiar environment is a luxury and one that pays dividends – each batch received will be in tip-top condition as they have had no major changes in their surroundings that might impinge on their flavour development.

ABOVE Chamrousse, French Alps

Comté d'Estive COMTÉ

Comté cheesemaking has been documented since the 12th century, but it has only begun to look like a dense Gruyère since the 1950s. Prior to this, the cheese was rather like Emmental, with large holes in the pate. However, the rich milk from the Montbéliarde cows could be matured like a Gruyère, a more expensive cheese than Emmental, and it made economic sense to develop this style of cheese. The *affineurs* (cheese maturers) have re-invented this cheese as one of the most popular hard cheeses in France, and due to the long ageing process, countries around the world are able to import wheels made with unpasteurized milk.

There is a strict code of practice to maintain all aspects of the cheese and inspectors regulate on a 20-point system. For scores 15 or above a green label is used around the outside of the cheese. Those scoring 12–15 get a red label, and any under 3 are not allowed to be called Comté. The perfect wines for Comté are Jura whites made with Chardonnay grapes, the local Savagnin grape and Vin Jaune with its almost sherry-like quality that is at once dry, fruity and sharp – a great foil for the Comté cheese.

BELOW AND OPPOSITE Comté d'Estive

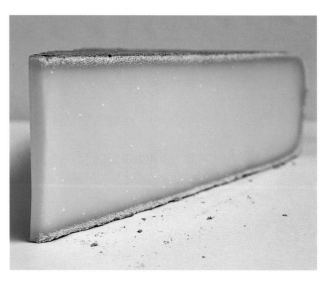

Beaufort Chalet d'Alpage

The mountain pastures, which in winter are ski runs, return to scented Alpine meadows in summer, and produce the perfect grazing land for the Abondance and Tarine cows.

Beaufort Chalet d'Alpage 🐄 SAVOIE

Beaufort cheesemaking takes place in the Beaufortain, Tarentaise and Maurienne valleys, plus part of the Val d'Arly. There are also high mountain or *alpage* pastures here too. Over 10,000 Abondance and Tarine cows graze these designated areas and it takes around 300 litres (530 pints) of milk to produce one 28–30 kg (61–66 lb) cheese. The cows are not over-milked and can only produce enough milk per year for about 300 cheeses. This not only ensures the quality of the cheese but also, just as important, avoids overworking the pastures, which would diminish their abundance of wild flowers and grasses. Whereas Comté cheese has salty/caramel deep flavours, the Beaufort has floral, almost sweet, nutty flavours that are rich but never abrasive on the tongue – even with the aged versions. Perfect with regional white wines from Chignin and Chasselas grapes, their freshness is bright and clear when partnered with the chewy fruitiness of the cheese.

ABOVE AND OPPOSITE Beaufort Chalet d'Alpage,
LEFT Grazing cows in the Savoie

BELOW, FROM BOTTOM CHEESE Tomme de Savoie, Abbaye de Tamié, Reblochon, Chevrotin des Aravis BACK CHEESE Emmental de Savoie Surchoix

OPPOSITE, TOP CHEESE Morbier BOTTOM CHEESE Bleu de Gex

Morbier  FRANCHE-COMTÉ

Ferme de Teigne, where Madame Chambon makes Morbier cheese, is off the beaten track. The Morbier cheeses she makes are quite different to any others I have tasted. The ash stripe through the cheese seems grittier, more like the original version of the cheese where the ash under the copper cauldrons on the embers was scraped off and mixed into a paste before being spread over half the cheese. In this way the morning milk cheese could be left to settle and then when the evening cheese was made it could be poured on top with the ash cinders providing a 'mat'. The cheese is mild with a nutty flavour when young, becoming richer and more pronounced with age.

Bleu de Gex HAUT JURA

This stylish blue cheese weighing around 5.4 kg (12 lb) has a lively taste and a rough natural thin crust. The unwashed curds have *Penicillium glaucum* added to encourage the blue to form. The cheese is allowed to drain naturally and is liberally pierced before going to the ripening room; this prevents the cheese from becoming too dense due to the richness of Montbéliarde cow's milk. The natural crust forms in the cold ripening room, and after about two months the cheese is ready. You can leave the maturing process longer, but I prefer this cheese on the young side so that its mild nutty flavour allows it to mix well on a cheeseboard with other softer cheeses of the region.

Tomme de Savoie SAVOIE

Many cheeses are labelled 'Tommes' in Savoie, as this word describes the smallish round shape of the cheese. Look out for *alpage* cheeses, those made with summer milk that have complex flavours of fruit and nut. The moulds around the cheese are grey/white/blue making it look like a small boulder. The morning and evening milk has some semi-skimmed milk added to help with the acidity, giving the cheese a sweet milky aroma mixed with the musty earthy crust. Enjoy with the local Gamay or Mondeuse wines.

Reblochon SAVOIE

The semi-soft disc weighing 500 g (1 lb 2 oz) has a washed and rubbed pinky-gold rind. The cheese has a supple chewy texture, with a lovely earthy aroma and rich hazelnut or fresh cobnut taste. The rind is all important to the overall flavour profile, but if the rind becomes hard or wet, cut it away as it will taste bitter. I like to add a few scoops of this cheese just before serving a fondue — it really gives it a glossy finish, although Reblochon is traditionally used in a classic Tartiflette (see recipe pages 252–253).

Chevrotin des Aravis HAUTE-SAVOIE

This is a plump goat's milk version of Reblochon, and is really delightful when properly ripened. Weighing around 300 g (10½ oz) the white pate should be supple and springy but not flowing or firm. The rind is washed to give a pale peachy bloom, and the goaty taste is both delicate yet rich and floral. A perfect late spring, summer and autumn cheese, it benefits from being served with a Savoie wine such as a red Mondeuse or a white Chignin Bergeron.

Emmental de Savoie Surchoix SAVOIE

This 80 kg (176 lb) Grand Cru cheese has a red cross on it to indicate that it is from Savoie. It is much like other pressed and cooked cheeses — Gruyère, Beaufort — and has that familiar fruity taste with a dense, chewy texture. The Grand Cru cheeses are more flavourful and better quality than the mass-produced versions. For cheese enthusiasts the size of the holes is very important — too big and you lose a huge amount of cheese when cutting, and too small, then there is a tendency to a wet, claggy paste — a skilled *affineur* can tell when the holes have reached the right size. Emmental is the main component of fondue and soufflés, as well as being used for sauces and toppings.

Abbaye de Tamié HAUTE-SAVOIE

The Cistercian monks first made this cheese in the Middle Ages; in 1861 the Abbey acquired more land and encouraged local farmers to sell their milk to the monks for cheesemaking. Now there are farms making the cheese for the Abbey, which then markets the cheese. The recipe is more or less a Reblochon, but thicker, weighing around 1.3 kg (3 lb) for the cutting cheese and 500 g (1 lb 2oz) for an individual version. It has the same rich creamy flavour as Reblochon with chewy density, but is perhaps a little less nutty though more robust and earthy in taste. The flavour of the cheese changes with each season. In the winter when the cattle are housed in smaller enclosures and fed on hay, the cheeses have a farmyard aroma and taste. In the spring and summer when the cattle graze on the mountain pastures, the cheeses develop nutty, mossy flavours.

Bleu de Termignon ☛ HAUTE-SAVOIE

From Haute-Savoie and weighing about 7–10 kg (15½–22 lb), this is one of the rarest cheeses made in the high mountain pastures, at 2,000 plus metres (6,600 ft) altitude. Made during the summer months only and ripened in mountain huts, this ancient cheese was almost forgotten until the early 1980s when a determined group of cheesemongers decided to help its continuing production. There is nothing forced, added or injected to achieve the blue – it simply forms by allowing the natural bacteria in the air of the maturing cave to filter into the cheeses that are freshly packed into their wooden moulds lined with muslin. Left over a period of time, the curds are pressed of their whey and then spiked with needles to create air pockets for the bacteria to work through the cheese. Once the cheeses are taken out of their moulds and placed on the wooden shelves the natural crust forms. The cheese has the texture of Wensleydale and the nutty flavours of the blue are quite different from any other blue cheese you will ever taste. The blue gives the flavour a sense of the cellar with its slight musty mineral quality, but the sweetness of the milk hits the roof of your mouth along with the natural blue tangle of flavours gleaned from the impact of air-borne bacteria in the maturing rooms. The best wine for this type of cheese is one that is not too heavy, and if you think of the lighter Rhône styles with their well-balanced acidity I think you will be on the right track. This is a 'particular' cheese as I call it, special and redolent of its place of origin, which is the heart of the Massif de la Vanoise, Praz Bouchet, located in Termignon-la-Vanoise.

Vacherin ☛ HAUT-DOUBS

I spent a morning making cheese at Le Fruitier des Jarrons, at Ville du Pont not far from the Comté cheesemakers in Les Fins. Monsieur Rene Boissenin and his three assistants were already busy heating up the early morning milk in three vats.

The Montbéliarde cow's milk is used from mid-summer until late autumn for Vacherin production. The milk will be particularly rich and fragrant during the months up to late autumn, an ideal time for making this soft, buttery cheese with its sappy aroma and taste from the pine-bark collar.

The short six-month season for Vacherin is important to respect, and cheeses made beyond this period cannot be called Vacherin du Mont d'Or, but other names like the Edel de Cléron, a pasteurized milk cheese that looks a lot like the Vacherin.

The flavour of Vacherin is superb with a meltingly rich verging on clotted cream taste. The billowy crust is washed pinky-peach with an earthy, sappy aroma. The bark around the cheese helps to achieve its distinctive texture and perfume.

This cheese is delicious when accompanied by a refreshing and zesty white wine. Try a Côtes du Jura produced in the Haut Jura region for the perfect patrnership.

LEFT **Vacherin**
OPPOSITE **Bleu de Termignon**

ABOVE, TOP CHEESE Tarentais MIDDLE CHEESE Abondance
BOTTOM CHEESE Besace

OPPOSITE, TOP LEFT CHEESE Grataron d'Arêches TOP RIGHT CHEESE Persillé
de Tignes/Tarentais MIDDLE CHEESE Grand Colombiers FRONT CHEESE
Persillé de Tignes/Tarentais

Tarentais ⌁ SAVOIE

This drum of goat's milk cheese weighing 200 g (7 oz)
or less has a natural rind that requires careful handling;
the white and grey/blue moulds are encouraged but so
are the darker yellow/gold moulds that cover the cheese
especially when it is at its fresher stage. This reaction to
the rind can be difficult to judge – if allowed to stay in
too high a humidity it will affect the flavours, causing it to
become bitter, but if the white and blue moulds flourish
on top of the gold then you will have a wonderful cheese,
closely packed and crumbly with a fresh nutty taste. The
goats are allowed to roam the rocky outcrops around the
farms during late spring and summer, and the cheese is
available only until early autumn.

Abondance ⌁ HAUTE-SAVOIE

This cheese takes the name of the valley as well as the
breed of cow used for the milk. The first cheeses were
made exclusively in the Haute-Savoie, as early as the 14th
century by the monks of the Sainte Marie d'Abondance
Monastery near the Swiss border. This high mountain
artisan cheese is made exclusively in Val d'Abondance in
the north of Haute-Savoie, which stretches to the Swiss
border; the farm-made cheeses are called Abondance de
Savoie and are made around the Massif du Parmelan. The
three breeds of cow used are Tarine, Montbéliarde and the
rather beautiful Abondance. Although the maturing time
is around 12 weeks, if you can wait longer, the flavours are

really rich and fruity with an almost melting quality and a
bitter nut taste rather like fresh hazelnuts. The best season
to eat cheeses made in late spring is late winter.

Besace ⌁ SAVOIE

A dome-shaped cheese weighing around 200 g (7 oz) and
moulded in fine muslin. With hardly a visible rind this
fresh, tangy and floral-tasting cheese has a delicious light
crumbly texture. Lovely when young, but if allowed to
dry out a bit it becomes more dense with age, developing
a mellow, nutty taste. It is only available during the late
spring and summer months.

Grataron d'Arêches ⌁⌁ SAVOIE

In the heart of the Beaufortain area and the village of
Arêches, this soft washed-rind cheese of around 200 g
(7 oz) is made with either cow's or goat's milk, although
it is the goat's milk cheese that is the rarer of the two.
Production is limited to spring through autumn when the
goats are allowed to roam the floral-strewn pastures. The
flavours of this cheese are soft but pronounced, and a
zesty white wine or a light Gamay are the most suitable
wine accompaniments.

Persillé de Tignes/Tarentais 🐐🐄 SAVOIE

This is a goat's milk cheese, which has varying amounts of cow's milk added to supplement the goat's milk when scarce. It is available during the spring and autumn while the animals are able to graze outdoors. Weighing about 1.5 kg (3⅓ lb) and looking like a small version of Wensleydale, the crust is studded with pale grey and white moulds. The texture is grainy with hints of sharp fruit and the merest shadow of blue showing through. Eaten young the sharp, crème fraîche flavours are delightful, but if you allow the cheese to mature further, more strident flavours will come forward and the blue will become more evident.

Grand Colombiers de Aillons 🐐🐄 SAVOIE

From the heart of the Beaufortain/Bauges region, this is another mixed goat's and cow's milk cheese weighing approximately 1.5 kg (3⅓ lb) with a lightly washed rind. Available during the summer and autumn months, the taste is soft, velvety and mellow. The rind should have a subtle aroma of mustiness and if too sticky will impart a bitter taste to the cheese. The well-balanced wines of the region, such as Mondeuse or a Pinot Noir would be an ideal partner, since there is a little vegetal spikiness coming through the flavours of the cheese and the clean style of these wines will be a good foil.

Swiss Alpine

The small grazing bells Swiss cows wear on the high mountain pastures are a necessity as each one has its own particular sound allowing the herdsman to locate every single creature. Switzerland is a landlocked country surrounded by high mountains, but these craggy cliff faces also allow for a temperate climate, which is probably the most satisfactory condition in which to make cheese. Mountains have pure

water systems trickling down into the valleys, and valuable minerals that feed the soil. This is probably why the large Gruyère and Emmentaler cheeses are so delicious, especially when they are made high up in the hills during the summer months. From the 13th century onwards, grazing rights and animal rights-of-way have been complex and led to the eventual privatization of communal grazing land, driving many cheesemakers to other European plains and overseas to America and Australasia. For many generations the right to use an Alp has been handed down within the family, and is owned by a single family or two families or an Alp co-operative, which is operated by all the farming families of the area. All the Alps are 'geyser', meaning that only a certain number of cows or other animals are allowed to graze during the summer in order to protect the land.

ABOVE The Pillar father and son making cheese, Swiss Alps

ABOVE The view of Charmey Mountains, Canton Fribourg

Gruyère 🐄 CANTON FRIBOURG

The high mountain cheeses weighing around 32–40 kg (70½–88 lb) are made between June and September by small independent cheesemakers such as the Pillar family in Charmey, using traditional methods and equipment in their mountain chalets. The flavours are savoury and almost toasty, from the unpasteurized milk being heated in large copper vats over open wood fires. Just two cheeses are made per day and maturing requires a minimum of 12 months although keeping longer will give a richer and fruitier taste to the cheese. Nearer to the village of Gruyère is Le Crêt sur Semsales where Jean Marie Dunand ages his cheeses up to two years, giving a fruity intensity to the flavours and a gritty crumble in the mouth. This cheese is used for a classic fondue. Or eat it on its own with a glass of white wine for an elegant finish to a meal.

OPPOSITE, TOP CHEESE Alpkäse Luven LEFT AND BOTTOM CHEESE Gruyére RIGHT CHEESE Alpkäse Luven

Alpkäse Luven 🐄 CANTON GRAUBÜNDEN

Dani Duerr decided to go back to his home town high up in the Alpine region of Graubünden in Luven, to make cheese just as his grandparents and father had done. However, he wanted to change the old traditional recipe of Toggenburg hard cheeses and make something with his own identity stamped on the cheese. Dani does extra brine washing to the cheeses to give a deep ochre colour to the crust, and learnt his craft from his father who was a traditional cheesemaker of Emmentaler. He adapted the recipe to make a much harder, close-textured cheese weighing about 5 kg (11 lb), and it tastes very fruity and nutty with a much earthier taste than other Swiss cheeses. He mostly sells his cheeses locally and to one or two major restaurants in Switzerland, and hopefully he will expand the maturing area to enable him to have enough cheeses to sell elsewhere in the world.

so it's best to eat it young before the flavours become very tangy and earthy. The delicious wines from around Lake Geneva and Vaud are the perfect foil for the dense, rich styles and flavours of Swiss cheese, in particular Le Sous-Bois produced by the Henchoz.

Alp Bergkäse CANTON GRAUBÜNDEN, CHUR

This is a similar cheese to Luven (see page 95), but whereas Luven is made by a single cheesemaker using his own cows' milk, Alp Bergkäse will be more readily available as the collective of farmers will club together and hire a cheesemaker for the summer season to make the cheeses in the high Alpine huts. They are ripened up to one year, and are really very seasonal.

Etivaz Gruyère
CANTON VAUD

This rarity is produced in a traditional way in copper vats over open fires. In the 1930s, the collective of farms and cheesemakers decided to break away from the strictures of the Gruyère administration to make a more 'authentic' style of Gruyère using older grazing and techniques.

During the summer and early autumn the cattle graze on more than 130 Alps between the glaciers of Les Diablerets and the vineyards of Lake Geneva. Maturing takes place in a modern cellar. All the cheesemaking is done in mountain chalets, giving the flavours a truly complex fruity and rich taste. Weighing around 18 kg (40 lb) and a little more expensive, they are really worth it.

Château d'Erguel BERNESE JURA, CANTON BERN
Made at the Fromagerie in Courtelary, the Kämpf family utilize the perfect Chasseral grazing areas at 1,300 metres (4,265 ft) where the cows are outside for eight months of the year. For the colder months they are inside but fed only hay with a supplement of dried legumes. Château d'Erguel is one of the oldest cheeses from this region. The Erguel, which weighs around 7 kg (15½ lb), is matured for five or six months until the spicy flavours are well developed and full.

Le Sous-Bois CANTON VAUD
The Henchoz family have lived and worked in Rossinière, high up in the hills of Vaud, Pays d'En Haut for generations. Their farm is totally organic and they also have a herd of sheep (which is unusual to see in Switzerland). The Swiss Vacherin cheesemakers think that Le Sous-Bois is very similar to Vacherin, but the cheese is smaller and the rind bloomy, unlike the Vacherin. The milk is unpasteurized and the Henchoz family only use their own milk.

The small 150 g (5½ oz) cheese is wrapped in a pine-bark collar to keep the cheese intact, and enhance the sappy flavours, which are rich, mellow and nutty. The very high humidity in the cellars encourages not only the bloom on the rind but the ripening of the cheese, and

Emmentaler 🐄 CANTON BERN
Weighing in at 100 kg (220 lb), Emmentaler is the largest cheese in the world. The more aged mountain-made cheeses have a darker rind and if you can get the 18-month cheeses from the *alpage* canton in Bern, this will taste strong and spicy and have fewer holes than the usual versions of this cheese.

It has an almost slightly wet appearance (it sometimes looks like little tears oozing out of the cheese), and a chewy density with a fine nutty texture. Perfect for eating as a table cheese, but also one of the main components for a Swiss fondue. Eat with a lighter-style, refreshing white wine with floral aromas to really bring out the flavours of this delicious cheese.

Fleurettes des Rougemont (Tomme Fleurette) 🐄
CANTON VAUD
Cheesemaker Michel Beroud, whose dairy production is based in the pretty valley of Rougemont, is something of an icon in the Swiss cheesemaking world. He has shown that it's not just Gruyère that is made in Switzerland, as his little cheese is such a success. This tender 170 g (6 oz) 'squared-off' disc of soft unpasteurized cow's milk cheese has been matured for 14 days to encourage its light bloomy white coat. The silky almost melting cheese within is nutty in flavour, with a light earthiness coming through. It is a perfect addition to the otherwise chunky, robust and heavier Swiss cheeseboard, and will partner both red and white wines wonderfully.

Stillsitzer Steinsalz 🐄 GÄHWIL, TOGGENBURG
In the Tilsiter style weighing around 4 kg (9 lb). Stefan Bühler is another renegade instilling his own style of maturing and production to the cheese. Unlike other cheesemakers in Switzerland who buy in cultures, Stefan creates his own starter and rennet to coagulate the cheese. Stefan also washes his cheeses in an untreated sea salt, which is more expensive. However, this gives the ultimate taste of rich dense fruitiness and slightly gritty texture to the cheeses.

Unterwasser 🐄 CANTON ST GALLEN
Made in Toggenburg/Unterwasser by the Stadelmann family, they decided to split with the Tilsiter Consortium to produce a cheese following an organic production. Since then a wide range of cheeses have been developed, one being the Unterwasser, weighing around 8 kg (17½ lb). You could believe that all these styles of cheeses would taste the same, but there are distinct differences in the milk from the different areas, and the cheesemaker himself imparts his style during the cheesemaking process that gives the cheeses their unique tastes. Thomas, who took control of the dairy from his father several years ago, leads his productions with passion and enthusiasm.

Raclette 🐄 CANTON GLARUS
Swiss Raclettes are much stronger than French, and there are two styles. Raclette Berghoff from Toggenburg has a dense texture and a supple body enabling it to melt quickly. Alp Raclette from Alp Luser-Schlossli in the Glarus Canton is made in the high Alpine region in the Mühlebach/Engi, and is much firmer textured with more brine washings and aged around five months. The flavours are nutty and almost smoky, and quite different in texture to the other Raclettes. The aroma when melting this style of Raclette will be much stronger and earthier too.

Alp Kohlschlag 🐄 CANTON ST GALLEN
Kohlschlag is just above Mels-Sargans, about 1½ hours from Zurich. This alp is run by a co-operative and every year they rent out the high summer pasture for cheesemaking. There are approximately 50 cows from different farms scattered in the lower villages, and as the season starts, the cattle are led half way up to start their summer idyll. As the summer progresses the cheesemaker follows the cattle higher up the mountain where huts and cheesemaking facilities are situated. After a few weeks the forms are brought down to Mels to be matured in a large cave where the humid environment and even temperature help the cheeses develop right through the winter months. The high mountain cheese is a little larger than the other St Gallen cheese and is for sale from three months.

LEFT, FROM TOP Fleurettes des Rougemont, Stillsitzer Steinsalz, Unterwasser, cut Raclette, Raclette rind, Alp Kohlschlag

ABOVE, FROM TOP CHEESE Scimudin, Formai de Mut, Branzi
OPPOSITE, FROM TOP CHEESE Scimudin, Formai de Mut, Branzi

ABOVE LEFT The Trentino countryside
ABOVE RIGHT Maturing cheeses

Italian Alpine

There are many national parks and protected regions within each country along the Alpine ranges. The Parc Nationale de Vanoise in the Rhône-Alpes is on the border between France and Italy and once through the Mont Blanc tunnel you are in Gran Paradiso National Park with the cities of Turin and Milan not too far away. Parco Veglia Devero is a natural Alpine area specifically for preserving pastureland. There are three mountain cheeses that you can find locally, but they are also transported to towns in Piedmont, as well as overseas. Parco dello Stelvio is the largest natural Alpine zone in Italy, encompassing many hamlets, small towns and mountain ranges. From Bitto, with its paler pitted pate and the inclusion of goat's milk in the summer cheeses made in the valleys of Albaredo and high mountain pastures of Sondrio, to the cheeses of the Valtellina hills, this is a region of outstanding beauty.

Scimudin 🐄 🐐 SONDRIO

This is a soft, richly creamy cheese made all over the Sondrio area, but there are still a few farms making a goat's milk version in the Val Codera, an isolated area north of Lake Como. Weighing around 1 kg (2 lb 4 oz), the milk has cream added to it before heating, then a *Penicillium candidum* added to encourage the white rind. The rich buttery texture is like clotted cream, but if allowed to ripen and become more fluid then a nutty sharpness will come through. The late autumn cheeses are the most rich and unctuous. The Valtellina wines of the region are ideal to drink with this cheese, or a Pinot Noir with a hint of nut.

Formai de Mut 🐄 LOMBARDY

The name implies 'mountain' or 'alpine' in the local dialect and that is exactly what this versatile cheese is — simple and delicate with a light floral taste in the manner of Branzi. It has a thinner, paler rind when young giving the cheese a more malleable texture, although with more brine rubbings during ageing the smooth rind becomes darker and very hard, and the cheese becomes a delicious fruity and fragrant morsel. The local community use this cheese for gratins, as a topping for soups and stews and *fonduta*, but it is the more aged cheeses that are served at the table to end a meal.

Branzi 🐄 LOMBARDY

This is a 12 kg (26½ lb) semi-hard cheese that becomes more brittle with maturity. The summer cheeses are made in the high mountain dairies and dry-salted, while winter cheeses are made in valley dairies and soaked in a brine bath. The cheese has a delicate flavour and aroma when made with the winter milk due to the cows' feed being more controlled, and in summer when grazing in the open pastures the flavours become more robust, vegetal and aromatic. It is a lovely table cheese but comes into its own when used to accompany polenta as the sharp, nutty flavours liven up the texture of the dish.

Franzedas Alpeggio 🐄 VICENZA/TRENTO

This is one of the rare cheeses made high up in the mountains only during the summer months. It is shaped like a flat stone, and the curds are wrapped in cloth and placed on shelves to dry out, before being hung up in the hut to mature. It has very fruity flavours and a dry, almost crystalline texture.

Asiago Pressato 🐄 VICENZA/TRENTO

This simple cheese is made on the low-lying areas of Vicenza and Trento. It has sweet, nutty, milky flavours and a springy open texture, and weighs around 12 kg (26½ lb). It is perfect for those who don't want an over-complicated-tasting cheese. The Asiago cheeses become much drier and crumblier with age, developing salty, gritty flavours and textures.

Carnia Altobut Vecchio 🐄 PADOLA

From the municipality of Comelico Superiore, in the province of Belluno, this is an age-old mountain cheese. Mild and delicate when young, the 6 kg (13 lb) cheese will age to give a fruity, sappy flavour to the close-packed pate with tiny breaks or cuts in the cheese. The rind is bathed in the brine tub and then rubbed and scraped during the ripening process. This cheese is easy to keep, and could even be kept out of the fridge during the cooler months.

Grana Val di Non (Trentingrana) 🐄 TRENTINO

Although under the same umbrella as the Grana Protected Consortium, the Grana Val di Non cheese has its own special mark on the rind to denote that it was made in Trentino.

Trentingrana is made in much the same way as Parmigiano Reggiano, although this cheese differs in that the aged versions do tend to have scatterings of tiny 'eyes' throughout the cheese. One of the main differences between Grana Val di Non and Parmigiano Reggiano is that the cattle are allowed to graze more freely, especially those on the higher pastures of the Trentino region, and the animals are not subjected to the strict dietary feeding rules as for Parmesan.

The flavours of the Trentigrana are rich and crumbly with a fruity flavour which is not as intense as Parmigiano Reggiano. A very versatile cheese that can be used both in the kitchen or as a table cheese, a sharp dry white wine is a perfect accompaniment, or even a sparkling fully dry Prosecco.

BELOW Franzedas Alpeggio
OPPOSITE, TOP LEFT CHEESE Franzedas Alpeggio TOP RIGHT CHEESE Asiago Pressato MIDDLE LEFT CHEESE Carnia Altobut Vecchio (cut and rind) MIDDLE RIGHT CHEESE Asiago Pressato BOTTOM CHEESE Grana Val di Non

Grasso d'Alpe Buscagna 🐄 PARCO VEGLIA DEVERO

Part of the Toma family similar to Gruyère, the Grasso, Rodolfo and Alpeggio have rough artisan-looking crusts.

Every 'alp' or mountain pasture has a cheesemaker to transform the milk into cheese, which is identified by the name of the alp. This particular grazing zone is a picturesque Alpine area for snow-shoeing rather than skiing, and the tiny hamlets dotted along the way are still very much like they were hundreds of years ago. Similar in style to the Ossolana but with a smoother texture and less rough 'artisan'-style rind. A good cheese for snacking, as well as grating for a *fonduta* or gratin.

Toma Ossolana Alpeggio 🐄 PARCO VEGLIA DEVERO

This is another Toma weighing around 5–7 kg (11–15½ lb). However, the Alpeggio has a deeper colour to the pate and a real fruity edge to the flavours, since it is the one made in the most basic of conditions, right down to hand-milking on the mountainside.

The chewy texture of the cheese is similar to Swiss cheeses but it has a little more oiliness with scattered eyelets. These cheeses are made in a protected area where grazing rights are carefully monitored to prevent the grass and flora diminishing.

Toma Ossolana Rodolfo 🐄 PARCO VEGLIA DEVERO

In the mountain Toma style, this cheese has had a longer maturing, and a slightly different method of making to the Alpeggio. The mountain pastures of Valdossola are where the Toma are made, and the golden straw colour of the pate has a slightly softer texture with a chewy savoury taste and a rough-looking crust.

The cheeses weigh around 5–7 kg (11–15½ lb) and have that simple quality to enjoy at the end of meal with walnuts or hazelnuts instead of fruit.

Bastardo del Grappa/Morlacco del Grappa 🐄
MONTE GRAPPA MASSIF

From the Monte Grappa Massif in the provinces of Treviso, Belluno and Vicenza, the cheese also takes its name from the river Grappa. The pastures in this region are poor and the Burlina cow, which was used for this cheese, has almost been surpassed by Friesian or Bruna Alpina breeds because of the better milk yields. The Bastardo version is called thus because poor grazing means that milk has to be obtained from outside the Morlacco area at certain times of the year. They are made with partly skimmed milk, and formerly were made only with skimmed milk, as the cream was used for butter.

The smooth, hard dry rind is brine-washed and rubbed in the usual mountain style, and the compact pate has scattered pinhead holes. The cheese is ripened for a minimum of six months, but the more aged versions (ripened for up to two years) are eaten in small quantities as they taste strong, or even grated.

A Valpolicella red wine is good with the less mature cheeses, but I love aged versions with Recioto di Soave, a dessert wine with a sweetly savoury sherry-like taste, or a fine Amarone with its deep complexity.

Monte Veronese Grasso 🐄 VERONA

Weighing around 6–9 kg (13–20 lb) and made with partly skimmed milk the Grasso cheese is well known throughout northern Italy as being a good table cheese after six months' maturing.

It is not too strong or bitter, and will age beautifully to a crackly texture and fruity, nutty taste. The flavours of a light and fruity Valpolicella wine work wonderfully with this delicious cheese.

LEFT, FROM TOP CHEESE Toma Ossolana Alpeggio, Rind of Toma Ossolana Alpeggio, Toma Ossolana Rodolfo, Grasso d'Alpe Buscagna

OPPOSITE, BACK CHEESES, FROM TOP Bastardo del Grappa, Monte Veronese Grasso, Grasso d'Alpe Buscagna, Monte Veronese Grasso FRONT CHEESES, FROM TOP Morlacco del Grappa, Stranghe di Lagundo

Stanghe di Lagundo TREVISO

This is a simple washed-rind semi-soft cheese, made
on farms around Vellau, Rio Lagundo, Rablà, Parcines,
the Table Mountain and the Sole di Naturno, high up
in the Treviso hills. It looks like a large rectangular loaf,
weighing around 2 kg (4½ lb), has a washed, soft pinky
rind with a musty, though not unpleasant aroma, and
not as farmyard-like smelling as other washed rinds. The
taste is milky and almost sweet, and perfect for thinly
slicing as a sandwich filling, or melting over pasta or
potatoes for a more hearty meal. It is a welcome change
from all the harder cheeses of the Alpine region, and is
a popular family favourite.

Fontina

This is the Val d'Aosta's most famous cheese. The region has a rugged beauty and backdrop of snow-capped mountains and fertile valleys for farming and vineyards.

Fontina 🐄 AOSTA

This very well-known cheese from Aosta looks as if it could be related to French Abondance (see page 92) with its curved 'waistline' and lightly washed and rubbed crust. A hugely popular cheese made in big quantities, it is, however, the mountain dairy cheese that is more prized, but also the most difficult to make.

Valdostana cow's milk from single milking is used, so cheeses are made twice daily. The milk is not skimmed – the high fat content may be one of the reasons why this cheese is difficult to make – and it is heated to no more

than 36°C (96.8°F) before the natural rennet is added. It is then left to curdle for around 50 minutes, then the soft curd is stirred and roughly broken up, and left to stand and settle. The curds are cut again to tiny granules, then again left to settle at the bottom of the vat, which is still warm to 'cook' the curds. When ready to be removed from the vat a muslin cloth is plunged into the mass and they are scooped up, lifted out and placed into a wooden band. The whey is pressed out, first by hand and then with a heavy weight for about 12 hours, and the cheeses are turned at regular intervals to release the whey evenly.

They are then transferred to a salting bath before going to the maturing rooms where more dry salt is added on alternate days by cleaning and brushing with brine. The cheeses absorb around 2 percent of the salt during the dry salt process and continual brine-washing and brushing, until the crust forms and the golden-brown colour becomes more evident, encouraged by the humidity and temperature of the cellars.

These maturing rooms can be in caves, grottoes, former army bases hidden in the mountains, or even in an old copper mine in one case; the natural flora and minerals in the air also contribute to the flavour profile of the cheese.

The cheese weighs about 8–12 kg (17½–26½ lb), and the flavours are sweet verging on fruity and robust; the more matured version has a texture that is chewy and dense. Fontina is a great melting cheese for Italian fondue, *fonduta*, and lighter red wines such as Pinot Noir or similar fruity but dry-edged wines are good partners.

LEFT Fontina rind
OPPOSITE Sliced Fontina
ABOVE LEFT The Aosta landscape
ABOVE RIGHT Mont Blanc, the Aosta Valley

ABOVE, FROM TOP CHEESE Romadur, Bavarian Blue, Butterkäse, Alp Bergkäse, Adelegger Urberger

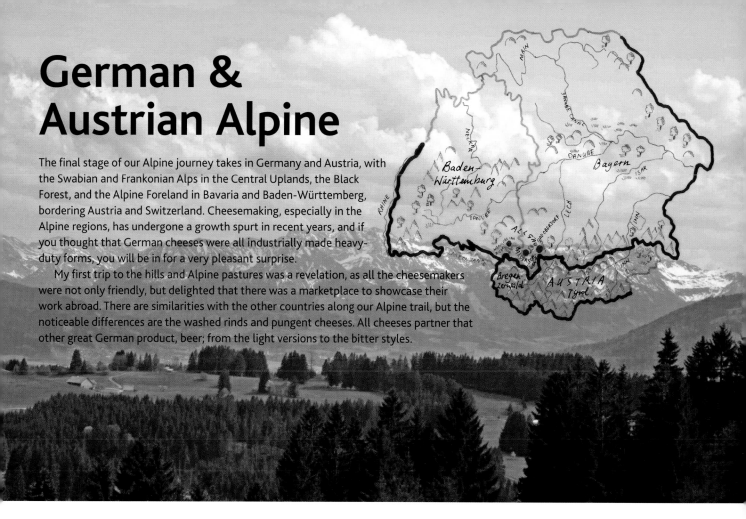

German & Austrian Alpine

The final stage of our Alpine journey takes in Germany and Austria, with the Swabian and Frankonian Alps in the Central Uplands, the Black Forest, and the Alpine Foreland in Bavaria and Baden-Württemberg, bordering Austria and Switzerland. Cheesemaking, especially in the Alpine regions, has undergone a growth spurt in recent years, and if you thought that German cheeses were all industrially made heavy-duty forms, you will be in for a very pleasant surprise.

My first trip to the hills and Alpine pastures was a revelation, as all the cheesemakers were not only friendly, but delighted that there was a marketplace to showcase their work abroad. There are similarities with the other countries along our Alpine trail, but the noticeable differences are the washed rinds and pungent cheeses. All cheeses partner that other great German product, beer; from the light versions to the bitter styles.

Romadur 🐄 ALLGÄU

Käserei Bremenried Co-operative works with 12 local dairy farms to make an award-winning Emmentaler and a delicious Romadur. The brick-shaped cheese weighs around 650 g (1 lb 7 oz) and has the familiar pungent aroma from the copious washings of the outside rind, which produce the 'Rotschmier Bacteria'. Basically, this is the sticky orange rind that forms on a cheese when washed in salty water and rubbed in raw salt over a period of time. The soft cheese is buttery with a nutty tang, and a perfect partner to beer.

Bavarian Blue 🐄 BAD OBERDORF

From the Obere Mühle Co-operative on the edge of the Alpe Engratsgund in Hindelang, this blue cheese weighing 2.5 kg (5½ lb) has a *Penicillium roqueforti* mould mixed into the curds; the cheese was invented by Basil Weixler in 1902 to rival his favourite Roquefort cheese. Bavarian Blue is really very different though, as it is creamier and denser with a mellow nutty taste making it a perfect morning cheese with toast and a blob of cherry jam, or as part of a cheeseboard selection.

Butterkäse 🐄 SOUTH WEST BAVARIA

Shaped like a loaf and without any rind, this is normally considered a melting cheese – I love it cut into small chunks, placed in the bottom of a bowl with hot vegetable soup poured on top. The northern German cheeses are very mild and basic, but the southern version has the familiar creamy texture but with a tart sharpness coming through. If you like Raclette but want something milder then this would be ideal. This family cheese is a staple in the high alps as well as all over Germany, but with a 50 percent fat content it should be used sparingly.

Alp Bergkäse 🐄 BALDERSCHWANG

At the Sennalpe Spicherhalde dairy, Fridolin Vogel has 30 Swiss Browns that graze Alpine pastures from May onwards when the whole family move up the mountain to make cheese throughout the summer. The cheese is ready to be sold at three months, but waiting longer allows the flavours to develop further and those high mountain meadows covered with flowers and herbs give the cheese a spicy end-taste.

Adelegger Urberger 🐄 BAVARIA

Isny Cheeses is not only the smallest dairy in Baden-Württemberg, it is also one of the best. This 7 kg (15½ lb) cheese is semi-hard with a dark washed and brushed rind, which, when allowed to ripen over nine months becomes a big, full-bodied-tasting cheese. The long maturing process allows the flavours to develop, and the rind, which is washed in a brine that includes wine, also helps deepen the taste.

Zigorome 🐐 ALLGÄU

Ulrich and Monika Leiner work together on their small farm, Ziegenhof Leiner, in Sulzberg in Allgäu. Their farm has been organic since 1989, when they received two nanny goats and two kids as a wedding present. The herd is now 60 nanny goats, and therefore the cheeses are mostly sold locally.

Goats thrive and produce plenty of milk during bright, sunny days; in the darker months they produce offspring and are not milked for cheesemaking, which is why true artisan-made cheeses are very seasonal. These days goats are often kept in 'artificial' daylight all through the year, in barns with daylight bulbs to give consistent milk production, but this means you don't get the character changes in the milk as you would with goats feeding on new spring grass or late summer grass.

The Zigorome takes its name from Romadur, another washed-rind cheese, but this small 150 g (5½ oz) cheese is sophisticated in taste, close-textured and almost sweet with its washed sticky rind that seems to lend a bitter-honey spiciness to the taste. Of all the cheeses from Bavaria, this one highlights the love of the animal and the land in complete harmony.

Emmentaler 🐄 ALLGÄU

This 90 kg (200 lb) cheese from the Käserei Bremenried Co-operative is quite unlike the commercial cheeses seen all over Germany. These monster cheeses require deft handling, arms of iron and a will of steel when it comes to lifting the mass of curds from the huge copper pan. They are usually sold from three months onwards, but the more aged versions give the most pleasure. The flavours are unlike Swiss or French versions, because the grazing areas have natural springs giving a very nutty and fruity intensity to the flavour.

Weisslacker 🐄 WANGEN IM ALLGÄU

From the Sibratsgfäll Co-operative (see Tilsiter, opposite), this is not a cheese for the faint-hearted – the aroma is pungent to say the least. The secret is the 20 percent salt water bath that the cheeses sit in for two days before going to the warm ripening room and hand salting twice a week. It takes about nine months to complete the maturing.

ABOVE LEFT Zigorome
LEFT Emmentaler
OPPOSITE, TOP LEFT CHEESE Tilsiter, **TOP RIGHT CHEESE** Weisslacker, **BOTTOM CHEESE** Rasskass

Serve this cheese in small pieces on top of thickly buttered rye bread with breakfast radishes with a strong beer. Traditionally, it is served with hearty sausages and spätzle.

Tilsiter 🐄 BREGENZ

The Sibratsgfäll Co-operative run by Hubert Eberle collects milk from 12 dairies around this picture-postcard pretty village on the edge of Bregenzerwald, and transforms the unpasteurized milk into super-dense, chewy textures with a hint of sourness that is pleasant rather than bitter. This flavour is essential as it provides heightened enjoyment especially at breakfast with toasted granary or rye bread, slices of cooked ham and really firm, slightly green tomatoes. What is more, pairing with beer is a joy — just think of those big flavoured wheat beers or dark amber rye beers or even a blonde — as that sour hint works wonders.

Rasskass 🐄 VORARLBERG/BREGENZ FOREZ

Anton Bader of the Dorfsennerei Langenegg Co-operative produces a 6.5 kg (14½ lb) cheese that is relatively low in fat. It is similar to Raclette (see page 97) when it is young at around three months and can be used in the same way. The cheese has small eyelets and slits running through, although the high mountain forms are smoother.

There is that familiar strong odour, its red washed rind that is dry and easier to handle, and the flavours are strong and robust. The milk used is unpasteurized and organic and the only feed the cows get other than fresh grass is sweet dry hay.

This cheese is the main ingredient used in Bregenz Forest cheese noodles (Käsespätzle, made with fresh egg noodles), a very hearty and tasty dish to serve alongside sausages from the region. It is a delicious partner to a light beer. The drinking milk and butter from this region are also exceptional.

Italy

When I started working with cheese I concentrated on France as I had spent so many summer holidays touring and winter breaks skiing there. My curiosity has never dimmed, but I also became interested in finding out about Italian cheese and why, with all the quaint Italian shops in London, the cheeses looked so processed. Surely there must be farm-made cheeses? Little by little I explored the regions and found a wealth of cheeses and producers who had never considered selling outside their immediate vicinity, let alone abroad or another part of Italy! Since my early foragings, the floodgates have opened and we see many handmade and small-production Italian cheeses not only in the UK and US but all over the world.

One way to really get to know rural Italy is to stay on a farm. Agritourism is big business in Italy and they offer an insight into the way the farm works, as well as a chance to enjoy the beauty of the region. Many of the small farms from which I purchase cheeses have installed these facilities, some vineyards have very fancy accommodation, and others are more modest. They produce much-needed revenue for the farms, as well as extra help should you feel the desire to get stuck in and do a little farmwork yourself. In France where the gîtes tradition has been going for many years, they don't offer that inspirational touch the Italians bring to the table – a welcome and a feeling of belonging right from the start, the joy of being able to cook, taste and buy the wonderful fruits of their labours.

LEFT An old water wheel in Tuscany
BELOW LEFT Maturing cellars in Trentino
BELOW RIGHT Italian cheeses in production
OPPOSITE TOP, MIDDLE AND BOTTOM The grazing pastures in Trentino

Blu di Langa ALBA, PIEDMONT

The cheesemaking dairy is based near Alba, right in the heart of the wine country. There is a mixture of cow's, goat's and ewe's milks in the cheese, which has *Penicillium roqueforti* added for blue moulds, and the outer rind is brushed with *Penicillium candidum* to encourage the white mould. The cheese, weighing around 1 kg (2 lb 4 oz), ripens very quickly and becomes almost melting at times, which for some is a virtue but for others a little difficult to control. The flavours are nutty and earthy, with a tingle from the goat's milk coming through. This makes a change from the classic Gorgonzola (see page 118), and is lighter too, making it a good match for lighter red wines.

Northern Italy has the river Po as its dominant force, coursing its way from the base of the Apennines to the Alps, right through to the Adriatic Sea some 320 km (200 miles) away, servicing Milan, Turin, Genoa, Venice-Padua and most notably Bologna. While the valleys possessed rich agricultural land, the mountain areas were left to scratch a living, but have now revived into farming communities as well as developing their vineyards and tourism.

The north is the economic and intellectual heartland of Italy, being historically influenced by its invaders. The cheeses have an identity with their French, Swiss and Austrian neighbours, and Ligurian cheeses share similarities with the South of France. However, one cheese stands out as the flag-bearer of Italy and that is the golden chunk, Parmigiano Reggiano.

From the glorious patchwork hills of the Piedmont where good wine and cheese mingle with the pungent aroma of truffles, to Venice, the centre of the spice trade in medieval times, there is so much to explore and to taste. Every season in Italy boasts something wonderful to celebrate.

Seirass Fresca 🐐 PIEDMONT

This is a delicate light and frothy ewe's milk Ricotta that is packed into a cotton cone sack. The whey is used from Toma cheese production and then whole raw milk is added before heating. Scoop it out of its sleeve and serve with fresh berries, or as a stuffing for pasta or chicken. Whip it with a little icing sugar, pile into coupe glasses and drizzle over a sweet dessert wine for an elegant and quick dessert.

LEFT Seirass Fresca
OPPOSITE Blu di Langa

Castelmagno 🐄 CUNEO, PIEDMONT

This is an ancient cheese from the municipalities of Monterosso Grana, Pradleves and Castelmagno in the province of Cuneo. It comes in various weights between 2–7 kg (4½–15½ lb), although the larger forms are more common. This is a semi-hard, mould-ripened cheese, rather like a Stilton, which is pierced to allow the air to infiltrate the cheese to encourage the blue (which is only really evident in the very mature forms). Very similar to Castelrosso (see below), but the grazing area is very specific and the mixture of milks to the laborious recipe makes it more expensive. The very young cheeses disappoint me and I prefer ripening them on to get that flaky texture and the earthy bitterness to the flavours. It is particularly good when paired with something special like a Barbaresco or Barolo red wine from the region.

Maccagnette alle Erbe 🐄 BIELLA, PIEDMONT

There are several shapes for this cheese, although nowadays it's mostly shaped like an oyster or clam shell. Its rind, once ripened, takes on this look; the cheese is scored on top to allow the herbs and black pepper covering it to permeate into the curd. Seen mostly around the Biella province and weighing from 500 g (1 lb 2 oz) to 1 kg (2 lb 4 oz), the milk type is mostly cow with additions of goat and ewe when available during the year. The flavours are dominated by the mountain herbs and the pepper, which is important not to cut away, and I would suggest maybe a local beer rather than a wine as an accompaniment.

Toma Maccagno 🐄 BIELLA, PIEDMONT

The Luigi Rosso family from the Biella province have been making cheese since the early 19th century. This part of Piedmont is favoured for skiing and the Rossos have a hut on the slopes to sell their cheeses to passing skiers. This lovely creamy, dense cheese weighing about 3 kg (6½ lb) has been brine-washed and rubbed to give a pale peach colour dotted with patches of grey and white bloomy moulds. The semi-hard pate is fruity and nutty with hints of smoky sweetness. I love this cheese teamed with a zesty Gavi di Gavi, or a more traditional Oltrepò Pavese red that's not too dry, or a young Barbera.

Seirass del Fieno 🐑 PIEDMONT

The word 'Seirass' is derived from the Latin *seracium*, which means whey, but in Piedmont and Val d'Aosta this word also means 'ricotta'. Del Fieno means that the cheese is wrapped in hay wisps, which used to help keep the cheese intact during transport. This cheese is made a little differently to other Ricottas – the whey is brought to the boil, then fresh milk and salt added before the solids are drained. The flavours will be much more interesting and nutty if you allow the cheese to dry to half its size; it is an interesting cheese to serve with a dry sparkling wine.

Castelrosso 🐄 BIELLA, PIEDMONT

This is a tubby Toma weighing around 5–6 kg (11–13 lb) from the Luigi Rosso family farm near Biella. It has a crumbly texture with lovely white and grey moulds on the naturally formed crust. Quite a moist cheese when young, and rather like a Wensleydale, it has a dry crumble although the cheese itself has a dewy quality when you cut into it. If you let it ripen slowly it will dry out to give a flakier texture. The flavours have plenty of mineral and herbal depth and the nutty, earthy tastes come through at the end. I really love the summer and autumn cheeses. This is good with a white wine like Gavi, or dry reds like Resiot, also from Piedmont.

ABOVE Castelmagno

RIGHT, BACK CHEESE Maccagnette alle Erbe FRONT CHEESE Seirass del Fieno

ABOVE, TOP LEFT CHEESE Seirass del Fieno TOP RIGHT
CHEESE Castelrosso BOTTOM LEFT CHEESE Toma Maccagno
BOTTOM RIGHT CHEESE Maccagnette alle Erbe

Caprino Tartufo 🐐 PIEDMONT

From the same producer as Caprini Freschi, but this time the fresh cheeses are topped with shavings of Alba truffles. The distinct bosky aroma give a luxurious element to the flavours, and if you cannot afford the high price of a knobbly truffle, then crumbling this cheese into a risotto or over pasta will give a real sense of their exotic perfume mingling with the delicate creaminess of the cheese.

Caprini Freschi 🐐 PIEDMONT

I love the cheeses from La Bottera situated in the heart of Cuneo near Morozzo, about an hour or so from Turin. The family estate is run both on traditional lines but with modern equipment, as the younger members of the family see the need to embrace both cultures in order to move forward. The resulting cheeses are always beautifully made and packaged well. The Caprini Freschi is delicate, just 100 g (3½ oz) of fresh goat's cheese with no visible rind. The flavours are light and nutty, but not insipid, as you do get that hint of goatiness coming through. Perfect with Champagne or a crisp white wine.

Robiola delle Langhe 🐄 🐐 🐑 PIEDMONT

Coming from between Bosia and Alba in the heart of Piedmont wine country, this cheese epitomizes the richness of the milk and the delicate flavours complement the fine wines. Robiola is famous throughout this region and uses a combination of cow's, goat's and ewe's milks to make a fudgy, soft cylinder weighing around 300 g (10½ oz); its thin natural rind has a hint of white bloom.

Truffle Cheese (Tuma Trifulera) 🐄 🐐 🐑 PIEDMONT

La Bottera's truffle cheese is made with mixed milk and weighs 500 g (1 lb 2 oz). The crumbly-textured cheese is slightly dry but this is necessary to appreciate the truffle pieces mixed into the curd. It is earthy and aromatic.

Fiore di Langhe 🐐 PIEDMONT

The smooth delicate pate has a soft bloomy rind to keep the cheese intact. The sweetly earthy, nutty flavours are light and delicate when young, becoming more pronounced with ripening. A lovely after dinner cheese weighing around 180 g (6 oz).

Caprino delle Langhe 🐐 PIEDMONT

A small medallion weighing 90 g (3¼ oz) with a natural thin rind hugging the close-textured pate. The Alta Langhe is in the heart of the Piedmont, which is also famed for its wines that work beautifully with this cheese, especially when ripened to give the flavours a more earthy quality.

LEFT, TOP LEFT CHEESE Robiola delle Langhe TOP RIGHT CHEESES Caprini Freschi and Truffle Cheese BOTTOM LEFT CHEESE Fiore di Langhe BOTTOM RIGHT CHEESE Caprino delle Langhe

BELOW Caprino Tartufo

RIGHT TOP Ricotta Carena BOTTOM Grana Padano

Ricotta Carena 🐄 LOMBARDY

Produced by Angelo Carena whose small farmhouse production is based in Piacenza, Lombardy. Angelo is famous for his Pannerone cheese, which has a protected place of origin (DOP), but his other fresh cheeses are a revelation if you have been used to supermarket-bought fresh curd cheeses. His Ricotta, made with cow's milk, is perhaps not quite as light and frothy as Seirass (see page 113) but nevertheless there is no sourness to the flavours, which are rich, dense and creamy.

Grana Padano 🐄 LOMBARDY

Piacenza is my chosen area in Lombardy for Grana. The dairy, No. 205, is situated in one of the designated zones, and is particularly prized for its taste and texture. Although often used as a young cheese as its Parmesan style has a creamier, crumbly texture rather than the grainy sharp Parmigiano, I like to have an aged version as well, around 18 months, to give a lovely fruity, gritty taste but still with that creamy density. Because the areas stretch from Trentino, through Piedmont and Lombardy the price of this 35 kg (77 lb) cheese is not as high as Parmigiano, but nevertheless it is still a taste to be reckoned with.

Gorgonzola

Gorgonzola is produced in the Piedmont and Lombardy regions. Both regions boast fertile and sheltered areas, like the valleys in Padana, which contribute to the complexity of flavours in the cheeses.

LEFT Gorgonzola Naturale

OPPOSITE TOP 'Combing' the curds

OPPOSITE MIDDLE LEFT 'Ironing' cheese during maturing

OPPOSITE MIDDLE RIGHT Cows in Lombardy

OPPOSITE BOTTOM Gorgonzola Dolce

Gorgonzola Naturale LOMBARDY

This 12 kg (26½ lb) cheese is traditionally made as a two-layered curd, using both the morning and evening milk, which is ladled in layers into the cheese moulds. The blue is from a *Penicillium roqueforti* added to the heated curds. The cheeses are brined in a salt water solution and left for a week or two before being pierced at the top, sides and bottom of the cheese to allow the blue bacteria mould to distribute evenly into well-spread blue-green veins. The taste is rich, fruity and sappy with earthy aromas. Perfect for the cheeseboard especially with a big, bold red wine, but also a favourite cooking ingredient.

I have tried Gorgonzola from both Piedmont and Lombardy, and there are subtle differences. While I like the rich buttery texture of the Piedmont Dolce cheeses, it is the Naturale from a small production in Valle de Padana, near Piacenza in Lombardy, that strikes a good balance. Everyone expects the flavours to be pronounced and nutty for the harder Naturale cheeses, but it is important that the blue doesn't have that aggressive, soapy attack, which can kill the taste of a wine stone dead. If you know the famous Grana Padano from this region with its sweetness and creaminess to the crumbly texture, you will also find the sweet, hazelnut, milky flavour coming through with the Gorgonzola too.

Gorgonzola Dolce LOMBARDY

Made in Piedmont and Lombardy, the Italians call it *erborinato* – Lombard dialect for 'parsley-green' – which is how the moulds look in the cheese. The Dolce is often termed 'Dolcelatte', which is a name given to a famous industrially made version, but in reality should not be associated with a true Gorgonzola. The Dolce cheese is really creamy and silky using milk from only a single milking per batch, weighs around 8 kg (17½ lb), and is cut into two half rounds, being such a soft cheese. The melting pate has blue veins gently bleeding into the curd, inducing a sweet nutty taste. As a table cheese it is sensational, but when used in cooking, such as spooning into pasta or risotto, it is delicious and unctuous.

Sottocenere al Tartufo Veneto 🐄

TREVISO

This is a compact smooth-textured cheese with flakes of truffle mixed into the pate before placing into moulds. The cheese is then brine-washed after a little ripening, left to dry before being rubbed in olive oil (to prevent moulds forming) and then rolled in fragrant ground spices including cinnamon and truffle essence. Fine ash cinders are then pressed onto the cheese to help retain all the delicious aromatic characteristics.

It is a difficult cheese to match to wine, due to all the spices, but perhaps a full-bodied dry red wine or a dessert-style wine from the region such as Recioto di Soave or a dry Prosecco di Valdobbiadene.

Pecorino Ubriaco 🐄 TUSCANY

(FINISHED IN TREVISO)

This is a Tuscan Pecorino that is shipped up to Treviso to be ripened and washed. The cheeses, which have been aged for three months, are plunged into a vat of Cabernet grape wine pressings, giving the rind a deep purple/burgundy colour. Left to marinate for at least 60 days and then dried out on wooden shelves in cool cellars, the resulting taste is deeply fruity and rich with a wonderful vinous aroma. There are cheeses made in this way in Tuscany and Umbria, but I believe the Treviso ones are much more elegant and refined.

Puzzone di Moena 🐄 TRENTO

The only rind-washed and rubbed cheese in this region, and although the name of the cheese is relatively new, the recipe dates to medieval times.

Maturing lasts for a minimum of 60 days but can go much longer — at least six or seven months. During the ripening time the cheeses are washed by hand once a week using a water-and-salt-moistened cloth, which is massaged over the cheese. This encourages the bacteria to form on the outside of the rind, and the intense, pervasive aroma or *puzzone* (meaning 'stinky') becomes more apparent as the bacteria also changes the colour of the rind to a pale golden apricot. This cheese has a chewy density and a nutty taste that is long and lingering.

ABOVE Pecorino Ubriaco
OPPOSITE TOP LEFT Sottocenere al Tartufo Veneto
OPPOSITE TOP RIGHT Puzzone di Moena, top cheese semi-mature, bottom cheese extra mature
OPPOSITE BOTTOM LEFT Strachitund
OPPOSITE BOTTOM RIGHT Taleggio

Taleggio 🐄 LOMBARDY

This is a washed-rind, soft, springy-textured square slab of cheese weighing around 1.7 kg (3¾ lb). The texture is creamy with a rich, melting quality that is not too salty, but has a lovely sappy, floral flavour, which marries well with firm, juicy cherries from Vignola (near Modena) as they have a slightly sharper taste but are delicious when partnered with certain cheeses. That salty-sweet grittiness to the cheese is a perfect partner to dry white and light fruity Valtellina wines.

Strachitund 🐄 LOMBARDY

The name of this cheese is derived from the local dialect meaning round (*stracchio*) and has been made in the Valbrembana area since the late 19th century. Weighing about 4 kg (9 lb), both morning and evening milk is used in the same way as Gorgonzola — the morning's milk is mixed with 25–30 percent of the previous evening's milk and then dry-salted before maturing for two months. The cheeses are periodically turned for even ripening, and at about 40 days they are pierced to allow a uniform growth of moulds. The blueing is hardly visible at first, and only after several months will you see the veining, which gives strength and nuttiness to the dry, crumbly texture. The natural crust develops its moulds, which have a mottled appearance, and careful monitoring is required as they can become wet and this affects the flavour.

Parmesan

Time is on Parmigiano's side, for it is this long, slow maturing stage where the environment works with the milk to produce the layers of flavour and texture that make this one of the world's most perfect cheeses.

Parmigiano Reggiano 🐄 EMILIA-ROMAGNA

The fact that Parmigiano Reggiano (Parmesan) is one of the healthiest cheeses, making it suitable for very young children, nursing mothers, the elderly and athletes, comes as no surprise. The long, slow ageing process helps the cheese to develop and disperse its goodness. Made with unpasteurized skimmed milk from accredited dairies within the allotted region of Emilia-Romagna, including Parma, Reggio Emilia and Modena, the crust of Parmigiano Reggiano is brine-washed, then rubbed with olive oil and slowly matured under strict supervision.

Only cheeses with the Consorzio Parmigiano Reggiano markings are the true Parmigiano, and there is a definite difference in flavours and textures between mountain or hill cheeses (with high numbers) and the valley and farms closest to the river Po (with lower numbers). Some believe that the low-numbered cheeses are the most prized, but they are also the most expensive. While my own preference is for the valley cheeses, mainly because I like this cheese to be at least three years of age, the mountain and hill cheeses are often more prized as their flavours are robust but not quite as gritty and salty.

The evening milk is left overnight in long, shallow metal troughs in a warm room. The cream will slowly rise to the top and the following morning is skimmed off, then the milk will be added to the morning's full cream milk, transferred to the vat where a starter is added and the milk is heated. This procedure is the kick-start to forming the curds and will also determine the flavour and texture profile of the cheese – too much or too little acidity in the starter can mean either too-dry or too-soft a crumble to the cheese. Next a traditional rennet is added and it takes 10–12 minutes for the curds to separate from the whey, ready to be 'milled' in the vat into tiny lentil-sized pieces. It continues 'cooking' until 55°C (131°F) is reached. The curds are placed into 'fascera' moulds, which have the characteristic markings that imprint into the cheese, then the ID showing the code number of the dairy is pressed on the outer rind, saying where it was made, the Consortium mark and the date of production. After immersing the cheeses in a brine bath for 24 days they are then ready for the maturing rooms.

I have forged connections with a very small producer called San Carlo who makes cheeses with milk only from his own herd and matures the cheeses in his own airy cheeserooms. This adds to the cost of the cheese since an inspector has to make regular visits to watch production, see that the cheeses are the right weight of 35 kg (77 lb), as well as test the cheeses as they ripen. Most producers prefer to take their cheeses directly to the Consortium maturing caves to be ripened by its professionals.

However, I can stipulate exactly what month and year of Parmesan I would like from San Carlo, and if he doesn't have what I want he will advise me what is at its peak. The butter they produce, which is made in very small quantities, is absolutely delicious – light and sweetly milky – perfect for making short pastry, and for mixing into a creamy risotto.

ABOVE LEFT The Italian countryside ABOVE RIGHT Carpineti Castle, Reggio Emilia
OPPOSITE Parmigiano Reggiano

Central & Southern Italy

Once into the central regions of Italy, you sense the influence of the Renaissance when visiting its beautiful cities, but travelling through the countryside, you can see why artists found this a paradise, and why tourists flock each year to soak up its history. The hams, salami and famous Chianina beef are prized in the regions of central Italy, and the cheeses that evoke this part are the Pecorinos – not just the hard, gritty, fruity ones, but also those that are soft and buttery, fresh and light, and others covered in bracken or vine pressings. The olive oils and wines of the region are also legendary.

   The Tiber River runs through Rome and is the major river of the southern 'boot' of Italy. The 'ankle' is Abruzzo and Molise and the southernmost part of Lazio, the 'toe' is Calabria and the 'heel' Apulia (Puglia), with the islands of Sicily and Sardinia off the coast. The weather is scorching in the summer, with rain and even snow in the winter – the arid rocky terrain and hills make farming difficult and transportation not easy. The cheese production here is Mozzarella from Campania where Indian buffalo were introduced to the marshy land, and the stretched curds of Caciocavallo 'gourds' hanging from the timbers, as well as strong and spicy Pecorinos. In Apulia you will find tomatoes and artichokes in abundance, olive groves and spicy olive oil, and all through this particular part of Italy the wines are big and bold.

Castagnolo 🐑 TUSCANY

This is one of these oddly shaped rounds of soft Pecorino with a natural thin crust, patted down to prevent too many moulds from flourishing. Weighing around 1 kg (2 lb 4 oz) the cheese has a smooth mellow richness with a sweet earthy taste, which can be matured for longer to obtain bigger flavours. The young cheeses are soft and springy, but if you ripen them quickly they become almost melting at the edges – if you are lucky enough to get them in this state, spoon some into a risotto.

Pecorino Marzolino Rosso 🐑

TUSCANY

This cheese is mostly seen with its natural rind still pristine white, achieved by placing the cheeses into cloths and then hanging them up to drain off any residue whey, and ripen. Weighing around 1.2 kg (2 ½ lb), the Rosso is removed from its muslin bag to have its rind rubbed in tomato paste and then olive oil before it is matured. The cheese is matured for 40 days giving it a light crumbly texture and a not too aggressive flavour, with hints of sweetness.

Casciotta Etrusca 🐑 TUSCANY

This is a soft ewe's milk Pecorino with a supple texture and a taste of milky sweet hazelnuts. Weighing about 1.5 kg (3⅓ lb) you will see these at the daily or weekly farmer's markets in all shapes and sizes. Melted into a sauce, or used as an accompaniment to young spring vegetables, it heralds the lighter foods for summer eating. Thinly slice the cheese onto piping hot bruschetta, for a quick and tasty lunchtime snack. Serve it with a smooth, dry white wine.

Capretta di Toscano 🐐 TUSCANY

This 2.5 kg (5½ lb) goat's cheese from around Maremma is very seasonal and not made in great quantity. It is a light sweetly milky, nutty-tasting hard goat's cheese, with the ridged rind rubbed in oil to give a deep ochre colour without any added bloomy moulds. It is especially good in the summer months when the sweetness of the milk really comes through.

Not to be aged too long as the gently earthy flavours are more desirable than the harsher more animal hints. It is especially good 'shaved' over a green salad or onto pasta with summer truffles.

Burrata 🐄 MOLISE/PUGLIA

This cheese is made elsewhere in Italy, but if you want to taste it at its best then make sure it comes from Molise or Puglia (Apulia). The cheese is so fragile that in summer it simply does not travel the distance on to London, so we stop selling it until autumn.

The cheese was invented by cheesemakers wanting to use up bits of cheese left over from their Caciocavallo and Provolone. They shred the pieces, add extra cream (from the cow's milk Mozzarella production) and place this into pouches made of Mozzarella curd stretched into a purse shape. The top of the pouch is squeezed together and tied with string, then dipped in a hot salty brine to cook it and make it more stable before being packed into a bag (although in the old days it was wrapped in the outer green leaves of leeks). Weighing around 300–500 g (10½–18 oz) this is a rich and creamy confection to eat as simply as possible.

OPPOSITE, TOP LEFT CHEESE Castagnolo TOP RIGHT CHEESE Pecorino Marzolino Rosso BOTTOM LEFT CHEESE Capretta di Toscano BOTTOM RIGHT CHEESE Casciotta Etrusca

ABOVE TOP The Tuscan countryside

ABOVE MIDDLE Burrata

Pecorino Tartufo 🐑 TUSCANY

Tuscany is the home of truffles, and in summer they are abundant and not too heavily priced. It is obvious that a small 500 g (1 lb 2 oz) truckle would be an ideal recipient of truffle pieces through the curd. The thin natural rind encases the cheese, which is flaky more than crumbly, but with a smooth mellow taste. The first impact is the sweetness of the ewe's milk with the follow-on of the truffles giving an earthy and aromatic taste. Lovely when fresh, but when ripened in cool humid rooms, it becomes richer and tastier with the truffle earthiness coming to the fore.

Pecorino Peperoncino 🐑 TUSCANY

Similar in size to the Tartufo, the fresh curds are mixed with chopped fresh red chillies to give the mellow-tasting cheese a spicy hot sweetness. Always look for cheeses made with fresh not dried chilli as the flavours will be fresher and livelier rather than too spicy. I love using this cheese when making pizza.

Pecorino Vilanetto Rosso 🐑 TUSCANY

This is another traditional-style cheese from Maremma made with unpasteurized milk to give a tangy flavour to the crumbly-textured cheese. Weighing around 3 kg (6½ lb), the young cheeses of early spring and late autumn have very different textures – spring cheeses are more crumbly and autumn ones smoother.

The ewes are allowed to roam and forage for their food on pastures studded with wild herbs and flora; by late summer the grazing areas are drier and very warm, which means that coagulation will be much quicker and will require only a light pressing. The caramel-coloured crust is achieved by lightly rubbing olive oil mixed with a little tomato paste into the rind before maturing the cheese in stone cellars. The Cuore cheeses are not quite as gritty with a softer more flaky texture, and flowery and fruity flavours to the taste.

Pecorino Vinaccia 🐑 PERUGIA, UMBRIA

This is a 4 kg (9 lb) farmhouse handmade ewe's milk cheese, which after a ripening period of three or four months is plunged into a vat of wine pressings including stems, skins, pips etc., and left for 30–40 days to macerate. The cheeses are then taken out and the vine pressings left on the cheese, and the maturing process continues in airy cellars on wooden shelves for another three months or longer. The resulting texture is hard with a moist crumble, the aroma is intense with the perfume of the wine pressings mingling with the salty-earthy cheese. The taste, as you can imagine, is strong, fruity and nutty.

RIGHT, FROM TOP RIGHT CHEESE DOWN Pecorino Tartufo, Pecorino Peperoncino, Pecorino Vilanetto Rosso LEFT CHEESE TOP AND BOTTOM Pecorino Vinaccia

Pecorino Affinato in Vinaccia in Visciola 🐑
APENNINE HILLS, UMBRIA

This 500 g (1 lb 2 oz) ewe's milk cheese has local cherries pressed on the outside rind. The Visciola cherry grows wild in Umbria and is rather like a Morello cherry. It is normally made into a sweet dessert wine, but this cheesemaker has taken the pressings after the juice is extracted and macerates three-month-aged cheeses for four weeks in the mixture. The result is a very intense fruity taste, making it strong but not bitter. The cheeses arrive with rather a sticky outside rind due to the steeping process, and if you find the aroma too powerful, then allow the cheese to dry out a little by placing on a tray in a cool room or cellar. Natural moulds will develop on the outside, which can be patted down to avoid becoming too thick. The cheese will become a little drier too, and will have a flaky texture with the flavour of the bitter cherry.

Pecorino Muffa Bianca 🐑 APENNINE HILLS, UMBRIA
From Gubbio, this 1.8 kg (4 lb) ewe's milk cheese is heated to just below pasteurization to help eliminate any unknown pathogens since the Sopravvissana and Sardinian sheep mostly graze on open pasture land with the addition of sweet dry hay during the colder months. The outside moulds grow naturally on the rind without any additional bacteria having to be added to the milk to encourage this process. The cheeses are aged for three months in stone caves in the hills, and the semi-hard texture has a lovely rounded taste with an aroma of wild flora and mushrooms. I prefer wines with a bit of bite and acidity with this cheese, especially the dry Chianti styles and Montalcino. You definitely need something that can cope with all the wild and fruity flavours.

Pecorino Montefalco 🐑 UMBRIA
From the town of Montefalco, this 1.2 kg (2½ lb) cheese is from a small family farm producing a limited quantity of cheese from their own flock of 150 ewes. Hand-milking is still valued and the traditional cheese recipe has not been altered. The cheese tastes earthy and nutty with a gentle sweetness, but with ageing there is a definite farmyard intensity, so we try not to keep it too long.

Formaggio di Fossa 🐑 UMBRIA
Weighing around 3 kg (6½ lb), this ewe's milk cheese, with additions of a little cow's milk, takes about ten months to mature fully. It is aged for five months in normal cellar conditions, then put into an Apennine *fossa* (which means hollow) for 90 days. The cheese is then matured for a further two months in normal cellar conditions to allow the deformed and softened cheese wheel to reshape and develop.

This is a rare, special cheese made according to Umbrian tradition: before placing it in the hollow, the rind is completely covered with herbs and spices from the hills — laurel, juniper, wild thyme, mint, rosemary and wild fennel. The cheese is then placed in a sack.

The flavours of Formaggio di Fossa are extraordinarily complex, fruity, aromatic, sapid and persistent. The cheeses are made in early summer, so the best time for eating is towards the end of the year or late winter. Because of the different flavours coming through with this cheese you need a well-structured red wine such as a Brunello di Montalcino or a Rosso Riserva from Chianti as an ideal accompaniment. Eat the cheese simply chipped into small pieces with a knife.

LEFT Formaggio di Fossa
OPPOSITE, FROM TOP CHEESE Pecorino Affinato in Vinaccia in Visciola, Pecorino Muffa Bianca, Pecorino Montefalco

LEFT Provola di Bufala Affumicate
OPPOSITE TOP LEFT AND RIGHT Provolone del Monaco
OPPOSITE BOTTOM RIGHT Mozzarella di Bufala
OPPOSITE BOTTOM LEFT Ricotta Salata

rather than put into moulds. Very fresh Mozzarella that is just 24–48 hours old has a tighter more chewy texture, and if you want to eat it this fresh you should really just keep the cheese in its own whey liquid at room temperature as you will taste the light, delicate qualities. However, keeping the cheese longer is not to be sniffed at as it becomes softer and creamier, and even after five or six days is still delicious. Just remember not to keep the cheese too cold as it is a hardier cheese than you think.

Provola di Bufala Affumicate
CAMPANIA

These small 300 g (10½ oz) Scamorze-style cheeses are made by heating up the Buffalo milk and adding the rennet and whey starter culture from the previous cheesemaking session. The curd is cut with wooden knives to expel as much whey as possible, and pressed together before slicing with steel knives into strips. After 24 hours the strips are placed into boiling hot water and large wooden spoons are used to stretch the cheese before being shaped and then dropped into a brine bath. The balls are tied with string made of wheat straw and smoked over wood chips whereupon the outside rind becomes a beautiful dark ochre colour. The aroma is intensely smoky and the taste is light and earthy with sweet oak-smoked flavours.

Provolone del Monaco NAPLES, CAMPANIA
This is an unpasteurized cow's milk cheese from Vico Equense, weighing 3 kg (6½ lb) from single milking only. The cheese is formed into its pear or cylinder shape, tied with string and left to hang in a cellar for 4–18 months with brine-washing in between. The outside rind is smooth and mottled with a few grey moulds and the flavours are sharp and herbal with a chewy density, redolent in both taste and aroma of the region.

Mozzarella di Bufala CAMPANIA
The humidity around the ancient town of Paestum and the Salerno province is perfect for the buffalo as they love to wallow in the muddy, swampy 'baths'. The term Mozzare comes from a Neapolitan word meaning 'to cut' as the stretched curds are cut into rounds or other shapes

Ricotta Salata PUGLIA, SICILY, SARDINIA
This is essentially a Ricotta that has been pressed of its whey, shaped into conical cylinders and is without any visible rind. Ricotta Salata's dried salty, firm texture makes it a good cheese for grating over pasta or as a filling for tortelloni. It is mainly made with ewe's milk, but also with buffalo and cow's milk. The cheese weighs about 300 g (10½ oz).

Pecorino Siciliano Peperoncino ⋒ SICILY

The addition of black peppercorns really spices up the flavour of the Pecorino, and the locals love this cheese with a glass of red wine. Shaving it over roasted artichokes is delicious, or even barbecued meats with thin slices of the cheese melting on top. It epitomizes summer, and toasted slices of country bread with tomatoes and slivers of this cheese are a great lunchtime snack.

Pecorino Siciliano ⋒ SICILY

The strong and spicy-flavoured Pecorino, weighing around 10–12 kg (22–26½ lb), is typical in Sicily and one farm, Casalgismondo, situated in the centre of Sicily close to the Greco-Roman site of Morgantina, produces an excellent cheese. The whole farm is run on organic principles, and the diet of the animals is supplemented by grain and hay grown on the farm. Maria Rita d'Amico and her dairymen make very traditional cheeses and this is the perfect example of how a sharp, salty Pecorino should taste. The Semi-Staggionati cheese is the one I offer when asked for a Romano style. The locals eat this cheese with a typical rough wine, but there are other ways of enjoying the cheese as a culinary ingredient. The Staggionati, which is very strong and salty, is lovely grated over pasta or vegetables instead of Parmigiano, and little nuggets with wine before dinner is a lovely appetizer.

Pecorino Siciliano Fresco ⋒ SICILY

The younger cheeses from Maria Rita d'Amico are really good as a simple snack, to chip away and serve with a full bodied 'meaty'-style red wine, especially those from the alluvial soil of Etna. The crumbly texture, with the outline of the reeded basket moulds just visible on the rind, is salty and sweetly earthy, yet has not acquired that aggressive 'catch in the throat' acidity of the older cheeses.

Formaggio Piacentinu Ennese ⋒ SICILY

Casalgismondo also make Piacentinu Ennese, an interesting local cheese weighing around 4 kg (9 lb), which takes on a deep gold or saffron colour from the infusion of saffron stamens. The curds have black peppercorns mixed in, then are strained into rush containers and placed into hot whey to cook. They are drained and covered with a weighted lid and left for two or three days to continue the draining before being dry-salted for a month and then matured. Best eaten fresh to experience the flavour of the saffron together with the hit of the peppercorn; pair with a sweet Sicilian dessert wine, although the Nero d'Avola red wines will also go well.

Ragusano 🐄 SICILY

The 10–16 kg (22–35 lb) squared-off loaf of stretched curd cheese is quite unique. Made in the same way as Provolone or Mozzarella, the cheeses are made from late autumn to spring, although winter-made cheeses are deemed to be the best. The grass is not so scorched and dry as in summer and the air is cooler, making this a perfect environment for the local cow breed Modicana to graze. Because of the increased production there are also Swiss Brown and Holstein cows to help keep up with the quota of milk required. The curds are worked by hand or with a stick and shaped into a ball, pulling and re-shaping to begin the stretching and splitting process. All

LEFT, TOP CHEESE Pecorino Siciliano Peperoncino LEFT CHEESE Pecorino Siciliano Fresco RIGHT CHEESE Pecorino Siciliano
BELOW LEFT Ragusano
BELOW RIGHT Formaggio Piacentinu Ennese

ABOVE LEFT AND RIGHT, FROM TOP CHEESES Caprino Sardo al Caprone, Pecorino Tinaio Moresco, Pecorino Saraceno

this turning and smoothing and rubbing in a little oil and vinegar solution gives the surface of the cheese its lovely smooth ochre finish. Best eaten at between 8–24 months, the complex flavours and aromas improve with time. You will sense fresh earthy mushrooms, toast, bitter orange, fresh cut grass and all the Iblei mountain flora coming into play, together with the typical sharp and slightly wild herbal flavours.

Caprino Sardo al Caprone ✍ SARDINIA

The season for goat's cheeses from Sardinia is very limited due to the scorching hot summers and often very cold, blustery weather in the winter. The aged cheeses from Oristano are some of the loveliest I have ever tasted; the spring, summer and autumn cheeses matured for three to nine months have gentle sweet flavours ranging to those with a more 'feral' scent. The cheese has the typical 'donkey-back' shape (flat top and bottom and vertical sides) with a dark brown smooth rind from rubbing with olive oil and cinders to prevent thick moulds. The compact texture with little eyelets gives an intense and persistent taste with an aroma of dry grass and earthy farmyard. The 2 kg (4½ lb) cheese is available up to Christmas when we get aged versions; this is probably the most stylish hard goat's cheese I have ever tasted.

Pecorino Tinaio Moresco ✍ SARDINIA

This cheese is from Oristano on the west coast of Sardinia, where the land is irrigated by Sardinia's largest river, the Tirso, which gives the grazing pastures a mineral richness. The full-flavoured Pecorino has a lovely salty sharpness and fruity edge. The cheeses are brine-washed for the first 48 hours and then rubbed in oil and tomato paste to keep outside moulds from appearing. The crust develops an ochre hue and the flavours of the milk come through with a tingle on the tongue. This is a perfect table cheese, although you can also shave over salads and risotto.

Pecorino Saraceno ✍ SARDINIA

There are matured, semi-matured and fresher versions of Pecorino, but the ones from the rugged mountain areas in the middle of the island have really powerful flavours. The versions with a blackened crust have been oiled and rubbed and then matured in mountain caves. There is a sweet mocha style in the fruity flavours, and dry red wines with mouth-puckering tannins work well with this cheese. The younger cheeses with more golden rinds have a smoother texture and are less gritty; you taste the sweeter, floral favours, which are delightful with both white and red wines. The artisan cheeses come in odd sizes, which can vary from 3–6 kg (6½–13 lb).

Spain & Portugal

The Iberian Peninsula (with Spain and Portugal making up a vast proportion of the landmass) has an unusual position on the world map — it is on the south-western edge of the European landmass with North Africa within sight at its narrowest point. Its geographical position gives rise to a huge variety of climatic conditions. The peninsula has a coastline of over 3,300 km (2,0050 miles): the Atlantic Ocean to the north and west allows humidity to sweep over the limestone peaks, the Mediterranean Sea to the hot east and south carries warming air. The dominant features of the central plateaus and mountains are temperature extremes as well as differing precipitation levels.

The biggest rainfalls happen twice a year and the summers are exceedingly hot causing droughts — these extremes of alpine climate in the Spanish Pyrenees and Sierra Nevada to the sub-tropical Canary Islands are reflected in the styles and flavours of the cheeses and are in tune with the terrain. The central plateau, where the most extreme temperatures occur, is referred to by Castilians as *nueve meses de invierno y tres meses de infierno* — 'nine months of winter and three months of hell'. Over the years the soil has been improved by diverting water sources, but for the small independent farmer and cheesemaker, life is still subject to often harsh climatic conditions.

There are many rivers coursing through Spain and Portugal but many are dry for most of the year. The longest river, the Tajus, starts off in the picturesque mountain region of Albarracín in Aragon, and flows right through Spain to its outlet in Lisbon, the capital of Portugal. The Duero commences in Picos de Urbión in the province of Soria and flows out at Oporto, in northern Portugal. In Andalusia, the Guadalquivir (its name derived from the Arabic translation of 'the great valley') is of immense importance to the irrigation of the 'fertile valley' of this rich agricultural area; it begins in Jaén and ends in Cádiz.

Spain was slow to develop a modern approach to agriculture, and unfortunately the Civil and World Wars intervened up until the 1950s. Following this, changes started to happen, albeit slowly until 1975 when a more open attitude to farming and the communities became possible. Hardship may have existed but the farmers and cheesemakers have held onto their cheesemaking traditions to produce such a diverse range of cheeses throughout the country.

The northern and western coastal regions and valleys have cows grazing with some mixed farming, while the hills and mountain areas concentrate on goats and sheep. The burgeoning wine market, where land is being nurtured, has meant that farms benefit from better grazing conditions. The cheeses from the northern regions are diverse and of differing textures and styles, while the more dry, arid and mountainous areas of the west and Canary Islands have goat's and ewe's milk cheeses with strong, spicy flavours. The Archipelago of the Azores with its microclimate created by its situation in the Atlantic about 1,500 km (930 miles) from Lisbon, produces the famous São Jorge (St George) cheese (see page 148), a strong Cheddar-style which, when fully matured, gives Cheddar a good run for its money.

The reason for grouping the two countries together is not only their close proximity, shared geography and climatic conditions, but also the similarity of some of the cheeses. Northern Portugal has rugged mountainous terrain, while the south is open and hilly with the extreme heat restricting the styles of cheeses being made. Although the cheeses of Portugal are not as widely exported as Spain's, the few that are regularly shipped abroad have made an impact, particularly alongside their wines and cured meats.

Although the wines of both countries are exceptional, it is the fortified wines such as sherry and port that are so distinguished and somehow fit perfectly with the food. These wines became very popular in England in the 18th century, and the port trade has British names such as Cockburn, Croft, Dow, Gould, Campbell, Graham, Sandeman, Taylor and Warre. Try a chilled white port or dry sherry as an aperitif with a wedge of Manchego (see page 144) or a scoop of Serra da Estrela (see page 147) for the unique tastes of these countries. Both Spain and Portugal have great seafaring and exploring traditions, and when the Spanish and Portuguese migrated to new lands, their cheesemaking skills went too; this influence can be seen in the New World.

OPPOSITE TOP LEFT Mountain sheep in the Spanish Pyrenees
OPPOSITE TOP RIGHT Artisan cheesemakers in the Pyrenees
OPPOSITE MIDDLE LEFT Churns on the mountain pastures
OPPOSITE MIDDLE RIGHT Cheeses collected from a mountain maturing cave
OPPOSITE BOTTOM A rushing stream in the Pyrenees

North & North East Spain

From the Spanish Pyrenees with its alpine climate to the Mediterranean warmth of the east and the verdant 'green' north with its Atlantic influences, the terrain in northern Spain is varied and

dramatic. The people are hard working and proud, and the food culture in Bilbao and San Sebastián has rocketed to stardom, whilst the incredible ingenuity of Ferran Adrià of El Bulli has shown the world a new way of cooking. Yet the cheesemaking here is so simple, with styles and flavours that embrace the land, and appeal to the eye, with some cheeses resembling craggy rocks and others smoky mounds. From the rugged beauty of the mountains to the seaside cliffs and the lush pastures straddling the rivers, the cheeses in this part of Spain really reflect the land that has produced them.

Garrotxa ⚲ CATALONIA

The once-isolated and neglected hills close to Girona have now been reclaimed and a community of farmers make this semi-hard 1 kg (2 lb 4 oz) cheese. Garrotxa, with a natural thin crust rubbed in charcoal and then matured to give a soft velvety coat, is also known as Pell Florida (pressed flower). I visited the Bauma farm because I wanted to see how they had managed to establish the dairy in what was barren wasteland. The simple stone and wood building has been in existence since 1980 and the herd of goats have been increased year on year. As an area more alpine in temperature than Mediterranean, the cheese is subject to limited production during the winter months.

The process of making cheese is quite quick, and the day I visited we spent the morning heating the milk, then curdling to form large pea- or hazelnut-sized grains before draining the whey, then replacing with hot water before draining off again. This practice is important in order to keep the texture of the cheese firm and moist, and reduce the acidity slightly, which helps the texture and taste. The high humidity not only in the dairy but also

outside, together with the cooler air highlight how careful you have to be to get the texture right. As soon as the cheeses are out of their moulds after the final draining, they are rubbed in charcoal ash and then placed in a cold room with fans to dry them very quickly and 'set' the rind. Once they have had an hour or so in the drying room they go straight to the maturing cellars to ripen.

The rinds are closely watched and patted and turned to encourage an even growth of moulds but also to encourage close contact to the cheese. The crumbly, flaky texture adds a sweetness to the gentle goaty flavours and because the animals are allowed to roam on scrubby grasses as well as flowers and wild herbs, the cheese has a wonderful bosky flavour. I enjoy the younger cheeses; the aged versions require a very robust red wine as the more wild goaty flavours evolve. I think this is where I first tasted the fine red Spanish Priorat wine, accompanied by a fully matured Garrotxa cheese – a great combination.

OPPOSITE Garrotxa
ABOVE Herding cows in the Spanish Pyrenees

Montsec 🐐 CATALONIA

This is a classic northern Spanish cheese, especially prized because of the fear that artisan cheeses would become extinct. It is a credit to Enric Canut, a pioneer who re-established cheesemaking skills in Catalonia, and then helped revive traditional cheeses all over Spain. The air in the northern mountains is humid, encouraging natural moulds; on cheeses such as the 300 g (10½ oz) Montsec, its flaky light texture is dusted with ash to allow the moulds to grow evenly, but also to dry the rind a bit so that unwanted spores don't develop. It has a creamy, nutty flavour that isn't too strong.

Turo del Convent 🐐

CATALONIA

I came across cheesemaker Formatges Monber in Agramunt when I was exploring the Spanish Pyrenees. Their cheesemaking facilities are next door to the shop and café serving their cheeses with local wine. The set-up smacks of Enric Canut's aspirations for this region as it is young, enthusiastic and eager to bring traditional cheeses back into circulation.

Vall de Meranges Cremos 🐐 CATALONIA

From Lérida in the Spanish Pyrenees, this cheese is made following a traditional country recipe. The smooth rind has been brine-rubbed to give a pale glow, and the sweetly earthy, floral flavour becomes more intense with age and takes on a smoother, creamier texture. The season to eat this cheese is late winter to early spring, and cheesemaker Albert Pons matures the handmade cheeses on wooden shelving in cool cellars.

Bauma Madurat 🐐 CATALONIA

This cheese is from Borredà in the alpine mountainous part of the region, which becomes more Mediterranean in climate on the coast. It is a large, rectangular 1 kg (2 lb 4 oz) 'log' cheese with an ash rind that develops white patchy moulds as it matures. The taste is light and sweetly nutty with a crumbly texture, and although the outside rind suggests a spicy and strong cheese as the aroma can be quite forceful, the surprise is that there is a delicate milky quality coming through. An aromatic dry white wine is the perfect accompaniment.

This delicious 400 g (14 oz) cheese with a white bloom has a close crumbly texture and a clean, fresh floral taste. The younger cheese (aged three weeks) is gentle and lemony-acidic, but with further maturing it becomes much more goaty and assertive with a definite edge to the flavours.

Roncal 🐑 NAVARRE

The fertile landscape which takes in Navarre to the border of Aragon, is the traditional zone for this cheese, using the milk of the local Latxa and Rasa-Aragonesa breeds. The hard, close-textured cheese has a smooth rind from washing and rubbing to inhibit the growth of moulds. The *tome* (cylinder) 1–3 kg (2¼–6½ lb) must be ripened for at least four months before selling.

The dense texture is pitted with tiny eyelets or cracks in the pate, and the pale straw/cream colour makes it look delicate, but in fact the flavours are nutty, with dried-fruit salty sweetness coming through, which reflects the milk style from this local breed. Serve this cheese with slices of coarse cured sausages and a glass of dry red wine with a robust edge.

Idiazábal 🐑 BASQUE/NAVARRE

The smoked version is seen in the higher mountain area encircled by the Aralar and Urbia ranges, while the valley areas around Navarre have the unsmoked version. This is a cheese that should be allowed to ripen and mature as the flavours will improve immeasurably given time. The milk from the Latxa (pronounced Lacha) or Carranza breeds has high acidity and low fat giving the cheese a sharp crumbly taste and texture. The unsmoked cheese is lighter and more delicate whereas the smoked has an earthy sweetness to the flavour.

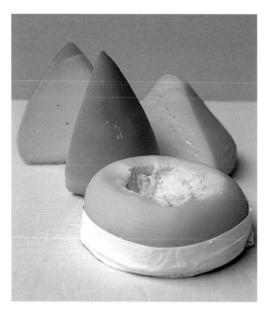

San Simón 🐄 GALICIA

A cone-shaped cheese weighing 375 g (13 oz) to 1.5 kg (3¹/₃ lb), formed using a special mould in a process similar to that of Tetilla (see below), but this cheese is smoked over birchwood which is native to the region. The flavours are not too strong or bitter, rather nutty and sweetly earthy, and it is popular throughout Spain. I love to partner this cheese with a pale, dry or even semi-sweet sherry, as the flavours match perfectly.

Tetilla 🐄 GALICIA

A cone-shaped cheese similar to the Arzua (see below) but a little more supple and scattered with a few small holes. Its origins are in La Coruña but nowadays it is made all over Galicia, and the milk from the local breed Rubia Gallega has had to be supplemented with other bigger milk sources in order to keep up with the demand. The 375 g (13 oz) to 1.5 kg (3¹/₃ lb) cheeses are mild and buttery and loved by children as it is almost spreadable. This versatile cheese is always used in tapas as it complements olives, cured meats, pickled and roasted vegetables, and also melts beautifully so is often used for gratins.

Arzúa Ulloa Arquesan 🐄 GALICIA

This is very typical of western Spanish cheeses, with its tubby shape, convex sides and its smooth washed and rubbed rind encircled with a cloth binding. Because this north-western region has such good pastureland, the cow breeds Rubia Gallega, Friesian and Brown Swiss are used for this cheese, which has a protected stamp of origin. The cheese, weighing between 500 g (1 lb 2 oz) and 2.5 kg (5½ lb), has brine washings to allow the rind to remain smooth and golden, and care is taken to prevent cracking of the rind by rubbing in a little olive oil. The cheese within is smooth and not as strong as you would find with goat's or ewe's milk, but there is a nutty complexity to the flavour from the brine washings. If matured the cheese becomes hard and has a much stronger flavour.

OPPOSITE, TOP LEFT AND MIDDLE CHEESES Vall de Meranges Cremos BOTTOM LEFT CHEESE Bauma Madurat TOP RIGHT CHEESE Montsec BOTTOM RIGHT CHEESE Turo del Convent

LEFT BELOW, LEFT CHEESE Roncal RIGHT CHEESES Idiazábal

LEFT ABOVE, LEFT CHEESE San Simón RIGHT CHEESE Tetilla FRONT CHEESE Arzúa Ulloa Arquesan

Peralzola Azul 🐑 ASTURIAS

This is a relatively new cheese made with ewe's milk. The style is leaning towards a French Roquefort, but less aggressive on the palate with nutty blue veins to give acidity. This delightful blue is excellent served with Pedro Ximénez, a dessert sherry, or port. Weighing around 2 kg (4½ lb), and with a slightly higher fat content since it is made entirely with ewe's milk, it is a welcome addition to the other Spanish blue cheeses, and although not actively exported yet, with increased production this cheese will be seen further afield.

Cabrales 🐄 🐐 🐑 ASTURIAS

This 2.5 kg (5½ lb) blue cheese is produced only in the village of the same name and three other villages. Principally a cow's milk cheese, but with additions of goat and ewe's milk in spring and summer when available, the texture is soft, but with a crumble that breaks down into a velvety pate. The cheeses are drained naturally, the salting is done by hand according to how the cheesemaker wants the flavours to expand. The cheeses are laid out in cool airy cellars for three to four weeks before transferring to limestone maturing caves that have a higher humidity than those of the Picos de Europa. The spread of the blue takes longer and can often be seen around the edges of the cheese, not all the way through. In this way you taste the metallic notes together with the salty, gritty crumble, which is very piquant and powerful. Match with the dessert sherry Pedro Ximénez for an amazing tasting experience.

Valdeón

The taste of this cheese reflects the landscape from which it springs. The limestone maturing caves found in Cantabria, the peaks of the Picos de Europa and even the trees in this landscape all influence the flavours of the cheese.

Picos de Europa (Valdeón) 🐄 🐐 🐑 CANTABRIA

The rich, creamy pate of this cheese with well-spread blue moulds has a mineral tanginess enhanced by the fruity zing from its sycamore-leaf wrapping. These are clues to the terrain of the majestically beautiful Picos de Europa mountains that cover the north and central section of the Cantabrian range. The peaks El Cornión to the west, Los Urrieles in the centre and Andara to the east are now part of the Spanish National Park and therefore protected, enabling tourists to explore the wild and picturesque landscape. Limestone caves, where the cheeses are matured, are key to the flavour profile of the blue cheeses from this area, and Picos de Europa is less intense than Cabrales, its other cheese. The leaf wrapping around the cheese gives the most stunning effect on a cheeseboard.

Picos de Europa is mostly made with cow's milk from sturdy Tudanca, Pardo-Alpina and Friesian breeds, with additions of goat's milk from the Pyrenees and Picos de Europa breeds during the spring and summer months. This is supplemented by a little Latxa ewe's milk, which can be detected in the flavours of the cheese. The cheese is dense and buttery with just cow's milk while more intense, sharp and spicy flavours are evident when the mixed milks are used.

Once the 2.5 kg (5½ lb) cheeses have been made and moulded, they are hand-salted, then pierced to encourage the growth of blue veins from *Penicillium roqueforti*, which was added to the curds. They are then wrapped in the leaves before being placed to ripen in the limestone caves with their natural humidity and cool temperature.

Allowing the cheeses to age for more than three months will encourage bigger flavours with a little more salty grittiness coming through. Drink a bold red wine with good tannins with this cheese, or even a port or Muscat if you wished to end a meal with just this cheese and a dessert wine.

RIGHT Picos de Europa (Valdeón)
OPPOSITE, TOP CHEESE Peralzola
Azul MIDDLE AND BOTTOM CHEESES
Cabrales

Central & Southern Spain

The climate in this area ranges from continental, then Mediterranean, with a little alpine in the mountainous areas to semi-arid along the south east corner. The Balearic and Canary Islands, although hot and sultry at certain times of the year, also enjoy good rainfall. For this reason the cheesemaking, especially on the Canary Islands with its rich volcanic soil, is very successful, and their semi-hard goat's cheeses have gained good recognition. The dusty Sahara winds and humidity inland with the sparse grazing areas do not see many cheeses produced here, although what there is on offer works very well with the great cured hams and meats. The southern zone, including the islands, also produces some very fragile, soft fresh cheeses, which are really delicious especially when served with strawberries or even peaches.

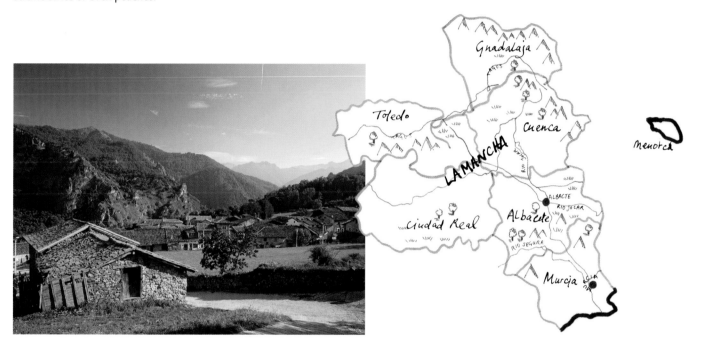

Murcia al Vino 🐐 MURCIA

The high milk quota from the Murciano-Granadina goat breed enables many styles of cheese to be made in Murcia. This traditional semi-hard, close-textured cheese weighing around 2.5 kg (5½ lb) is made both with a plain brine-rubbed rind and also dipped in wine and vine pressings to give a beautiful dark-red coating. The sweet flavours of the milk come through instantly, but having the wine wash means there is also fruit and acidity too. There are many hard and semi-hard goat's cheeses in Spain but this one is among the most popular with my customers.

Mahón 🐄🐑🐐 MENORCA

The island of Menorca has a microclimate allowing for lush pastureland and cheese producers are able to graze cows as well as a few sheep and goats. If you want to taste an interesting version of this cheese, look for those from

the hills named 'Llumena'. The artisan cheeses weighing around 2.5 kg (5½ lb) are made with raw milk from the unique Menorcan breed and Friesian cows, although goat's and ewe's milk are added at certain times of year when quantities are available.

The curds are wrapped in a cloth, suspended to drain off the whey, before being placed on a table and pressed of any remaining water. The bag is then swiftly placed in a brine bath before being transferred to the maturing rooms. The odd shape of the rounded edges and markings of the cloth on the cheese denote the real artisan cheeses. I love the younger *tierno* cheeses of summer with their paler crust smooth from being rubbed in oil to prevent moulds growing. In autumn I can't wait for the aged or *curado* cheeses with their toasted hazelnut flavours and salty, gritty texture to enjoy with the season's new crop of apples. The fresh, semi-mature and mature cheeses are also rubbed in paprika to give a darker finish to the rind, although I do not believe this adds to the flavours.

OPPOSITE, TOP AND MIDDLE CHEESE Murcia al Vino BOTTOM CHEESE Mahón

Manchego & Membrillo

The matching of a ewe's milk cheese like Manchego with the sweet density of slow-baked fruit such as quince (Membrillo) really enhances the flavours of the cheese. The milk used in Manchego is rich and earthy with an almost lanolin silkiness which, when made into a hard cheese, almost cries out for something sweet to highlight the richness but also temper the 'animal' flavour profile.

Manchego 🐑 LA MANCHA

The whole of La Mancha is devoted to Manchego, from the provinces of Albacete, Ciudad Real, Cuenca and Toledo. With its protected origin in place, this cheese is recognized throughout the world and the increased demand for it has placed the regulatory body under pressure to change the specified areas of the designation of origin.

This harsh, arid, rocky landscape was named Al Mansha, meaning waterless land, by the Moors when they were here; it exactly describes the extremes of climate – from freezing winters to unbearably hot summers with little rain and variable wind patterns – throughout the vast expanse of plains. The Manchega sheep are completely acclimatized to the extreme climate, as well as being able to digest the scrubby vegetation and grasses and what little vegetable and cereal fodder is grown for them. They are natural foragers, and take refuge under trees in the scorching heat of the day, or in makeshift shelters and caves in the winter.

The cheeses are ripened to varying degrees of strength; to enjoy the experience of Manchego you should buy a mild and medium, or medium and strong, or even a little of all of the types, to allow you to explore the flavour profiles. Shops often only sell one Manchego, which is a pity since the distinctive tastes evolve with maturity.

The cheesemaking process is slow: the fresh milk is cooled before being transferred to the heating vats where the rennet is added and the milk gently warmed. The curds are cut to very small rice-like grains and then heated again before the whey is drained. The curds are then placed into the moulds with the familiar basket pattern and pressed to drain off any remaining whey. Once scored with the Manchego seal, the cheeses have a further pressing, then are removed from their moulds, turned upside down and returned to the mould for another pressing. The cheeses are then plunged into a salt water bath for 2–4 days depending on the quality of the milk, the season and the fodder. Maturing takes place in cool rooms with high humidity and the cheeses are turned and rubbed to avoid unwanted moulds growing on the surface rinds.

The smaller cheeses, weighing around 1.5 kg (3^1/$_3$ lb), will take about 30 days, and larger forms around 60 days. However, the fully matured cheeses can take two years to reach their ultimate taste. Once you cut through the hard rind, the cheese is a pale creamy yellow with a few eyelets and cracks formed during the maturing, the aroma is sweetly earthy and sharp, and the flavour is not buttery but savoury with hints of caramel and hazelnuts.

This cheese is copied all over the world, even down to the decorative outside pattern, but do not be confused as only Manchego will have the name emblazoned on top of the cheese.

The perfect accompaniment for Manchego is Membrillo, a quince jam. The fruit when eaten raw is sharp and bitter, but if cooked slowly with added sugar it turns into a dark brick-red-brown shiny jam or paste with a taste that is fruity with a good acidity to serve alongside cheese or cured meats.

ABOVE The Manchego stamp
BELOW, LEFT Membrillo quince block RIGHT CHEESE Manchego
OPPOSITE LEFT The maturing caves for Manchego
OPPOSITE RIGHT The fields of La Mancha

ABOVE, TOP CHEESE Serra da Estrela,
BOTTOM CHEESE Terrincho
OPPOSITE The landscape in São
Miguel, Azores

Portugal

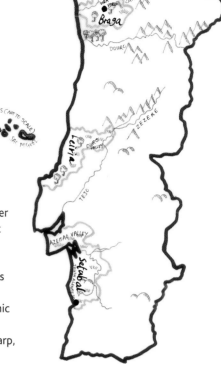

Portugal is split by its major river, the Tagus. This creates a clear demarcation of the landscape as the northern terrain is mountainous where rivers course through the valleys, and the south features a rolling landscape of plains and hills and a hotter, drier climate. The summer weather in the mountainous areas is very arid and blazingly hot with the animals huddling under what trees or bushy shelter there is for shade. The islands of the Azores and Madeira produce fine cheeses as well as the famous dessert wine, and the Duoro wines from the north with their rich style and savoury sweetness are a great partner for the cheeses. Even though Spain is so closely connected, the cheeses of Portugal have their own very distinct flavours and textures, and the volcanic soil composition rich in minerals means the grazing areas give a really interesting structure to the milk. Portuguese cheeses have a very definite identity as they are sharp, yet rich, but with a herbaceous tingle quite unlike other European cheeses.

Serra da Estrela 🐑 NORTH

This cheese is named after a mountain between the Dão and Mondego rivers, a landscape of rugged natural beauty, spreading down to fertile orchards and vineyards producing some of Portugal's most popular table wines. The cheese is probably the most famous with a protected place of origin (DOP), and while similar cheeses are made in Spain, it is the Portuguese Serra da Estrela that most stands out. This is because of its delicous and unique flavour, and the very small designated area where this cheese can be made.

Local Bordeleira or Churra sheep provide the milk, and the spring cheeses are rich and herbal, whereas the late winter versions are more intense and dense. The curdling of the milk is not done with the traditional rennet but with cardoon thistles (*Cynara cardunculus*) that grow wild in this region. This imbues the cheese with a peculiarly earthy, lemony, bosky herbal flavour that is very unusual, and is absolutely delicious when paired with a fortified wine such as port or a Duoro red wine. There are similar cheeses in other regions of Portugal probably due to the migration of shepherds to warmer climates in deep winter.

Transforming the unpasteurized milk means that great care has to be taken with hygiene at this crucial stage. The milk is strained and heated, and the cardoon rennet is added to curdle the milk. The whey is drained, the curds washed a little and then broken down by hand before being placed into muslin-lined moulds and slowly pressed by hand, which gives a dense, elastic texture to the cheese. They are rubbed with salt and left overnight before being placed in the cold but humid maturing rooms. The cheeses are ready after 30–45 days for the Amanteigado or buttery-textured style and after at least six months for the matured or Velho style.

Terrincho 🐑 UPPER DOURO VALLEY

Weighing between 800 g (1 lb 12 oz) and 1.2 kg (2½ lb), this protected place of origin cheese is made entirely of milk from the local Churra da Terra Quente ewes. Popular throughout Portugal for its strong, vegetal flavours and its harder texture, which is a foil for the softer-style spicy cheeses. Ripe after 30 days, although the flavours are more pronounced in cheeses aged for 60 days or more. The brine-rubbed rind is sometimes worked with paprika to add another dimension to the flavours.

Cabra Transmontano and Quinta dos Moinhos Novos Serrano 🐄 VILA VERDE

New developments from the company Quinta dos Moinhos Novos include the Cabra log, which has a French-style bloomy rind tasting surprisingly sweet and nutty, given the almost melting edges hugging the rind. The Serrano is a close-textured hard cheese still retaining a juicy crumble, which is presented either with a simple smooth white rind, or washed in wine giving a lovely fruitiness to the flavours. Both these cheeses suit the local light, sparkling white wine perfectly.

São Jorge 🐄 AZORES

One of Portugal's rare cow's milk cheeses, as well as the largest, it is a magnificent-tasting hard cheese. Unpasteurized cow's milk is mostly used for São Jorge cheesemaking from late spring to summer. The hard cheese has a sort of waxy texture, but it is rather like a Cheddar, with sharp, nutty flavours and crumbly texture, and if aged over a year, is really delicious. If you make a Portuguese fondue, use this as the base cheese, and add softer cheeses at the end of cooking.

Graziosa 🐄 ILHA GRACIOSA

Ilha Graciosa, called 'White Island', is known for its wines as well as meat and agriculture. The semi-hard cow's milk cheese is similar to São Jorge (see above), but simpler and rustic with a sharper, fruitier quality that almost tingles on the tongue.

Serpa 🐑 SOUTH ALENTEJO

These protected place of origin cheeses vary in size from 120–500 g (4–18 oz). This cheese is made with predominantly Lacaune ewe's milk, although there are still a few local Merino herds. The heated milk is passed through a cloth filled with salt, which means no other salting process is needed, the thistle liquid is added and then after about 40 minutes the curd is ready to be cut, drained, moulded and then ripened. The Amenteigado (softer) curd is often thought to be the more preferred way of eating this cheese (like spooning out a Serra da Estrela). If you allow the Serpa to mature to a harder consistency the flavours develop to become powerful, strong and spicy.

Évora 🐑 ALENTEJO

This ewe's milk cheese, with its protected place of origin place, is produced in small rounds of 120–200 g (4–7 oz); traditionally the cheeses are placed in a stoneware pot filled with olive oil to preserve them through the year. However, today, there are very tiny, softer cheeses to be eaten at a fresher stage; the larger versions are aged 60 days or more to give a dense, almost brittle texture with scattered holes due to the slow draining procedure. They have a strong, spicy, tangy taste, making the cheeses suitable as an *entrada* or appetizer.

Azeitão 🐑 AZEITÃO

This is another protected place of origin cheese, which includes the areas of Palmela, Sesimbra and Setúbal. The cheeses are ripened for 23 days to form a semi-soft creamy texture to the smooth, full, rich fruity flavours. The Assaf breed of sheep is used for the milk and cardoon thistle for the coagulant; the curds are shaped by hand to form the rounds and pressed of as much whey liquid as possible before going to the ripening rooms, where further moisture reduction will take place. The 250 g (9 oz) cheeses are eaten with a spoon, and the taste is sweetly earthy and not too strong.

Castelo Branco 🐑 🐐 CENTRAL

Similar in style and flavour to the Serra da Estrela (see page 147) insofar as the true artisan cheeses are made from ewe's milk using thistle flower as rennet, while the mixed milk cheeses using both the ewe's and goat's milk are similar in style and appearance but called Beira Baixa Amarelo (medium – 40 days matured) and Beira Baixa (strong – 120 days aged) and use traditional rennet. The region around Castelo Branco is protected by a microclimate giving the pastures a lushness that is evident in the flavour of the cheese. Although similar to Serra da Estrela, these cheeses are a little more yellow in colour.

Nisa 🐑 ALENTEJO

These cheeses, weighing around 300 g (10½ oz), have a protected place of origin. The area is commonly known as the 'bread basket' of Portugal, a vast open countryside with a softer, undulating landscape and rich fertile soil. The cheeses have the cardoon thistle coagulant, and the flavours have a somewhat sweeter and less fermented sour taste than other similar-style cheeses.

Barrão 🐑 ALENTEJO

These little cheeses weighing around 150 g (5½ oz) with the familiar yellow waxy-smooth rind and 'sheepy' aroma are very similar in flavour to neighbouring cheeses such as Nisa (see above). However, being smaller they are harder and therefore stronger – a perfect aperitif cheese to serve with a chilled white port. The Monte Barrão, in the northernmost part of Alentejo, is well suited to cattle rearing, and sheep and goats can be seen grazing on the open plains or gathered under the trees.

OPPOSITE TOP LEFT, BACK CHEESE Novos Serrano **FRONT CHEESE** Cabra Transmontano

OPPOSITE TOP RIGHT, TOP CHEESE São Jorge **BOTTOM CHEESE** Graziosa

OPPOSITE BOTTOM LEFT FROM TOP Évora, Évora second round, Serpa, Azeitão

OPPOSITE BOTTOM RIGHT, BACK CHEESE Castelo Branco **MIDDLE CHEESE** Nisa **FRONT CHEESE** Barrão

The Rest of Europe

The distinctive cheeses from the following European countries serve as symbols of identity for those nations included and have also had a great influence on New World cheesemaking. Cross-border movement of people in Europe has often resulted in cheese being made in one country that is evocative of and influenced by the taste and style of cheeses produced in neighbouring countries.

The land and climate obviously play a big part in the style of cheeses produced by these different countries, but the necessity to produce food that will keep well from the land to the table also plays its part. These countries do not produce a vast array of styles like France or Italy, but somehow the cheeses through their shapes and flavours give you an instant snapshot of the places, the people and their cuisines.

THE NETHERLANDS

Protecting the land from flooding has always been a priority in the Netherlands. Reclaimed marshy areas demonstrate how the land can be managed and adapted for dairy farming and agriculture. Cheese plays a huge part in the country's economy and there are five main cheese markets: one in Woerden with a modern commercial format, and four that are still based on the traditional way of selling from stalls in Alkmaar, Gouda, Edam and Hoorn.

Gouda 🐄 GOUDA

The name 'Gouda' has never been registered or trademarked and is therefore used throughout the world wherever this style of cheese is made. Gouda accounts for about 50 percent of the cheese production in the Netherlands and is done on a huge commercial scale. However, the *Boerenkaas*, or farmer's cheese, is made from unpasteurized milk from the dairies' own herds with additional milk from no more than two other farms operating on similar lines. This ensures the hands-on production and slow ageing of the cheeses.

The cheeses take on an amazing range of flavours as they age. A seven-month-old cheese (*belegenkaas* meaning young) will have a smooth texture with a gentle nutty flavour and creaminess to the light, salty, tangy taste. This is a perfect cheese for breakfast or for shaving slices on toasted granary bread topped with tomatoes. In a two-year-old cheese the texture is a little more dense and has

hints of crystallization where the proteins in the milk give a salty tang. This is a delicious lunchtime cheese to serve with slices of baked ham and pickled cucumbers as well as on a cheeseboard. These cheeses are *oude kaas* or old. At four years old the cheese becomes darker and more solid with the crystals of protein more evident, and the flavours are caramelized and rich with a brittle texture. This super-aged cheese is great with fine red wines from Bordeaux.

Some Goudas have cumin, nettles and mustard seed added to them and are generally eaten younger, although ageing gives the flavours a bigger spicy taste. The flavoured Goudas are interesting and complex, and again a perfect companion to beer.

In recent years goat's milk Gouda has appeared, and the sweetness of the milk is totally different in style to any other goat's cheese. There are also Goudas with truffles incorporated into the curd giving the milk a gamey taste that is delicious with a glass of dry champagne.

RIGHT, TOP LEFT CHEESE Two-year-aged Gouda TOP MIDDLE CHEESE Cumin Gouda TOP RIGHT CHEESE Four-year-aged Gouda WHOLE CHEESES, FROM TOP Nettle Gouda, Mustard Gouda, Two-year-aged Gouda, Seven-month-aged Gouda BOTTOM LEFT Goat Truffle Gouda

SCANDINAVIA

The term 'Scandinavia' is commonly used for Denmark, Norway and Sweden, and all have long cheesemaking traditions. The Scandinavian climate is very varied: ranging from typical western European weather for Denmark and southern Sweden and along the west coast of Norway; humid continental weather from Oslo to Stockholm in the centre; and subarctic conditions further north. The areas with dairy farming have perfect grazing conditions and clean, clear air giving the grass a sweetness that is reflected in the milk and the cheese.

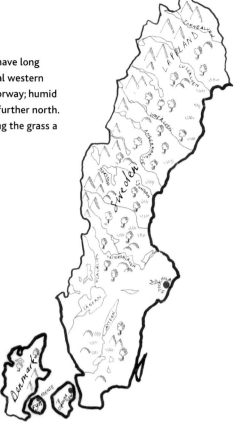

Svecia ☞ SWEDEN

This is a semi-hard cheese weighing around 12–15 kg (26½–33 lb) with a waxed rind that is then foil-wrapped. The smooth, firm paste gives a soft buttery, dense texture and a lovely mellow taste yet nutty sharp finish. Svecia is a typical cheese from the low-lying areas all over Sweden and is sometimes seen with added cumin or cloves. This is quite a low-fat cheese at 28 percent and is particularly favoured at breakfast on a dark rye bread, or as part of a meal with Swedish herring dishes and a glass of Schnapps.

Greve ☞ SWEDEN

This is a semi-hard cheese rather like the Norwegian Jarlsberg, weighing around 15 kg (33 lb), although it also has similarities with a Swiss Emmentaler (see page 97). The dense texture has scattered cherry-sized holes and is best eaten at around ten months when the flavours will be rich and buttery but also have a zingy, tangy finish. This style of cheese suits beer and lager perfectly, but also a fruity zesty white wine works works very well with this cheese.

Kryddost ☞ SWEDEN

This is a semi-hard cheese weighing around 12 kg (26½ lb) with a softer paste that is densely packed with cumin and cloves. It is a real delicacy in Scandinavia

OPPOSITE, FROM TOP CHEESE Svecia, Greve, Kryddost, Havarti

where it is served as part of a buffet-style meal with herring and pickled vegetables, fish and meat, but also thinly shaved onto dark rye bread. These styles of cheese can be eaten young, but if matured will become very tangy and spicy in flavour. Try serving this cheese with a glass of strong Schnapps for the perfect accompaniment to the flavour profiles.

Havarti ☞ DENMARK

There are lovely old stories surrounding Havarti, which was originally created by Hanne Nielson in the 19th century as a cottage industry on her family's farm Havarthigaard in Øverød, north of Copenhagen. She had travelled around Europe and wanted to try to create a cheese that was somewhat like a semi-hard Swiss style. Today this cheese is sold as a major commercial brand both plain and with all sorts of flavour additions; when you find a more artisan version you will be pleasantly surprised by the flavours.

The cheese has a really sticky orange rind and a high aroma, but straight from the fridge the texture will be dense and the flavours quite mellow. I prefer it at room temperature with the edges starting to melt and the taste becoming nutty, sharp and tangy.

Serve this cheese with a selection of smoked and cured fish and meats and thinly sliced rye bread with unsalted butter. It works perfectly with a glass of light fruity red wine or a Pilsner beer.

POLAND, GREECE & GERMANY

Agriculture accounts for more than 60 percent of the land in Poland. The cheeses produced are influenced by other European countries, although Poland has its own traditional cheeses. Greece, in the Mediterranean, is a diverse country with mountains as a backdrop and the beauty of the islands. From north to south, Germany is a cheese country. A third of the production is exported and influences from neighbouring countries have resulted in a diversity of cheese styles.

Ser Korycinski 'Swojski' 🐄 NORTH EAST POLAND

A traditional family-style cheese, it was mainly produced by the Jewish population until the Second World War and sold throughout the country. Nowadays, this local cheese is made in bigger quantities yet still retains its 'homely' appeal of uncomplicated clean, light flavours.

The cheese is mainly served fresh without any visible rind and has a flaky texture like a pressed Ricotta, which is either plain or with herbs or black peppercorns. It can be spread on rye bread with a sprinkling of sea salt, or used to make fillings for a salty cheese pastry as well as being used for a drier-textured cheesecake.

Feta 🐑🐐 GREECE

The wide fertile plains of Thessaly are one of the seven protected regions for Feta production and each region has its own unique tasting style. The Peloponnese Feta is harder, drier and more salty than the one from Thessaly, while Macedonian Feta is much creamier and mild in flavour. This is also due to the individual production style and if you have previously thought the cheese to be a rather uninteresting salty affair, then search out the barrel-aged cheese, which is far superior.

The time of year will define whether more ewe's or goat's milk is available, although the ewe's milk will give a richer, earthier and more complex taste profile, and the goat's milk a lighter, lemony sharp style. The perfect accompaniment to have with this cheese is a delicious fresh Retsina wine, which copes beautifully with the salty, sharp flavours of the cheese.

Bachensteiner 🐄 GUNZESRIED CO-OPERATIVE, GERMANY

The cheese styles in Germany have associations with cheeses from surrounding countries: for instance Tilsiter and mild Gouda have a Dutch ancestory and Limburger is related to both the Netherlands and the Belgian Herve. Monasteries were instrumental in creating the cheese recipes as well as the beers, and cheeses like Bachensteiner with its washed rind are typical.

This brick-shaped washed-rind cheese of 200 g (7 oz) has the familiar high aroma typical of smear-ripened cheeses, but the chewy, soft texture is quite mild and buttery with a mellow finish. You can cut Bachensteiner into small squares or shave into long curled slices and sprinkle over caraway seeds and top onto rye bread. A blonde beer works well with the flavours of this cheese.

Münster 🐄 ZURWIES CO-OPERATIVE, GERMANY

Near the historic city of Wangen im Allgäu in south east Baden-Württemberg, this biodynamic dairy makes a classic Münster cheese, both large, 500 g (1 lb 2 oz), and small, 200 g (7 oz).

Unlike its French counterpart, the German cheese has a lighter, more delicate taste, almost like soft, fresh, bitter almonds. The sticky washed rind can be further enhanced by massaging a Gewürztraminer wine into the cheese and then leaving it for a day or two until it becomes very aromatic and gives the cheese a lovely nutty richness to the flavour profiles.

Some people can be put off tasting this cheese as it has a very strong aroma. This is due to the rind-washing and the damp, cold cellar conditions during maturing to encourage the development of the rind. This process creates the beautiful, warm, orange-apricot glow to the outside of the cheese, but also a very high almost farmyardy odour. Münster is a perfect example of not judging a cheese by its smell, as in reality this cheese is rich and mellow, and its strength is really only found in its scent on the outside rind. The dry Riesling and the aromatic flamboyant Gewürztraminer wines are good matches, as are Pinot reds or even a northern Rhône.

Limburger 🐄 ZURWIES CO-OPERATIVE, GERMANY

Making a Limburger that is so different from the mass-produced cheeses has been a work in progress for cheesemaker Anton Holzinger, and it has paid off. The simple-style cheese, weighing 200 g (7 oz), is great for lunch with a thick slice of smoked ham, but it is only when tasting an artisan version of such a well-known cheese that you get the real pleasure of the flavours.

This cheese has a high aroma due to the bloomy rinds coming into contact with the salty brine solution. The flavours of the cheese are mellow, rich and creamy. Partner with a rich, dry Chardonnay, or other full-bodied white wine.

OPPOSITE TOP LEFT, LEFT CHEESE Bachensteiner RIGHT TOP CHEESE Small Münster RIGHT BOTTOM CHEESE Large Münster

OPPOSITE TOP RIGHT Ser Korycinski 'Swojski'

OPPOSITE BOTTOM LEFT Limburger

OPPOSITE BOTTOM RIGHT Barrel-aged-Feta

USA & Canada

There is a cheese revolution taking place in America: a pastoral movement where a spirit is rippling through an already substantial cheesemaking tradition. I realized that the times were a-changing when I tasted the prototype Vermont Shepherd cheese from the Major's farm, Putney, Vermont back in 1993. It was a revelation; it was only a matter of time before I would be hearing more about new cheesemakers and the vivid response to the usual bland and ordinary offerings.

Every time an American customer came into my shop and bemoaned the fact that their country's cheeses could never be compared to European counterparts, I have defended farmstead cheesemaking, and guided them to the best US cheese shops in their part of the country. The incredulity that such things existed highlighted how shopping had become a weekly trawl in a supermarket rather than a daily visit to local shops and a weekend forage in a farmer's market. Although US farmer's markets have been going for many years, it is only recently that urban dwellers have taken them to heart — even in the centre of Manhattan. Shoppers can now indulge in the joy of buying local, seasonal and reasonably priced foods at famer's markets in cities all over the US. A favourite market takes place in Union Square, in New York, where you can find an incredible selection of salads and vegetables as well as cheeses coming in from small farms just outside the city.

These new American cheesemakers have a definite entrepreneurial mindset — some have left the fast lane to return to their country roots, others just want to get back to the land and see what nature provides. Some producers have big operations, then decide to scale down with another small artisan dairy alongside to make a completely different style of cheese. My initial expectations of American cheeses were modest, but what I have found is a myriad of flavours and really good maturing practices.

In order to assess the cheeses of the United States and Canada, I needed to understand how the countries are divided by culture. In Canada the early settlers were French and Scottish, while along the West Coast of America they were Italian and Hispanic. The Midwest was settled by the Germans, Scandinavians, Norwegians, Dutch, Welsh and Cornish, and the East Coast by the British, French, and Dutch as well as the Amish, Greeks, Armenians, Eastern Europeans and Italians. It is interesting to note that in the 1960s and 1970s when new irrigation techniques were implemented, the explosion of artisan or farmstead cheesemaking started in earnest.

There are literally hundreds and hundreds of cheeses, but what I have detailed here are just some notable varieties by both artisans and larger producers. I can't wait to go back to the States and search out more cheeses. It is indeed miraculous what is now available not only at local farmer's markets but also in delis and supermarkets.

BELOW LEFT The fields at Andante Farm, Petaluma, California
BELOW RIGHT Sheep at the Three-Corner Field Farm, Shushan, NY
OPPOSITE TOP LEFT The barns at Three-Corner Field Farm
OPPOSITE TOP RIGHT A goat at Rawson Brook Farm, Massachusetts
OPPOSITE BOTTOM LEFT The barns at Three-Corner Field Farm
OPPOSITE BOTTOM RIGHT Sheep in the barn at Three-Corner Field Farm

West Coast

Along the west coast in California, great swathes of desert precluded any agricultural farming until irrigation brought water for grazing and pastureland. Fruit and vegetables were the first major crops, and dairy farming started thereafter. Everyone knows California is sunny and hot, but in the north it is bitterly cold and mountainous. However, from Los Angeles to San Francisco and further north, cheese production has blossomed and the temperate climate is perfect for producing some of the best goat's cheeses you will ever taste.

Moving into Oregon, the valley around the Willamette River in the western part of the state is where most agriculture can be found. The Pacific coastline is gloriously scenic and windswept, with huge Douglas firs and Redwoods, which contrast with the rugged Cascade mountain range in the north. The weather on the West Coast is mild and with good rainfall, but in the northern and eastern region the winters become bitterly cold, whilst dry and hot in the summer.

Washington is the most north-westerly of the states (except for Alaska), and borders Canada. It is a land of contrasts, from the temperate rainforests of the Olympic Peninsula to the semi-desert found east of the Cascade Range. The mostly temperate climate and good rainfall has allowed dairy farming to flourish for over 150 years, but cheesemaking is relatively new, although making a big impact with quality, stylish flavours and textures.

CALIFORNIA

California is bordered by Oregon to the north, Nevada to the east, Arizona to the south east, Baja California (Mexico) to the south and the Pacific Ocean to the west. The major rivers serving the Central Valley flowing out to the Pacific are the Sacramento and San Joaquin, and in the north the Klamath with the Colorado to the south east. Cheese production in California is expanding, and the goat's cheeses are excellent.

BELOW Goats in the fields at Andante Farm, Petaluma, California
OPPOSITE TOP AND BOTTOM Vella Cheese Company, Dry Jack Special Reserve

Dry Jack Special Reserve  VELLA CHEESE

COMPANY, SONOMA, CALIFORNIA

Much of the milk comes from Mertens Farm which is close by, and although the majority of the milk is from Holstein cows, this cheese also contains at least a 30 percent Guernsey milk for its rich, buttery qualities.

Dry Jack Special is a more aged version of Vella's original Jack cheese that was produced to take account of the new refrigerators in the late 1930s onwards and housewives wanting to be able to keep the cheese longer. When the Italian population grew in the 1950s, a drier, harder version was made so that it could be grated in the style of a Parmigiano. However, the super-aged versions are gold-medal winners, and the long, slow ageing gives the flavours a big hit and a dry, almost crystalline crumble. The 3.5 kg (8 lb) cheese is brined and left to dry naturally for some days before a special mixture of oil (soya or safflower but without colour or flavour), bitter cocoa powder and black pepper covers the cheese. After 18 months or even longer these shiny brown wheels reveal their lovely flavours of fruit and nut but never that slightly bitter sharpness of Cheddar. Perfect for both white and red wines, especially the Sonoma County style, Zinfandel.

Fiscalini Farms 🐄 STANISLAUS COUNTY, CALIFORNIA

The farm is situated rather comfortably between the
Sierra Nevada mountains to the east, and the California
coastal range to the west, giving a perfect climate and
environment for the Holstein cows to graze.

San Joaquin Gold is a 12.27 kg (27 lb) natural rind cheese,
which has been bandaged to hold back the mould growth.
Although it has a Cheddar style it was supposed to be based
on a Fontina recipe with a smoother, chewier texture.
Ultimately it falls between the two, and is a delightful
'snacking' cheese with its nutty and buttery flavours.

Cloth-bound 18-month-Aged Cheddar On cutting, this cheese
is mature and has a good crumble to its golden pate with
a nutty almost sweet and toasted balance of flavours. This
24 kg (52 lb) cheese isn't in competition with British
Cheddars since it has enough personality of its own. Look
out for the imprint of the cow stamped on top of these
cheeses, and enjoy with the Pinot Noirs of California.

Point Reyes 'Original' Blue 🐄 POINT REYES, CALIFORNIA

The Giacominis run a family farm and use only their own
milk for cheesemaking. They developed their famous
blue with the aid of Monte McIntyre who refines the
2.5 kg (5½ lb) cheeses for five or six months in humid
cellars aided by the salty Atlantic breezes that sweep across
the farmland. The flavours are strong and meaty with
richness to the moist almost gritty texture. A strong full-
bodied wine would be best but this cheese is also a perfect
component to a blue-cheese butter or as a dip.

Cowgirl Creamery 🐄 POINT REYES STATION, CALIFORNIA

Peggy Smith and Sue Conley left their former jobs in
catering to become cheesemakers; their milk supply comes
via the farm of Bill Straus, which goes to make all the
cheeses and fresh curd, crème fraîche, Fromage Blanc and
quark. The two cheeses listed below are the best known,
and have receive numerous awards. These are perfect
partners to hard, sharp cheeses and buttery blue cheeses
as well as the myriad choice of Californian wines.

Red Hawk is a 250 g (9 oz) triple cream, brine-washed
cheese with a buttery richness and top notes of savoury
meat juices. This is no mean feat since washed rinds are
notoriously difficult to ripen without becoming too sticky
and rancid tasting. This cheese is a must on a cheeseboard
selection that brings together hard, fruity-tasting cheeses
and blues and softer, sharper cheeses. It's all about
achieving a balance.

Mount Tam is a 250–300 g (9–10½ oz) buttery rich cheese whose bloomy white rind is a cross between a thick chunky Coulommiers, with a chewiness of a Pont l'Évêque. However, being a *Penicillium candidum* rind it has an earthy mushroom aroma – the best way of enjoying the cheese is with the rind still white and downy, with a hint of beige ridges coming through from the shelf grids, and the cheese within still springy with scatterings of tiny eyelets.

Bellwether Farms   PETALUMA, CALIFORNIA
Since 1992 the Callahans at Bellwether Farm have been making ewe's milk San Andreas, which has a very seasonal production, and a buttery, dense Jersey cow's milk cheese called Carmody. Both of the cheeses are the result of trips the Callahan family took to Italy, where they were inspired by the cheeses. Petaluma is situated just 20 km (12 miles) from the coast, giving the grazing land whiffs of iodine and sea spray that, in turn, give the cheeses their

ABOVE, TOP LEFT CHEESE Point Reyes 'Original' Blue TOP RIGHT CHEESE Bellwether Farms, San Andreas FRONT LEFT CHEESE Carmody FRONT RIGHT CHEESE Cowgirl Creamery, Red Hawk MIDDLE CHEESE Mount Tam
OPPOSITE, TOP CHEESE Fiscalini Aged Cheddar Gold, BOTTOM CHEESE San Joaquin Gold

salty sweetness. As with many small dairies in the US, a selection of other cheeses are made – crème fraîche, Fromage Blanc, yoghurt and a peppercorn cheese as well as Ricotta are available in small quantities.

San Andreas has a definite sweet earthiness of a Pecorino. It has a smooth, full flavour and is delicious with red wine, crusty bread and olives.

Carmody, especially the Reserve, has a chewiness along with the rich creaminess of younger-style Italian cheese with its washed and rubbed-smooth rind. This particular cheese is a simple table or family cheese and can be enjoyed as part of a cheeseboard. The name Carmody was given after the road that runs adjacent to the farm.

Goat's Leap ☛ SAINT HELENA, CALIFORNIA

In the heart of the famous wine country of Napa Valley, Barbara and Rex Backus live out their dream that started back in 1972. The small Spanish breed of sturdy LaMancha goats thrive in the Californian climate, and all the cheeses have a lovely sense of flora and herbs as background flavours.

Barbara thought up the names, which relate to her passion of all things Japanese, and the toppings really do reflect their style. The milk is slowly pasteurized to retain all the flavours of the milk, and by using a traditional rennet all the cheeses reveal a clean taste with subtle and zesty tang.

As Goat's Leap is a small producer you will see these cheeses locally and at farmer's markets as well as good restaurants. Alongside the ones listed, they also produce a hard Tomme style with a natural dried crust called Carmela, and very fresh small cheeses made to order.

Eclipse is a tubby drum with a bloomy coat clinging to the ash-dusted covering, topped with a star anise spice. Cut into the cheese and you will see a vein of ash running through the centre of the cheese, which explains the name as Barbara and Rex likened it to the sight of a lunar event in the sky. The flavours of this cheese are bright and lemony, perfect for the local crisp, fruity white wines or softer reds.

Dafne is a delightful 200 g (7 oz) tubby, slightly flattened top cheese with a pale almost translucent *Penicillium candidum* mould rind, in the French style. The topping of bay leaves gives a clue to the name, but it also indicates the herbal and floral notes of the cheese as the goats graze on the open, unpolluted hills aound the farm for as long as the season allows.

Kiku is a seasonal 'Banon'-style cheese, with a covering of fresh vine leaves that have been dipped in Sauvignon Blanc, wrapped around the cheese and tied with raffia string. This gives the cheese a really tangy taste, with edges that are just melting. This cheese is a perfect summer cheeseboard choice.

Sumi is a lovely truncated 200 g (7 oz) pyramid with an ash coat covering the downy white, bloomy rind. Once cut the sparkling white interior has a flaky, dewy texture and lovely nutty crisp flavours.

Hyku Noir is a delicious cheese dusted with ash and topped with a pomegranate blossom. This opulent flower motif is an unusal topping for a cheese – toppings of this nature are rarely found on European cheeses. However, it does add a beautiful element of surprise as well as reflecting the landscape.

Hyku is like a large Crottin (see page 63) with patchy white, bloomy moulds and a fudgy texture that will start to melt further after cutting. If allowed to become too soft its flavours will be compromised and become a bit bitter. This is a perfect cheese to enjoy with a Pinot Noir, particularly those of the region.

Redwood Hill Farm and Creamery ☛
SONOMA, CALIFORNIA

Jennifer Bice and her partner Steven Schack are leading breeders of dairy goats and have been making cheese since 1978. The farm is located in Sebastopol, which is right in the heart of wine country, with a beautiful green landscape of apple orchards, forests and meadows as well as the world-famous vineyards.

Their breeds include Alpine, Nubian and Saanen goats, which all produce good quality and quantity milk. The goats are left to roam and forage outside during the fine weather, and when the rain and wind become uncomfortable as the season changes the animals are brought inside to keep warm.

They make a large selection of cheeses in small batches, mostly in a fresh, zingy style, but there is also a lovely creamy one too. Apart from the softer cheeses, they also make a goat's milk Cheddar-style cheese, which is aged for 5–6 months and is good for grilling and as a table cheese. In addition, they produce a smoked version of the Cheddar, Feta and a new cheese called Gravenstein Gold, which has a 'smear' or washed rind using a local cider made with the Gravenstein apple variety.

Fresh Chevre can be literally scooped out of its pot; these 150 g (5½ oz) cheeses can be spread on crackers or bread, and taste light and gently earthy. It is a lovely young cheese, which you can use in cooking for cakes or as a filling for pasta, and is also a perfect introduction to goat's cheese. By allowing them to ripen and age further, the bloomy rind dries and the texture within becomes crumbly and nutty. The more aged cheese is perfect for light red wines and dry whites.

Camellia is a Camembert-style cheese weighing around 200 g (7 oz) with a soft white *Penicillium candidum* mould with a downy-fluff style. There is a yeasty and creamy taste coming through in the flavours of the softer, riper cheeses, while the younger cheeses are rather gentle and can be a good starter cheese for those who want to avoid 'goaty' flavours. I would eat the rind and all with this cheese as the light nutty flavour of the crust is a good foil for the mild creamy interior.

California Crottin, a multiple award-winning cheese, weighs about 150 g (5½ oz) and has a fudgy yet crumbly texture that dries out beautifully to a small hard ball and is perfect for grating. The flavours of lemon zest are gently earthy and you can either eat as is, or perhaps dust with a little black pepper and grill to top a mound of baby green salad leaves.

Andante Farm

Petaluma still retains its old world charm, and the countryside around Andante Farm is unspoilt, quiet and lush even though it is only 51 km (32 miles) from the cosmopolitan city of San Francisco.

Andante Farm 🐄🐐 PETALUMA, CALIFORNIA

Soyoung Scanlan has a musical background, and it is no surprise that the names of her cheeses express this part of her life. I met Soyoung when she visited London, and she spent a day or two in our cheese room tasting some of her favourite French cheeses. What marks her cheeses out among many others is the finesse and delicacy of not only the inner cheese, but also the rinds. The milk is pasteurized due to the 60-day minimum ripening in the US for unpasteurized milk cheeses, but this does not detract from the flavours, as according to Soyoung, it is the starter cultures that give the milk curds their flavour and texture at this vital first stage.

Soyoung has an academic and methodical way of working, and production is small, so she sells locally and also at a few favoured restaurants. Her cheesemaking facility is based next to the Volpi farm where she sources the goat's milk, and the Jersey milk she gets from Spring Hill farm in Petaluma. There is nothing high tech about her cheesemaking — it is pure and simple, and relies entirely on her expertise and delicate touch.

Cavatina is made as small- and larger-sized goat's milk logs with ash coating, similar to a Sainte-Maure (see page 62) from Touraine, but with a lighter crumble to the texture. I am bowled over by this cheese mainly due to the fine rind and the scattering of the soft, downy white bloom.

Cadence is a mixed cow's and goat's milk cheese with extra cream added. This cheese is similar in style to Saint Félicien (see page 69) and is perfect for the cheeseboard. The flavours are rich and creamy with a little tangy aftertaste from the goat's milk addition.

Minuet is a goat's milk cheese with cow's milk crème fraîche added at curdling stage to give a rich density to the texture. The light white bloomy rinds give a gentle earthy aroma to the cheese. Match with a Chenin Blanc white wine to help cut through the density of the cheese with a crisp, refreshing zing.

Figaro is a mixed cow's and goat's milk cheese, wrapped in fig leaves that have first been dipped in white wine. Available only during the summer when figs are in season. The texture is rich, and the flavours have an astringent quality from the wine-soaked leaves.

ABOVE, BACK ROW LEFT CHEESE Minuet BACK ROW RIGHT CHEESES Cavatina
(large and small) FRONT ROW LEFT TOP CHEESE Cavatina FRONT ROW LEFT BOTTOM
CHEESE Figaro FRONT ROW RIGHT CHEESES Cadence

BELOW The barns at Andante OPPOSITE TOP LEFT Cheesemaking at Antante OPPOSITE TOP RIGHT
AND BOTTOM LEFT Goats at Andante OPPOSITE BOTTOM RIGHT Cheesemaker, Soyoung Scanlan

Sierra Mountain Tomme ✍ LA CLARINE FARM, SOMERSET, CALIFORNIA

This farm is the perfect setting for the cheesemaking and now the vineyard that encompasses this 4 hectare (10 acre) enterprise. Caroline Hoël, who trained in France as a cheesemaker, and Hank Beckmeyer have the right attitude to farming and cheesemaking. Their classic 1.2 kg (2½ lb) hard goat's cheese is sweet, nutty and full of the flavours of the meadows and pastures. The crust forms naturally over the minimum three months ripening, and the pure white crumbly pate is perfect just on its own or maybe grated or shaved over salad or vegetables. The crust is beautiful with patches of white and pale grey moulds and beats European cheeses in terms of purity of flavours.

Cypress Grove ✍ MCKINLEYVILLE, CALIFORNIA

Much has already been written about Mary Keehn since she is a pioneer of the Californian artisan cheese phenomenon, and her signature cheese, Humboldt Fog, still looks as unique today as it did in the late 1980s, when it suddenly jumped into the spotlight. Today, Mary doesn't have goats herself, but the same care and consideration goes into every batch of cheese she makes, and like most American small producers she makes numerous cheeses of different styles. Humboldt County is a huge Redwood-encrusted area close to the ocean that is known for its natural beauty.

Truffle Tremor is a white bloomy-rind cheese weighing 1.3 kg (3lb) and is a rather sophisticated tasting sensation with the scattering of black truffles through the curd. The flavours are light and frothy with that earthy quality of the truffle giving a truly decadent taste.

Humboldt Fog is stunning with its ripple of ash through the centre of the flaky white crumbly cheese, and the outside ash coat thickly scattered with white moulds, is like the wafting mists that filter through the woodland. The edges of the cheese just begin to melt and that contributes to the lemon-zest tang of the flavours.

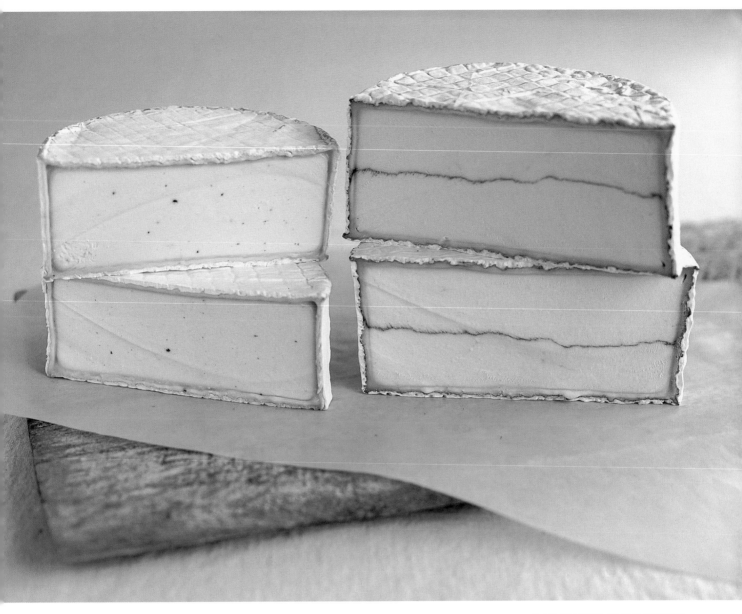

St George 🐄 MATOS CHEESE FACTORY,
SANTA ROSA, CALIFORNIA

Joe and Mary Matos hail from the island of São Jorge in the Azores. The famous cheese of the same name produced on the island (see page 148) gave them inspiration to make their own version when they made their home in Santa Rosa in the 1970s. St George, weighing between 5–10 kg (11–22 lb) has that familiar sharp crumbly texture and taste. The Atlantic salty breezes give the definition to the flavours much like their Portuguese counterpart. This cheese always wins prizes, mainly because it has further depth to the flavours that are both rich and spicy. Match St George with local wines such as a spicy full-bodied Zinfandel red.

RIGHT Matos Cheese Factory, St George
ABOVE, LEFT CHEESE Cypress Grove, Truffle Tremor RIGHT CHEESE
Humboldt Fog
OPPOSITE La Clarine Farm, Sierra Mountain Tomme

OREGON

Oregon is situated in the Pacific Northwest on the Pacific coast, with Washington to the north, California to the south, Nevada to the south east and Idaho to the east. The major rivers are the Columbia and Snake, which cross through the northern and eastern boundaries. The eastern region of the state has evergreen forest and pine and juniper woodland, and a semi-arid scrubby landscape and prairies, which stretches from Central Oregon.

Rogue Creamery 🐄 CENTRAL POINT, OREGON
A big investment in time and effort went into creating the custom-built maturing caves at Rogue Creamery, to ensure the right degree of cold and humidity.
Smokey Blue, one of the notable cheeses of Rogue Creamery, is the original Oregon Blue recipe (the first blue cheese made on the West Coast) that is then cold-smoked for 16 hours over hazelnut shells, giving a sweet caramel nuttiness to the sharpness of the blue.
Rogue River Blue is wrapped in local Syrah and Merlot vine leaves that have been marinated in a pear brandy. The year-long-ageing gives the flavours a big, fruity twang and a creamy dense texture. This cheese is made with late summer milk only and therefore availability is limited.

Up In Smoke 🐐 RIVER'S EDGE CHÈVRE, THREE RING FARM, LOGSDEN, OREGON
Cheesemaker Pat Morford makes up to 20 different styles of cheese. The herd of goats graze on 5 hectares (12 acres) of pasture and woodland. Up In Smoke is a small 150 g (5½ oz) hand-moulded rindless cheese, wrapped in maple leaves that have been smoked and then dried. The cheeses are smoked over alder and hickory chips, but first the outer leaf wrappings are sprayed with a little bourbon, which keeps the leaves moist and imparts a smokey flavour.

BELOW Rogue Creamery, Rogue River Blue

Juniper Grove Farm 🐐 REDMOND, OREGON
Pierre Kolisch's farm enjoys a climate of cool nights and sunny days, with mineral-rich volcanic soils, clean air and pure water from the Cascade Mountain, contributing to the perfect environment for the herd of 110 goats. Pierre, like many farmstead cheesemakers, prefers to make a range of cheeses as well as the ones listed.
Bûche is a 150 g (5½ oz) log, with a wheat straw complete with flower head through the middle. The close texture and crumbly mouth feel are perfectly ripened, and the flavours are rich with the complex nutty and tart combinations. The rinds on all the cheeses I tasted were absolutely right and I suggest you do not cut them away.
Tumalo Tomme is a 1.5 kg (3⅓ lb) semi-hard cheese in the French mountain style, with a natural crust that has been rubbed during ripening in the cellar. The texture of the cheese is slightly moist and crumbly with scattered eyelets from the drying during ripening. The flavours have a sense of the wild flora with full-bodied, earthy qualities.
Pyramid is a 150 g (5½ oz) classic in the style of Pouligny-Saint-Pierre, with a perfect thin and delicious rind that really comes into its own when ripened for 8–10 weeks. The drier, crumbly style has an elegant almost restrained taste, which is perfectly suited to dry white wines.

Pholia Farm 🐐 ROGUE RIVER, OREGON
What is important to this cheesemaking team is their commitment to the land and to their animals. Allowing the goats to forage and graze in the open pastureland means they have an ever-changing choice of food.
Elk Mountain is very much like a Pyrénées Tomme d'Aydius (see page 75), with its washed and rubbed rind giving a smooth finish to the crust and patches of natural white bloom. The 2.5–3 kg (5½–6½ lb) cheeses need three or four months of slow ripening to reach their potential.
Hillis Peak looks very much like a Spanish hard cheese with a herbal acidity and a gentle salty tang. The basket-mould pattern on the outside rind, which has also been rubbed with oil and smoked Spanish paprika, acquires a dusting of white bloom during the 6–8-month ripening period.

Pondhopper 🐐 TUMALO FARMS, BEND, OREGON
This semi-hard, pressed cheese weighing 4 kg (9 lb) has a smooth texture with scattered eyelets due to the addition of the local microbrew made with Cascade hops. The waxed outside rind holds the flavours intact; the ripening and daily rub help develop the hoppy yet sweet flavours.

ABOVE, MIDDLE CHEESE Rogue
Creamery, Smokey Blue
VINE-WRAPPED CHEESES River's
Edge Dairy, Up In Smoke

RIGHT, FROM TOP Juniper
Grove, Bûche, Tumalo Tomme, Pyramid

BELOW LEFT, TOP CHEESE Pholia Farm, Hillis Peak
BOTTOM CHEESE Elk Mountain

BELOW RIGHT Tumalo Farms, Pondhopper

WASHINGTON

The landscape of Washington State is quite varied, with forests and mountains, the highest being Mount Rainier. The climate is mostly temperate, which has encouraged successful dairy farming. Cheesemaking is a fairly new development, although there are now some very interesting cheeses coming out of Washington.

OPPOSITE Beecher's Flagship Reserve ABOVE LEFT Mount Townsend Creamery, Seastack ABOVE RIGHT Sally Jackson Cheeses

Flagship Reserve 🐄 BEECHER'S, SEATTLE, WASHINGTON

This is a cloth-bound truckle weighing around 7.5 kg (16½ lb), and is my cheese of choice for macaroni cheese! Although in looks and crumble Flagship resembles Cheddar, because the culture used is reserved for Gruyère and Emmental, this pushes the nutty aroma and creamy texture forward and lessens the tangy sting you sometimes find in Cheddar.

Seastack 🐄 MOUNT TOWNSEND CREAMERY, PORT TOWNSEND, WASHINGTON

Matt Day and Ryan Trail have only been making cheese a few years but their clean flavours and terrific way with ripening rinds have given their cheeses an elegance and depth. Seastack is one such cheese, which is a 150 g (5½ oz) disc covered with charcoal ash and then ripened to allow the white *Penicillium candidum* moulds to blend in with the ash. It is obvious that the cheesemakers are tipping their hats towards France, but giving the cheese a few more weeks ripening will allow the earthy and nutty flavours to come forward.

Sally Jackson Cheeses 🐄🐐🐑 OROVILLE, WASHINGTON

Sally Jackson and her husband Roger are pioneering spirits who exactly reflect the commitment and energy required to not only master artisan cheesemaking, but also allow it to develop modestly.

Sally doesn't follow a strict rule of thumb and is self-taught, preferring to use her eyes, rather than reading from a technical book. Her cheeses are wrapped in locally collected chestnut and vine leaves, and the moulds are made by a local potter. The cheese production is small, since they only have around 25 sheep and goats and a few dairy cows.

The cow's milk cheese is around 1 kg (2 lb 4 oz), the goat's is a smaller round weighing 300 g (10½ oz) and the ewe's milk is a hexagonal shape of 300–400 g (10½ –14 oz). The flavours of Sally's cheeses are fruity and bosky from the leaf wrapping, but the milk has a gamey sweetness to it, reflecting the farm's environment of grasses, edible weeds and alfalfa. I would serve a bold and dry, fruity red wine with these cheeses and it would complement the flavours perfectly.

Central United States

The United States is a vast country with a huge diversity of landscape within its central region – good dairy farming and good cheesemaking abound in such far-flung states as Wisconsin, Minnesota, Iowa, Illinois, Indiana and Colorado. The many different styles of cheesemaking take into account the settlers from all over the world who have made these states their home.

WISCONSIN

Known as America's Dairyland, this state is north-central but considered part of the Midwest, bordered by Minnesota to the west, Iowa to the south west, Illinois to the south, Lake Michigan to the east, Michigan to the north east and Lake Superior to the north. The land is rich if somewhat rocky, and the weather patterns suit dairy farming with an emphasis on cheese. Blessed with a good river system right through the state and Lakes Michigan, Superior and Winnebago, all the elements for good dairy farming are present and there is a justifiable pride in the way this is supported by the various associations offering information, tours and festivals all to do with cheese. The many different styles of cheesemaking take into account the settlers from all over Europe who have made Wisconsin their home, and it is hard not to fill a whole book just with cheese from Wisconsin, but here is a good selection.

Bleu Mont Dairy 🐄 BLUE MOUNDS, DANE COUNTY, WISCONSIN

About 50 km (30 miles) from Madison, the dairy is situated between Blue Mounds State Park and Brigham County Park where Willi Lehner and Qui'tas McKnight have honed their craft. Willi learned cheesemaking from his father, who first gained experience as a cheesemaker in his native Switzerland. The milk for the cheeses is supplied by local organic farms utilizing a rotating pasture system for feeding the cattle.

Bleu Mont Cloth Cheddar This is a perfect example of farmhouse cheese with its distinctive musty aroma on the crust, which has been brushed free of any tiny cheese mites that gather during the long ageing process. The crumbly texture is perfect, not too dry and not too moist and acidic, and there is a sweetness and nuttiness with a long lingering finish. The more aged cheeses have that crystalline density somewhat like Parmesan, but even so, there is no hint of bitterness coming through, just lovely beefy caramel flavours. The 5 kg (11 lb) cheeses are wrapped in fine muslin in the traditional manner and then brushed with a solution of clean water mixed with moulds from the rinds of aged cheeses to seal the wrappings. Once in the maturing room with its high humidity and cool temperature the natural airborne bacteria will filter into the cheeses.

Lil Wil's Big Cheese is a Swiss-style cheese with a smooth, dense texture and a brine-rubbed rind. The 1 kg (2 lb 4 oz) cheese is brine-washed using the method of mixing soil from the farm with fresh water, then filtering. The cheese itself is a Havarti style with a rich texture that is almost melting at the edges. After the brine washing, the cheese is rubbed, then placed in the maturing rooms for ripening where a white bloom grows on the rinds. A micro-brewed beer from the state works with this cheese.

OPPOSITE TOP LEFT, TOP CHEESE Bleu Mont Dairy, Lil Wil's Big Cheese **BOTTOM CHEESE** Bleu Mont Cloth Cheddar

OPPOSITE TOP RIGHT Bleu Mont Cloth Cheddar

OPPOSITE BOTTOM PICTURES The Bleu Mont Dairy

Fantôme Farm 🐐 RIDGEWAY, WISCONSIN

Anne Topham and Judy Borree with their herd of 12 goats make just enough cheese to sell at the local Dane County market. Goat's cheese is not a familiar sight in Wisconsin and so it is to their credit that the cheeses have made such an impact, gaining medals at prestigious cheese awards.

Fleuri Noir is lightly dusted with charcoal, the curds are hand-ladled and left to drain in muslin cloths, then salted and whipped before placing into moulds. The sparkling white cheese is light, almost frothy, and fresh in taste with a clean acidity.

Small Plain Chevre is delightful as a very fresh cheese, or you could let it ripen a little to dry out the texture and give a flakiness. It has very simple crème-fraîche acidity and creaminess.

Ridgeway Ghost, with just a hint of speckled ash, is perfect fresh or if left to dry out a bit, becomes more dense. A perfect end-of-meal cheese.

Moreso is completely coated in dark ash, which gives a nutty flavour to the cheese, and would ripen up well to give a more complex taste. All these cheeses would be perfect with a white Sauvignon wine.

Brunkow Cheese Co-op 🐄 DARLINGTON, WISCONSIN

Karl Geissbuhler's family have been associated with dairy farming in Wisconsin since 1899, and today Karl and his partner Greg Schulte work with the help of over 30 dairy farmers who form the co-operative.

The Brunkow Cheese dairy used to churn out staple cheeses for the mass market, but have diversified to produce new artisan cheeses that are handmade and matured in an underground cellar on wooden boards, like those given below.

Avondale Truckle, made with unpasteurized milk, is a 9–10 kg (20–22 lb) cloth-bound truckle aged 6–18 months to develop layers of flavours that are fruity, dry, earthy and vegetal when mature, although more buttery when young. It has a lovely crumbly texture, and red full-bodied dry wines are a good match, although beefy beers and ales are a good partner too.

Little Darling is a 1.5 kg (3⅓ lb) truckle, aged for six weeks, that has naturally evolved outside moulds and a lovely grassy aroma with a rich flaky texture that is sweetly earthy. A red wine that is fruity and round rather than robust would work, as would craft-style beers.

Dunbarton Blue 🐄 ROELLI CHEESE HAUS, SHULLSBURG, WISCONSIN

The Roelli cheesemaking tradition started with Adolph, who hailed from Switzerland, and three generations later Chris has taken over, producing Emmental, Havarti, Cheddar, Gouda, Jack and other styles. In 2007 Chris developed a blue Stilton-style Dunbarton Blue. On tasting it you find a creamy richness with a fine crumble, and the blue is not intense but adds a nutty mineral quality. I would like to keep it a little longer to see how the flavours develop. Enjoy with a glass of dry red wine.

Ten-Year Aged Cheddar 🐄 HOOK'S CHEESE COMPANY, MINERAL POINT, WISCONSIN

Tony and Julie Hook's award-winning ten-year aged cheese, weighing 20 kg (44 lb) has a complexity of calcium crystals giving the crumble a lovely sharpness but with a full-bodied, rich and creamy finish. Enjoy this cheese with a red Bordeaux.

Mobay 🐐🐑 CARR VALLEY CHEESE COMPANY, LA VALLE, WISCONSIN

This dairy has been operating for over 100 years and Sid Cook is the fourth-generation family member to run the business. The 2 kg (4½ lb) Mobay cheese is based on Morbier cheese (see page 89) but combines goat's and ewe's milk with a stripe of emulsified grapevine ash to separate the two layers. The sharpness of the whiter goat curd contrasts with the sweetness of the ewe's milk, and the hint of fruitiness from the grape-vine ash stripe finishes off the taste.

OPPOSITE, TOP LEFT CHEESE Fantôme Farm, Fleuri Noir TOP RIGHT CHEESE
Small Plain Chevre MIDDLE RIGHT CHEESE Ridgeway Ghost BOTTOM
CHEESE Moreso

ABOVE, TOP RIGHT CHEESE Brunkow Cheese Co-op, Avondale Truckle
TOP LEFT CHEESE, ABOVE Carr Valley Cheese Company, Mobay TOP LEFT
CHEESE, BELOW Hook's Cheese Company, Ten-Year Aged Cheddar
MIDDLE RIGHT CHEESE Roelli Cheese Haus, Dunbarton Blue FRONT CHEESE
Brunkow Cheese Co-op, Little Darling

Marieke Foenegreek Gouda 🐄

HOLLAND'S FAMILY FARM, THORP,
WISCONSIN

Rolf and Marieke settled in Thorp
from the Netherlands in 2002,
first to become dairy farmers and
then to make a proper farmhouse
Gouda. The traditional recipe has
the addition of fenugreek, a seed
native to Asia much used in Dutch
cooking, and has a nutty, spicy/sweet
flavour. The fresh unpasteurized
milk is pumped directly from the
parlour to the dairy and straight into
the vats. The curds are made into 8
kg (17½ lb) forms and then pressed
before being taken out of their forms
and placed in a salt-water bath for
60 hours. The maturing rooms
have Dutch pine planks, which are
scrubbed daily to prevent moulds
growing, and these help absorb the
liquids that seep out of the cheeses as
they mature. For the first 14 days the
cheeses are turned daily and rubbed
to prevent moulds; during this stage a
waxy coat is painted by hand onto the
cheeses. Further maturing continues
with the cheeses being turned twice a
week until ready for sale.

Trade Lake Cedar 🐑 LOVETREE FARMSTEAD,
GRANTSBURG, WISCONSIN

Mary and Dave Falk practise a sustainability programme,
including creating their own cross-bred sheep in order
to develop a strain that is hardy to their region, grass-fed
only and still able to produce a high butterfat milk to give
the cheeses their unique flavours. The typical Trade Lake
Cedar weighs around 2.7 kg (6 lb). I was impressed by
the fruity deep flavours and the bosky aroma, due to the
cheeses having a platform of cedar branches in the 'fresh
air' ageing rooms.

Dante 🐑 WISCONSIN SHEEP DAIRY CO-OP, SPOONER,
WISCONSIN

Spooner's natural wild beauty not only boasts woods, lakes
and rivers, but also the hill grazing for sheep is ideal.
Dante is made with ewe's milk, which is sweet and nutty,
and its texture is slightly dry with a lovely flaky crumble.
The rind has a plastic coating, somewhat like a Gouda
without the waxing, it is there to prevent moulds growing
and a crust forming, and during the six-month maturing
time the cheeses are turned and wiped with a wet cloth
to keep the moulds at bay. A light Beaujolais-style wine
would be good with this cheese or a dry Riesling.

Petit Frère 🐄 CRAVE BROTHERS FARMSTEAD CHEESE,
WATERLOO, WISCONSIN

Thomas and Mark have 950 very pampered Holstein cows
and in 2001 they decided to become cheesemakers as well
as farmers. Their Petit Frère is a very good attempt at a
European washed rind and the small 250 g (9 oz) cheese
comes in a box rather like a Camembert. The brine-
washed rind is a deep apricot, and little patchy white
moulds grow to give a delicate mottled effect. The cheese
is at its best when the pate begins to melt around the edges
and the flavour is sensational – earthy, fruity and sweet. If
you like Munster, Epoisses or Ardrahan cheeses then you
will definitely love this.

Big Eds 🐄 SAXON HOMESTEAD CREAMERY,
CLEVELAND, WISCONSIN

The Kelssig family have farmed here since the 1850s,
having emigrated from Germany; the present family
members run the dairy farm and the creamery producing
five different varieties of cheese, all made with
unpasteurized milk. Big Eds, named after the founding
father, is 7 kg (15½ lb) of buttery texture with a mild,
sweet hazelnut taste that is instantly enjoyable. It has a
joyous appeal, which is especially good for those hesitantly

entering the world of artisan unpasteurized cheese tasting and is a true family favourite. The cheese is 'cooked' in the Asiago and Emmental style, pressed and ripened for 120 days although it can mature on up to six months. It is very versatile as both a table and cooking cheese.

Pleasant Ridge Reserve 🐄 UPLANDS CHEESE,
MADISON, WISCONSIN

Mike and Carol Gingrich together with Dan and Jeanne Patenaude started the farm in 1994. The cheese is modelled on Pyrénées cheeses such as Ossau, with particular attention to the washing and rubbing of the rinds during the maturing process, and replicating the temperature and humidity levels you would find in the stone caves of that region.

The fresh unpasteurized milk is processed into cheese directly after the last cow has been milked, and traditional cultures are used in the coagulation into curds. The slow ageing of the reserve cheese, 12 months minimum, gives a really layered flavour profile of fruit, nut, cream and acidity that is not only incredibly delicious but also lingering and sweet. This is an expensive cheese, but worth every penny and highlights the level of expertise from independent cheesemakers.

RIGHT TOP, LARGE CHEESE Saxon Homestead Creamery, Big Eds
SMALL CHEESE Crave Brothers Farmstead, Petit Frère

RIGHT BELOW, BOTTOM CHEESE Holland's Family Farm, Marieke Foenegreek Gouda TOP CHEESE Wisconsin Sheep Dairy, Dante

BELOW Uplands Cheese, Pleasant Ridge Reserve

OPPOSITE Lovetree Farmstead, Trade Lake Cedar

MINNESOTA, IOWA, ILLINOIS, & MICHIGAN

Often known as 'the land of 10,000 lakes', the soil in Minnesota is full of nutrients and mineral elements that give the cheeses their richness and depth of flavour. The land in Iowa is generally flat, although there are several natural lakes that give rise to good soil conditions and drainage. Illinois and Michigan both have fertile land and agricultural traditions, although cheesemaking is still a small production.

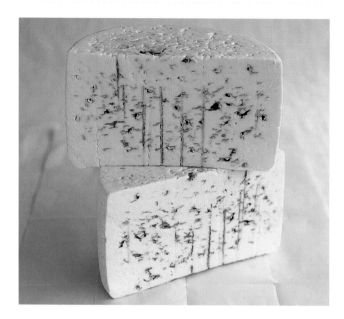

Faribault Dairy 🐄 FARIBAULT, MINNESOTA

This area is blessed with ancient St Peter sandstone caves along the Straight River overlooking Faribault. They have been used to age beer, and since 1936, to age cheese. Faribault Dairy produces French-style crumbly blues but have added a new cheese to their selection, which is a Gorgonzola. It still remains the only US cheesemaker to cure in natural stone caves.

Amablu, weighing 2.7 kg (6 lb), is a rich and creamy-textured cheese with well-defined veins that has been aged for 75 days to give a good acidity and crumble, together with a strong and vibrant blue mould. As the cheeses age, salt and mineral crystals form on the outside, which have to be scraped off to allow the air to penetrate and create the blue moulds. The cheese goes well with dry red wines, port or sweet dessert wines with a savoury edge.

St Pete's Select is a 2.7 kg (6 lb) cheese aged for up to 110 days giving it a darker yellow colour and a deeper, more assertive flavour. The ageing rooms burrow deep into the caves, where the cheeses mature in the murky darkness until ready for sale.

Prairie Breeze 🐄 MILTON CREAMERY, MILTON, IOWA

Rufus Musser arrived in Milton in 1992 with his wife Jane to start a farm. They now make numerous styles of cheese including Colby and Cheddar, along with 'squeaky' fresh cheese curds. Prairie Breeze may look like a simple large block Cheddar aged over six months, but due to the quality of the milk, and the respect for grazing and

maintaining a seasonal approach to rearing the cows, the flavours of the cheese are really delicious and fruity. I think many lessons can be learned from this style of production and the results that can be achieved by a considered approach. This simple-style table or cooking cheese is great with a dry cider or a hoppy beer.

Prairie Fruits Farm 🐐🐑 CHAMPAIGN COUNTY, ILLINOIS

Champaign is located in an area known for its farming communities, but Wes Jarrell and Leslie Cooperband started Illinois's first farmstead cheesemaking production in 2005. With just 50 goats, the production is small, but the range of styles diverse; they have also started to get ewe's milk from a nearby Amish dairy in Arthur, Illinois.

Roxanne is a ewe's milk cheese with a lovely natural rind and patchy blooms, and its fudgy, crumbly texture is sweet and earthy. The pale rind develops darker patches as it matures, and the flavours become richer and nutty. This is perfect for a full-bodied white, or a fine dry red wine.

Krotovina is styled on a French truncated pyramid, and has a layer of goat's milk curd topped with a thin layer of ash, then ewe's milk curd placed on top. The cheese is close textured with a very delicate bloomy rind. The sweetness of both milks and the acidity of the goat and earthiness of the ewe's milk are delicious, and I suggest a Pinot-style wine or something with a dry edge.

Little Bloom is a 175 g (6 oz) Camembert-style goat's milk cheese aged 4–5 weeks with a dense creamy texture and soft downy white rind. Perfect with light fruity red wines that will not overpower the flavour of the milk.

RIGHT, FROM TOP Prairie Fruits Farm, Roxanne, Krotovina and Little Bloom

OPPOSITE LEFT, TOP CHEESE Faribault Dairy, St Pete's Select BOTTOM CHEESE Amablu

OPPOSITE RIGHT Milton Creamery, Prairie Breeze

Capriole Farmstead

Capriole is situated in Greenville, Indiana, the smallest Midwest state. The great soil conditions on the 'till plains' and the flow of rivers and streams all make for great farming. An area known as Kentuckyana, the Big and Little Indian Creeks thread their way through the township.

LEFT, MIDDLE AND RIGHT
The goats of the Capriole Farmstead at feeding time

Capriole Farmstead 🐐 GREENVILLE, INDIANA

Judith Schad and her husband Larry bought their farm in 1976 and later found out that the property had once belonged to Larry's great-great-grandfather. At first the intention was to have a mixed farm without the ubiquitous horses and run on sustainable practices, until the goats won their hearts and Judith was determined to make cheese from their milk. Although Judith had vague farming roots, she is the first of the family to take it up seriously and embrace fine-quality goat's cheesemaking. She and Mary Keehn from Cypress Grove (see page 166) revolutionized the thinking around artisan small-production handmade cheeses in the early 1990s. Both she and Mary travelled through France, learning along the way, and by the time they returned, they knew exactly how and what they wanted to produce. Today, Judith's herd of 400 Alpine, Saanen and Nubian goats produce a varied selection, with a definite nod to the classic French styles, but with the flavours and aromas of the land. Outside grazing takes place for as long as it is possible, but come winter – which is harsh – they live inside and eat sweet hay. Her maturing and ripening skills are flawless and any new cheesemaker coming onto the scene will always look to Capriole goat's cheeses for inspiration.

Old Kentucky Tomme This unpasteurized, white mould rind 1.3–2.25 kg (3–5 lb) cheese has an earthy mushroom aroma coming from the rind, and with ageing of around five months develops a richness to the pate and a smooth mellow creaminess. It falls between a classic mountain-style Tomme and a crumbly nutty freshness of Chaource (see page 59). I would partner definitely with a Chardonnay wine, but not too oaked.

Julianna is an aged unpasteurized 350 g (12 oz) cheese covered with herbs and spices rather like a Corsican cheese, and then aged to produce the lovely patched white moulds on the rind. The flavours are dense and herbal with a sweet woodland aroma, and are aged for around four months.

Sofia is a closely packed 250 g (9 oz) log dusted in charcoal, which grows billowy white moulds that need to be patted down during the cheesemaking process to ensure they don't become too thick. Inside, the cheese is marbled with ash layers that give a tangy note to the creamy texture and flavours.

O'Banon was inspired by a trip Judith and Larry took to Provence. The curds are hand-ladled for a slower, even draining, then wrapped in chestnut leaves that have been soaked in Old Forester or Woodford Kentucky bourbon. The cheese is then tied with raffia string. The 175 g (6 oz) cheeses are made with pasteurized goat's milk since they are sold before 60 days old, but their creamy texture will become drier and more fruity in flavour if allowed to ripen for one month.

Mont St Francis This cheese in particular reveals Judith's ripening prowess with a lovely washed rind, very gently attaching itself to the 350 g (12 oz) unpasteurized milk cheese. It is important that the rind is not allowed to become too sticky nor too dry. The flavours of the milk become sweetly earthy as the ageing process continues for up to six months.

Piper's Pyramide is very much in the style of Pouligny-Saint-Pierre (see page 62), but the dusting of paprika lends a spicy, meaty note to the flavours of the cheese. Allowing it to dry out a bit will make the texture more flaky and give a lovely tartness too.

Wabash Cannonball is a lumpy-looking Crottin (see page 63) with an ash coat that is quickly covered in white fluffy moulds during the ripening stage. It is always best to eat this cheese when the texture is flaky and slightly drier in the French style.

OPPOSITE, TOP LEFT CHEESE Capriole Old Kentucky Tomme TOP RIGHT CHEESE Juliana SECOND ROW, LEFT CHEESE Sofia, cut SECOND ROW, RIGHT CHEESE Mont St Francis THIRD ROW, LEFT CHEESE Sofia, cut THIRD ROW, RIGHT CHEESE O'Banon FRONT ROW, LEFT CHEESE Piper's Pyramide FRONT ROW, RIGHT CHEESE Wabash Cannonball

Zingerman's Creamery ANN ARBOR, MICHIGAN

The name Zingerman is held in great esteem in Ann Arbor, a major university city situated on the Huron River. There is good agricultural farming and fruit growing in this region, as well as a fertile green landscape. It was originally a super-deli with its own bakery to supply the daily sandwich production for the shop. However, in 2000 John Loomis who was working as the cheesemonger in the shop was chosen to head a new venture with a goat farm in Manchester to make fresh cheese. The success of the fresh cheeses soon saw the dairy move next to the bakehouse, where new cheeses were created, including a cow's milk Cheshire. These much-loved and unique cheeses are just another important part of the Zingerman philosophy and apart from being sold in their own shops, are shipped to both the East and West Coasts to specialist cheese shops and restaurants.

Garlic with Chives is a fresh rindless goat's button flavoured with garlic and topped with chives. This cheese is a perfect spreading cheese.

Manchester is a hand-ladled soft, fudgy-textured cheese with a snowy-white bloomy rind and a rich creamy, gently tangy taste that has had the addition of a little extra cream to the milk. This cheese is lovely at 3–4 weeks but can be aged a further four weeks when it becomes more solid and flaky.

Lincoln Log is a simple log-shaped goat's cheese with a bloomy white rind, patted close to the cheese in order to prevent it becoming too fluffy and separate. This is a rich-tasting morsel with a lovely citrus edge and a little mushroom earthiness.

Great Lakes Cheshire it has taken a lot of trials to get the acidity levels right for this cow's milk classic crumbly hard cheese.

City Goat is a fresh button of gentle, frothy goat's cheese achieved from hand-ladling the curds to keep them super light; it's topped with a fresh herb motif.

Detroit Street is a small goat's milk brick shape with bloomy rind and coated in freshly cracked green peppercorns, tasting sharp and spicy, and aged ten days to one month.

Little Napoleon hand-ladled curds gives the cheeses time to drain and develop their flavours. The bloomy white rind becomes mottled with grey/blue moulds during the maturing process. The flavours of this cheese are gentle and acidic when aged for two weeks, becoming drier and nuttier with a more goaty aroma when matured for one month.

Bridgewater is made from the same recipe as Manchester (opposite), but contains black peppercorns to spike up the flavours a little. The fluffy white bloom will become a little drier with ripening, which also increases the spiciness of the flavours.

BELOW, BACK ROW, LEFT TO RIGHT Garlic with Chives, Manchester, Lincoln Log, Great Lakes Cheshire
FRONT ROW, LEFT TO RIGHT City Goat, Detroit Street, Little Napoleon, Bridgewater, Garlic with Chives and Plain Cheese on bread

COLORADO

The state of Colorado is known for its magnificent scenery taking in mountains, rivers, lakes and plains. The climate is one of contrasts with high mountains sheltering the valleys. The eastern side of the state is principally made up of farmland with many small farming communities.

Haystack Mountain Goat Dairy 🐄🐐

NIWOT, COLORADO

This dairy is located just outside of Boulder. Cheesemaker Jim Schott started making cheese in March 1992 with just 25 Nubian goats. Today, although retired, his influence still remains, even though the goat's and cow's milk is now brought in from several nearby farms to make their Buttercup mixed milk cheese. All the goat's cheeses they produce have a clean-tasting, simple style.

Queso de Mano, a 1.8 kg (4 lb) semi-hard cheese with delicious nutty, hearty yet sweetly herbal flavours that stand out, primarily because the mineral-rich pastures add to the flavours.

Haystack Peak, a pyramid-shaped cheese with a close texture and nutty character.

Snowdrop is a 175 g (6 oz) light and delicate cheese with a creamy interior. It has a soft, white bloomy rind that is edible and contributes to the flavours.

BELOW, TOP RIGHT CHEESE Haystack Mountain Goat Dairy Queso de Mano **MIDDLE CHEESES** Haystack Peak **FRONT LEFT CHEESE** Snowdrop

The East

This part of the US is a tremendously varied and large region, encompassing the New England states of Vermont bordered by Massachusetts to the south, New Hampshire to the east, New York to the west, as well as Connecticut, all of which have well-established agricultural industries that stretch back to the 18th century. In the south of this region are the states of Tennessee, Virginia and Georgia, with a climate and landscape that is very different from their northern counterparts, with hot, humid summers and coolish, but not cold winters that make for ideal grazing land.

BELOW A goat at Rawson Brook Farm, Massachusetts

LEFT The barns at Rawson Brook

VERMONT

Agriculture is an important industry in Vermont, and cheesemaking, especially artisan small-scale enterprise, is very much in evidence, with many farms offering tours and tastings. The colours of the trees and forests are vibrantly green, which is probably due to the mica-quartz-chlorite schist – that glistening decomposed shale formation in rocks – the minerals leach into the soil and rivers, which then give the flora their extremely bright colours. This is particularly evident in the autumn, when flaming reds, oranges and golds light up the deciduous forests, especially the Sugar Maples.

Jasper Hill Farm

The ripening rooms at Jasper Hill Farm, which are ideal for all types of cheese, are used not only by the farm, but also by other small independent cheesemakers in and around the region.

Jasper Hill Farm 🐄 GREENSBORO, VERMONT

Mateo and Andy Kehler, who started cheesemaking in 2002, have invested a huge amount to create the first US state-of-the-art underground network of ripening rooms, which serve not only their farm but also other small independent cheesemakers in the region.

Constant Bliss is a bloomy white-rinded cheese not dissimilar to the French Chaource (see page 59), weighing 200 g (7 oz), made using the naturally cooled milk from Ayrshire cows, which give a rich milk if not a huge yield. Using unpasteurized milk, the cheese has to be ripened for 60 days under US law, and in that time the outside rind will become closely matted to the cheese with some grey/blue moulds appearing. The flavours are rich and dense, but with lovely floral, grassy tones.

Bayley Hazen Blue is made every other day with morning milk only, as the fats in the Ayrshire milk are lower at this milking. This facilitates the ripening process, which takes 4–6 months, and gives a drier texture to the pate as well as bringing out the full flavours of the milk rather than the overpowering minerality of the blue moulds. A red wine with body and not too powerful tannins would be ideal to drink with this cheese.

LEFT CHEESE Jasper Hill Farm Bayley Hazen Blue RIGHT CHEESE Constant Bliss

Weybridge 🐄 SCHOLTEN FAMILY FARM, MIDDLEBURY, VERMONT

This cheese is produced by the Scholten family whose approach to farming combines environmentally friendly practices with husbandry and family values. Their small herd of Dutch Belt cows and Holstein-Friesians (both native to the Netherlands) produces the single cheese Weybridge that is taken to the Jasper Hill Cellars (see page 185) for ripening. It weighs around 225 g (8 oz) with a delicate white bloomy crust, and houses a rich almost melting buttercup-yellow cheese within. The cheeses are ripened for up to 30 days. They have the nutty, earthy taste of a Camembert, but are more fluid and lighter in texture and depth, which works well with the mushroomy aroma of the rind.

Vermont Ayr 🐄 CRAWFORD FAMILY FARM, WHITING, VERMONT

The Crawford family are fourth-generation farmers on their 134-hectare (330-acre) farm overlooking the Adirondack and Green Mountains in the fertile Champlain Valley. They have 60 Ayrshires, 24 of which are milked for cheesemaking, and an historic barn with its original slate roof has been converted as a parlour with a small maturing room. The farm produces just one style of cheese based on an Alpine Tomme, made by hand.

Vermont Ayr weighs 1.8 kg (4 lb) and is made with unpasteurized milk; only a small quantity of rennet is added to the milk to form the curds, which are cut and stirred by hand for an hour while the vat continues to heat the whey. The curds are placed in moulds lined with cheesecloth, lightly pressed and turned every few minutes before being removed from the moulds and salt-brined overnight. They are aged slowly for several months, forming a natural crust with a light white bloom. The flavours are earthy and nutty, like fresh milky-sweet hazelnuts, and perfect with crisp white wines or light reds.

Sarabande 🐄 DANCING COW CHEESE, BRIDPORT, VERMONT

Steve and Karen Getz moved from eastern Pennsylvania in 2003 to become dairy farmers and raise their family in Vermont. After winning awards for their high-quality organic milk, they decided to make cheese. As their success grew, they teamed up with Jasper Hill (see page 185) in 2007 to use their cellars to age their cheeses as well to enable them to reach new markets

and increase sales. The pair are now able to diversify into other farm-made products to add to their three cheeses – Menuet, a semi-hard Tomme style, Bourrée, a semi-soft washed rind and Sarabande.

Sarabande weighing around 225 g (8 oz) is an unpasteurized single-milked cheese in a truncated pyramid shape that is lightly washed. The golden pate has a slightly chalky centre and flavours of dewy, sweet grass, fresh nuts and a little earthy complexity, which comes from the ripening time in the high-humidity cooled rooms. This is a perfect cheese for red wines with light tannins and forward fruit flavours.

Cabot Clothbound Cheddar 🐄 CABOT CREAMERY, CABOT, VERMONT

Cabot Creamery is a dominant feature in this part of Vermont. Started in 1930 as a collective, it has developed into a major conveyor-belt-style dairy, churning out basic cheese seen in all the supermarkets and shops. However, times change and cheesemaker Marcel Gravel decided to have a separate unit to make a cloth-bound cheddar. With help from Jasper Hill Farm (see page 185) with its fine ageing facilities, they have, quite magically, created a magnificent cheese in Cabot Clothbound Cheddar, weighing 17 kg (38 lb). There have been a few tweaks along the way, notably to turn the sweeter flavours into a more robust fruity flavour. The traditional wrapped cheese is rubbed in lard to resist mould growth but this also allows the cheese to breath through the cloth during its 12-month maturing process at Jasper Hill.

OPPOSITE, FRONT CHEESES Scholten Family Farm, Weybridge
BACK, BOTTOM CHEESE Crawford Family Farm, Vermont Ayr
TOP CHEESE Dancing Cow Cheese, Sarabande
RIGHT Cabot Creamery, Cabot Clothbound Cheddar

Twig Farm 🐐 MIDDLEBURY, WEST CORNWALL, VERMONT

Michael Lee and Emily Sunderman are 'first-generation' cheesemakers who have made a concerted effort to understand their surroundings and what it has to offer, but have also chosen to be very hands-on in their approach. The people who farm in these parts are called 'flat-landers' locally, for the most obvious of reasons, but Twig Farm is hidden down a track through what is like a magic forest of tall, spindly pines and scrubby bush. Here on the stone ledges and outcrops the goats wander and forage. With just 25 goats of their own the pair supplement their milk supply with goat's milk from a farm in Bridport. They produce three simple styles of cheese

that reflect the skills of the cheesemaker. I would choose either a dry cider or a straightforward country-style red wine to serve with all three of these cheeses.

Twig Farm Square is an unpasteurized goat's milk cheese (using only milk from their own herd) weighing 900 g (2 lb). It is an irregular square due to it being wrapped in muslin and then having the ends tied in a knot in the middle of the cheese. After weighting down and pressing it takes on its homely shape; it is then aged for 80 days during which time pretty moulds form on the natural crust. The flavours of this square cheese are earthy and nutty, and there is a real taste of 'foraged' fodder such as leaves, twigs and bracken.

Twig Farm Washed-Rind Wheel is an unpasteurized 500 g (1 lb 2 oz) goat's milk cheese, with additions of cow's milk from Joe Severy's farm in Cornwall, Vermont at certain times of the year when the goat's milk yield is low. It is aged for 80 days, and during the ripening process a whey-brine is used to wash the cheeses giving a pale apricot glow to the sticky surface rind. The pungent aroma of the rind and the fudgy texture of the cheese, which is almost melting at the edges, has a full-bodied earthy, rich and sweetly savoury flavour.

Twig Farm Tomme is an unpasteurized 1 kg (2 lb 4 oz) cheese using milk from the Twig herd and from Dan Robertshaw's herd in Bridport. It is aged for 80 days, forming a lovely natural crust mottled with bloomy moulds from the ripening rooms, which have high humidity and cool, even temperatures. The clean, bright interior of the cheese has a flaky, semi-hard texture and a nutty, slightly sharp rusticity with a lingering finish.

Vermont Shepherd ☛ VERMONT

SHEPHERD FARM, PUTNEY, VERMONT

This 2.7–3.5 kg (6–8 lb) cheese has inspired cheesemakers to develop European techniques and incorporate them into their surroundings, especially with underground ripening rooms. Cheesemaker David Major has lived on the farm all his life, and his 250 sheep are on rotational pasture with special care shown to improving the soils, pastures and water resources. The simple shape of the cheese is achieved by packing the curds into two domestic style colanders and pressing them together. This unique example of the sweetly earthy almost feral quality of the milk requires a wine with good body and depth, such as Madiran.

Tarentaise ☛ THISTLE HILL FARM,

NORTH POMFRET, VERMONT

This 9 kg (20 lb) wheel is matured for a minimum of four months but can be further ripened for a year to give the sweet, hazelnut creamy texture and rich fruit flavours more depth. As the cheeses are made from spring to autumn with the cows grazing with only a little home-grown organic hay and grain supplement you get a true taste of the *terroir*.

OPPOSITE, LEFT CHEESE Twig Farm Square RIGHT
FRONT CHEESE Twig Farm Washed-Rind Wheel
RIGHT BACK CHEESE Twig Farm Tomme
RIGHT TOP Vermont Shepherd
RIGHT BOTTOM Thistle Hill Farm, Tarentaise

Summertomme  WILLOW HILL FARM, MILTON, VERMONT

The unique maturing cave at Willow Hill is 2.5 metres (8 feet) underground and has a wall of natural bedrock that allows water to seep through the cracks, thus creating moisture and humidity in the air. This helps the rinds on their cheeses to develop beautiful moulds. This 225 g (8 oz) ewe's milk cheese has a delicate crumbly texture with the sweet, earthy almost emulsified flavour mingling with the floral herb coating.

Boucher Blue 🐄 BOUCHER FAMILY FARM, HIGHGATE CENTER, VERMONT

Weighing around 1.5 kg (3⅓ lb) this unpasteurized cow's milk cheese has a smooth texture with a mellow blue hit rather like a Fourme d'Ambert on which the recipe is based. Enjoy this with a sweet dessert wine or a fruity red.

Two-year Cheddar Block 🐄 SHELBURNE FARMS, SHELBURNE, VERMONT

Although this is a 1 kg (2 lb 4 oz) block style with a waxed coat, all the elements of cheddar are present, and the acidity is very forward with this handmade unpasteurized milk cheese. There is a memorable nutty richness of the milk, with its distinctive tangy finish on the aged cheeses.

Vermont Butter & Cheese Company 🐐
WEBSTERVILLE, VERMONT

Allison Hooper started the business with colleague Bob Reese in 1984. She is a maker of cheese not a farmer, with a network of 25 family farms supplying the milk. I would serve a fine Sauvignon Blanc with these cheeses.

Coupole weighing 185 g (6½ oz) is dense yet creamy with a full-bodied flavour achieved right at the start with a warm drying room and then a cool ripening room. It can be ripened for up to eight weeks.

Bonne Bouche is 115 g (4 oz) and has an intriguing mixture of light mousse textures when young at around two weeks, becoming more dense and dry after 45 days of ripening. The rind is achieved by high temperatures in the drying room immediately after making, and then ageing at a lower temperature to develop the wrinkled appearance and bring the flavours forward. The ash and salt spread on top of the cheese helps prevent the rind becoming too thick, which would affect the natural drying as it ages.

Bijou is a goaty, gamey button of 55 g (2 oz) similar to Coupole. When young it is quite citric and floral, while the more aged cheeses are dense but creamy in the middle, with pronounced goatiness.

Fresh logs are frothy fresh, mild and not yeasty cheeses, and should be served young, given their lack of salting at the curd stage to keep the fresh purity of the milk. The coatings of peppercorn or herb give added dimension, and are lovely when sliced into a salad.

LEFT, FRONT CHEESE Willow Hill Farm Summertomme BACK LEFT CHEESE Boucher Family Farm, Boucher Blue
BACK RIGHT CHEESE Shelburne Farms, Two-year Cheddar Block

BELOW, BACK LEFT CHEESE Vermont Butter & Cheese Company, Coupole BACK RIGHT CHEESE Bonne Bouche MIDDLE LEFT CHEESE Coupole MIDDLE CHEESE Bonne Bouche MIDDLE RIGHT CHEESE Fresh Log - Peppercorn FRONT LEFT CHEESES Bijou FRONT RIGHT CHEESES Fresh Logs - Plain and Herb

ABOVE, FRONT LEFT CHEESE Consider Bardwell Pawlet FRONT RIGHT CHEESE Machester BACK RIGHT CHEESE Dorset

Consider Bardwell Farm 🐄🐐 PAWLET, VERMONT

The name of the farm is taken from the original founder Consider Stebbins Bardwell who set up in 1864. Over 100 years later, Angela Miller, Russell Glover, Chris Gray and cheesemaker Peter Dixon continue the tradition of farmhouse cheesemaking with milk from their herd of 100 Oberhaslis goats and cow's milk from Lisa Kaimen's herd. Nine different styles of cheese are made ranging from Alpine-inspired to Italian Toma to unpasteurized goat's milk feta, and aged cow's milk and goat's cheeses. The goats graze on organic pastures in the rotational fashion and all the cheeses are handmade in small batches.

Pawlet is an unpasteurized 4.5 kg (10 lb) Jersey cow's milk cheese with a lightly washed rind and scattered white moulds. The texture is supple and chewy like an Italian-style Toma with a sweet richness that is perfect for sandwiches or for melting on toast. A great appetizer to serve with a floral white wine or blonde beer.

Manchester is an unpasteurized 1.2 kg (2½ lb) semi-hard Tomme with the flavours of the farm coming through and a nutty, earthy finish. The cheeses are aged to give perfect patchy grey and white moulds to the crust, and I think a dry cider would be a good partner.

Dorset is an an unpasteurized Jersey cow's milk cheese of 1.2 kg (2½ lb) with a washed rind. The aged cheese has a rich, buttery texture and a deep savoury taste, and is perfect for Riesling-style wines. The aroma from washing the rind will be more pungent at certain times of the season according to what the pastures offer.

Dunmore 🐐 BLUE LEDGE FARM, SALISBURY, VERMONT

Greg Bernhardt and Hannah Sessions have a mixed herd of 75 Nubian, Alpine and LaMancha goats that graze outside all through the year, coming inside only when the cold becomes too intense. The unique flora and fauna of the Champlain Valley together with the wetland and woodland pastures are organically managed, with a rotational grazing system to allow nature's resources to flourish. Although the goats produce milk for ten months of the year, milk is supplemented during the busy Christmas season from nearby Burnell Pond Farm. Dunmore is a 500 g (1 lb 2 oz) soft buttery-textured cheese with a bloomy white rind, barely able to contain its almost Brie-like contents.

It has a lovely richness yet slightly sharp nutty flavour too. Eat the rind with this cheese to get the full effect of the milk's herbaceous qualities combined with the mushroom earthiness of the rind. This is a perfect cheese for Rhône-style wines.

Woodcock Farm 🐄🐐 WESTON, VERMONT

Mark and Gari Fischer's flock of East Friesian sheep graze on 18 hectare (45 acres) of lush organic pastures. As soon as the snows cover the grazing pastures, the sheep are brought indoors to rest, recuperate and produce their lambs – an important hiatus in their working year.

The Fischers buy in cow's milk from Taylor Farm nearby. Several cheeses are made including a Bulgarian-style unpasteurized milk Feta, and the Fischers have established themselves as cheesemakers of individual styles, textures and flavours, and their cheeses require a rather robust-style wine.

Summer Snow at around 200 g (7 oz) is an oozing, melting ewe's milk Camembert-style cheese available only during the summer months. The thin bloomy white rind is perfect and adds a lovely mushroom earthiness to the rich, sweetly fresh nut flavours of the cheese.

Timberdoodle is a new cheese made according to milk availability with either cow's and ewe's milk, or just cow's milk. Weighing about 800 g (1 lb 12 oz) in the Havarti-style with a washed rind and chewy, dense texture with scattered holes, the flavours are earthy and nutty with a tangy sharpness coming through the buttery finish. This is a good addition to the cheeseboard.

Weston Wheel is about 2.25 kg (5 lb) and is made with unpasteurized ewe's milk. It has a natural washed and rubbed rind and is aged up to six months. This distinctive-tasting, award-winning cheese with its earthy, nutty and almost dark caramel salty sweetness has a long finish to the flavours, and is perfect for well-structured red wines.

MASSACHUSETTS

This pretty New England state lies on the Atlantic Coast. To the east is the Atlantic Ocean with the large sandy, arm-shaped peninsula of Cape Cod and to the south, the fashionable holiday islands Martha's Vineyard and Nantucket. The historic city of Boston is at the innermost point of Massachusetts Bay at the mouth of the Charles River. Even though it is a small state, there are significant climate differences between the eastern and western sections. The entire state has cold winters and quite warm summers, but the west has both the coldest winters and the coolest summers.

Hillman Farm ⚑ COLRAIN, MASSACHUSETTS

Carolyn and Joe Hillman have what is termed a micro-production of goat's cheeses, with their 40 American, French Alpine and Nubian goats grazing on a 18-hectare (45-acre) organic farm – a perfect sheltered environment for the animals to explore the woodlands and rocky ledges. The cheeses are made from spring to autumn, both soft and matured, using simple farmstead techniques. This includes using a 1945 Cherry-Burell pasteurizer that Joe rebuilt into a cheese vat, which heats the milk at a low slow rate, setting overnight to a lactic fermented curd. This curd is then hand-ladled into different shapes or cheesecloth bags to drain.

Harvest Cheese is a hard goat's cheese, and this 3.5 kg (8 lb) washed and rubbed rind cheese has toast in the flavours, sweet on first impact, then the body of the milk comes through with a myriad of fruit and herbal flavours. The cheeses are matured for 4–6 months to acquire these nutty, grassy flavours, and further ripening will see the flavours become richer, sweeter and earthier. I think even an off-dry white wine may work with this cheese.

Birch Hill Cakes are 225 g (8 oz) cheeses dusted with charcoal prior to ripening, and acquire their scattered bloomy moulds during the stages of development. There is a lovely earthiness to the aroma on the rind, and once opened the cheese has a rich creamy texture that is nutty and goaty.

It can be ripened further to a dry, crumbly texture where the sweetness of the milk and the complex goat's milk structure comes forward. It is worth trying a micro-beer as well as dry red wine with this cheese.

Flora Pyramid is a 175 g (6 oz) truncated pyramid, with a mixture of *Geotrichum candidum* and *Penicillium candidum* cultures used to grow white moulds on the dewy, moist fresh cheeses, which have first been dusted with charcoal. The cheeses are aged to become firmer and crumblier; they taste nutty when young becoming more goaty and strong in flavour with a little maturing.

Ripened Disc is a 140 g (5 oz) round that gathers its moulds not only from the *Penicillium candidum* but also from the natural flora in the air of the ripening rooms. The flavours are goaty and nutty – in early spring and summer the milk is sweetly sensitive to the acidity, but by autumn you will be getting deeper, more fruity flavours coming through the milk.

Maggie's Round 🐄 CRICKET CREEK

FARM, WILLIAMSTOWN, MASSACHUSETTS

The Sabot family bought one of the region's oldest active dairy farms in 2001, and when Jason DeMay and Amy Jeschawitz took over as cheesemakers they added their own herd of Brown Swiss to the farm's Jersey's. This is an unpasteurized semi-hard cheese weighing 500 g (1 lb 2 oz) and aged four months to give a supple, buttery, rich texture with a mellow nutty flavour. The crust has beautiful striated sides with woven patterns from the moulds the curds are put into prior to draining and pressing. This is in the alpine or even Manchego style, and as the natural crust forms, moulds grow in the grooves making a very decorative pattern. I would suggest a lighter red wine with clean Pinot fruit and soft tannins.

Great Hill Blue 🐄 GREAT HILL DAIRY,

MARION, MASSACHUSETTS

On the shores of Buzzard's Bay south of Boston, Tim Stone makes this cheese using the rich buttery milk from his outstanding herd of Guernsey cows. The unpasteurized as well as unhomogenized milk is also sourced from other local farms. Once the milk is heated and turned into curds, the moulds are filled by hand to ensure proper draining of the whey and the delicate curd structure is kept intact. The 2.7 kg (6 lb) cheeses have a good scattering of blue veins, not overly dense, and release their lovely nutty, mineral flavours through the buttery rich texture of the cheese. A classic match for this cheese would be a fine Burgundy with medium tannins.

Classic Blue Log 🐄🐐 WESTFIELD FARM,

HUBBARDSTON, MASSACHUSETTS

Debbie and Bob Stetson started making cheese in 1996 when they took on the working farm. Even without previous cheesemaking skills they quickly learned how to make delightful goat's cheeses, as well a few cow's milk cheeses, obtaining milk from local farms since they just concentrate on making cheese, rather than rearing the animals too. Located just a few hours drive from Boston in 8 hectares (20 acres) of unspoilt land, the Stetson's beautifully preserved wood-clad farmhouse dates back to the first Pilgrim settlers. This 125 g (4½ oz) small log has a very interesting 'coat'. It is soft, almost like a pashmina scarf with a grey/blue mould, which is actually a Roquefort blue mixture. This gives the cheese a unique intense flavour to the rind, but within is a soft, velvety-textured cheese that is tangy and fresh with a bright, clean finish. This is a very individual style of cheese that I would partner with a full-bodied dry white wine or a Pinot Noir.

OPPOSITE, BACK CHEESE Hillman Farm, Harvest Cheese LEFT CHEESE Birch Hill Cakes RIGHT CHEESE Flora Pyramid, FRONT CHEESE Ripened Disc

ABOVE Cricket Creek Farm, Maggie's Round

BELOW, FRONT CHEESE Westfield Farm, Classic Blue Log BACK CHEESE Great Hill Dairy, Great Hill Blue

Rawson Brook Farm

Just three hours from Manhattan, and down a gravel drive, there is a little bit of heaven right here on earth. Rawson Brook Farm may be close to the metropolis, but it couldn't be more remote and tranquil.

Rawson Brook Fresh Chevre ♝ RAWSON BROOK FARM, MASSACHUSETTS

Just three hours from Manhattan, Susan Sellew retreated from the rat-race to become a 'homesteader' on a farm in northern New York. This desire was discovered during a trip to France. Susan stayed on a farm and was taught the cheesemaking process by a French woman who made fresh goat's cheeses from her small herd, which were just for her own family's use. It didn't take Susan long to realize that she not only loved goats but also the simplicity of life on a farm, and she found Rawson Brook tucked away in the Berkshires in Massachusetts where she had been brought up. She transforms the milk very quickly into fresh curd, either plain or with herbs or garlic, and you can buy her cheeses at the farm door or at local stores, and you may even be lucky enough to see it in Manhattan and Boston.

What makes this cheese very special is the care that Susan brings to her work. There are about 70 goats, mostly American and French Alpines, but also several white-haired Saanens and one Nubian, with around 12 babies in a low-fenced paddock — a sort of kindergarten. The milkers are let out on the pastures during the day, but need to return to the safety of their paddock and barn in the evening, although they are free to graze wherever they wish to roam during daylight — close to the farm or foraging further afield.

The key to the fine milk quality is the milking, which is done three goats at a time, causing no stress to the goats and no heavy-handedness by the milkmaid. While being milked, the goats nibble some grain that is kept in old army helmets at each milking station. As soon as the milk is in the pail it is taken through to the parlour and poured into the vats, heated up, then cooled slightly, then heated again until the curds have formed. The curds are then lifted out into muslin cloths to be hung up to drain out the whey. It is as simple as that. The light, sweet-tasting curds are packed into 200 g (7 oz) or 450 g (1 lb) tubs and go out for sale within 48 hours of being made.

ABOVE Rawson Brook Fresh Chevre, whole and spread on bread
OPPOSITE TOP A grazing goat at Rawson Brook Farm
OPPOSITE MIDDLE The entrance to Rawson Brook Farm
OPPOSITE BOTTOM LEFT Fresh curds draining in muslin bags
OPPOSITE BOTTOM RIGHT The milking parlour

NEW YORK & CONNECTICUT

The landscape of New York state consists of farms, forests, rivers, mountains and lakes, and the climate is governed by two continental air masses – a warm, humid one from the south west and a cold, dry one from the north west giving long and cold winters, and warm summers in the higher elevations turning to very warm almost sultry conditions with high humidity further south around New York City. Connecticut's landscape varies from 'colonial' green belt, to hills and mountains as well as industrial areas, including stone quarries of both limestone and granite, which indicates the soil is rich in minerals and well drained. The climate has seasonal extremes on the coastline, inland the winters are cold with hot, humid summers and the autumn with its mild and sunny days is ablaze with colour right across the state.

Cato Corner Farm 🐄 COLCHESTER, CONNECTICUT

Elizabeth MacAlister and her son Mark have been making cheese since 1997; they have 13 different styles, which are seen in cheese shops and restaurants on the East Coast.
Brigid's Abbey is a monastery-style 1.5 kg (3⅓ lb) cheese with a lightly rubbed rind and aged around 2–4 months. The flavours are mellow and buttery when young, and will mature to a nuttier flavour. As with all cheeses using milk from grass-fed cattle, the taste and texture changes with the season. I suggest a Pinot Noir with this cheese.
Hooligan is a salt-washed-rind 600 g (1 lb 5 oz) cheese with a lovely rich, buttery texture to the pate and patches of white and grey moulds on the rind. The pungent aroma on the orange, slightly sticky rind gives way to the sweet and savoury flavours. I suggest an Alsace-style wine.
Drunken Hooligan is available in winter, when the 600 g (1 lb 5 oz) Hooligan cheeses are dipped in a bath of grape must and young red wine from Colchester's Priam Vineyard. The vinous aroma is not quite as gamey as the Hooligan, but the flavours of the vine definitely come through to give this cheese a unique taste.

Old Chatham Sheepherding Company 🐑 🐄

OLD CHATHAM, NY

This may be the largest sheep herd in the US with 1,200 East Friesian, of which there are 400 milkers. The farm is run by Tom and Nancy Clark along traditional lines.
Ewe's Blue is a Roquefort-style cheese using pasteurized ewe's milk and weighing around 1.3 kg (3 lb) with sharp blue veins mingling with the sweet earthiness of the milk. The crumbly texture is perfect as a partner to dessert pears

BELOW, BACK CHEESE Cato Corner Farm, Brigid's Abbey FRONT RIGHT CHEESE Hooligan FRONT LEFT CHEESE Drunken Hooligan

BELOW, RIGHT CHEESE Old Chatham Sheepherding Company, Ewe's Blue, LEFT CHEESE Nancy's Camembert

and sweeter white wines; it is also good crumbled into a salad with toasted Pecan nuts or with ripe figs.

Nancy's Camembert is a 900 g (2 lb) cutting Camembert made with ewe's milk from the farm and a neighbouring farm's cow's milk. The rich creaminess of the cheese coupled with savoury hints of the ewe's milk have a slightly denser texture than traditional Camembert.

Nettle Meadow Farm 🐄🐐🐑 THURMAN, NY

Lorraine Lambiase and Sheila Flanagan make these two cheeses and a variety of fresh goat's cheeses.

Kunik is a triple-cream using both goat's milk and Jersey cow's milk cream to give a richness but also a tangy flavour. The soft downy rind has the merest whiff of mushroom, and the 250–275 g (9–10 oz) cheese is a perfect foil to sparkling wines or a dry cider or perry.

Three Sisters are small 115 g (4 oz) cheeses made with cow's, goat's and ewe's milk with a thin bloomy rind; the earthy, nutty taste has a definite tang at the finish. I would pair this with a fruity dry wine.

Sprout Creek Farm 🐄🐐 POUGHKEEPSIE, NY

This 80-hectare (200-acre) working farm was founded by nuns in the late 1980s as a place for children to enjoy the countryside and agriculture. Today the cheesemaker Colin McGrath produces award-winning cheeses with a herd of grass-fed Jersey, Guernsey, Milking Shorthorn and Brown Swiss cows as well as a small goat herd.

Sophie is a 200 g (7 oz) goat's milk cheese available from spring to early autumn, which has a delicate alabaster pate and a soft downy white rind. The flaky, fudgy texture is fresh and tangy with a light herbaceous taste perfect for Sauvignon white wines or a lighter red.

Rita is a 200 g (7 oz) cow's milk cheese available autumn to spring, with a soft downy rind that is well balanced with the rich, buttery texture. The earthy aroma on the rind offsets some of the dense texture with the tang providing a lovely finish.

Three-Corner Field Farm

The hamlet of Shushan is just outside Salem in the eastern region of the state. It is the very essence of rural charm, preserving its history with agriculture remaining a vital part of the area's economy.

Three-Corner Field Farm 🐑

SHUSHAN, NY

Karen Weinberg and Paul Borghard's farm lies in an unspoilt area in the Battenkill River Valley close to the Green and Adirondack Mountains. The farm is much as it was when the original settlers farmed the land in the 1840s, and even the Revival farmhouse is much as it was, with the cellars now turned into the maturing rooms. The family fell into farming through giving a loving home to a few sheep, and before she knew it, Karen had learned to become a farmer and cheesemaker. Today, the 150 sheep and over 300 lambs provide cheese, meat and other products, and by living 'light on the land' they offer a natural healthy environment for the animals, not over-farming and keeping the approach simple. I watched the gathering of the ewes for milking, and then the transforming of the milk into curds in the cheesemaking room, which is really no bigger than a large kitchen. Karen chatted away as she stirred the curds, then cut them, then broke them down, drained them and packed them into their moulds.

Battenkill Brebis is aged in the cellars below the farmhouse to acquire its wondrous live cultures, which go to making the crust of this 2.7 kg (6 lb) cheese. The unpasteurized milk curds are prepared meticulously with some of the whey removed and water added during the cutting process; the curds are broken down by hand to form the right-sized nuggets before being packed by hand again into the moulds. This gives a lightness to the texture and the flavours are sweetly earthy with a brace of mineral and grassy flavours. It is a perfect example of a farmhouse made cheese, to be enjoyed with either a fruity dry white or red wine, or even a dry cider.

Shushan Snow is a 225 g (8 oz) or 600 g (20 oz) Camembert-style cheese that has a delicate white bloomy rind hugging a dense, richly creamy interior.

The pasteurized milk is heated slowly to retain as much character as possible, and if ripened the cheese becomes soft and creamy with the flavours a little more earthy and bold against the wild mushroom aroma on the rind. This is definitely for a red wine with character.

Feta is really worth trying, made with unpasteurized ewe's milk, and ripened in a brine bath for 60 days. The taste is quite unlike any other Feta you will buy ready-packed, and is perfect crumbled over a salad or served as an aperitif with olives and a crisp dry white or rosé wine.

OPPOSITE TOP Breaking down the curds in the vat
OPPOSITE BOTTOM The gathering of the ewes for milking
BELOW, BACK CHEESE Three-Corner Field, Battenkill Brebis RIGHT CHEESE Shushun Snow LEFT CHEESE Feta
BOTTOM The barns at Three-Corner Field

TENNESSEE, VIRGINIA, GEORGIA & CAROLINA

The state of Tennessee is close to the Appalachian Mountains and Valley where the spring is warm followed by hot humid summers, and warm, pleasant autumn months. Even the winter is mild, only getting the odd snow shower. This area was also known as 'marble country' so the soil has good minerals for grazing pastures. Virginia is Blue Ridge Mountain country, and much of the state has a subtropical climate, with very humid summers and very mild winters. The weather in Georgia is glorious through spring and summer, with the autumn and winter months temperate and cool but never freezing, making ideal conditions for grazing and agriculture.

La Mancha  LOCUST GROVE FARM, KNOX COUNTY, TENNESSEE
This is an unpasteurized 3 kg (6½ lb) cheese based on the Spanish Manchego with the familiar striated 'basket-weave' pattern from the cheese moulds. The handmade cheeses are slightly sweeter than their namesake as the starter used gives a more rounded complexity and brings out the flavours of the sweetly scented grass, especially in the more aged versions.

Grayson MEADOW CREEK DAIRY, GALAX, VIRGINIA
This unpasteurized milk washed-rind cheese weighs 2 kg (4½ lb) and its golden-yellow pate derived from the high betacarotene content in the milk, as well as the diversity of flavours from the grazing pastures through the season. The inspiration for the recipe came from a visit to Wales and Ireland in 2000, and while it is not dissimilar to Taleggio, there are distinct flavour comparisons with Livarot, Reblochon and Durrus. I think this is one of the most perfect cheeses for a cheeseboard selection with its earthy farmyard flavours and soft, chewy texture.

Everona Dairy RAPIDAN, VIRGINIA
Dr Pat Elliott turned part of her kitchen into a dairy laboratory and learned how to make cheese. By 1998, a small dairy had been built and she had taken on a couple of helpers, with Carolyn Wentz as head cheesemaker.
Shenandoah Dr Pat and Carolyn created this in 2008 to a Swiss-style recipe to give a tangy flavour with that familiar chewy crumble and long lingering finish. Dr Pat is eager to tell you that ewe's milk is special because it has twice the protein, twice the vitamins, twice the solids of cow or goat's milk and good medium chain fatty acids.
Everona Piedmont has a beautiful nutty flavour, weighing around 2 kg (4½ lb), and with the French cultures it has a lovely chewiness to the texture, and a nutty, floral, sweet earthy style showing all the fine aspects of ewe's milk.

Sweet Grass Dairy THOMASVILLE, GEORGIA
This beautiful 57-hectare (140-acre) farm surrounded by woodland is farmed by Al and Desiree Wehner. In 2005 Jeremy Little, their son-in-law and chief cheesemaker, and his wife Jessica bought the farm and continued the good farm practices, including rotational grazing pastures.
Hopeful Tomme is an unpasteurized 2.25 kg (5 lb) mixed cow's and goat's milk cheese with lovely natural moulds on the crust in the style of a Pyrénées Tomme. The process involves hand-salting using Atlantic sea-salt, and actually came about when a storage tank failed to keep temperature and all the milk had to be used quickly. They 'hoped' it would work and to everyone's relief it did, which resulted in a new cheese style for the list. Accompany with full-bodied white wines as well as dry reds.
Thomasville Tomme is an unpasteurized cow's milk Pyrénées Tomme with a natural crust mottled with delicate moulds, and a buttery, mellow flavour from the higher butterfat contained in the milk. The layers of flavours are perfect for a cheeseboard and will partner a fruity red wine.

Goat Lady Dairy CLIMAX, NORTH CAROLINA
In 1995 Steve Tate and his sister, Ginnie, decided that goat's cheesemaking would be successful in North Carolina. This pioneering spirit has been so successful that they have had to supplement milk from other local farms to increase the supply.
Old Liberty is an unpasteurized milk Tomme-style semi-hard cheese weighing approx 1.5 kg (3⅓ lb). It retains a lightness with a lovely crumble to the texture, which is not too dry, and the aroma on the rind is quite powerful but the cheese within is sweetly savoury.
Sandy Creek The pasteurized milk has been slowly heated to retain the nuances of the milk and its bloomy rind thickly coats the grapevine ash outer rind. Within, the denser texture still retains its softness and flavours of dry fruit. I would suggest a Pinot-style wine.

TOP LEFT Locust Grove Farm, La Mancha

TOP RIGHT, BACK LEFT CHEESE Meadow Creek Dairy, Grayson BACK RIGHT
CHEESE Everona Dairy, Shenandoah FRONT CHEESE Everona Piedmont

BOTTOM LEFT, RIGHT CHEESE Goat Lady, Old Liberty LEFT CHEESES Sandy Creek

BOTTOM RIGHT, BOTTOM CHEESE Sweet Grass Dairy, Hopeful Tomme
TOP CHEESE Thomasville Tomme

Canada

The second largest country in the world in terms of area, Canada has a vast expanse of land, with a huge diversity of terrain and landscape. The climate is very harsh in some areas, but the large expanse of the land across the southern belt of the country is given over to agriculture. The Atlantic provinces of Prince Edward Island and Nova Scotia have a strong farming and fishing heritage.

Quebec and Ontario are the most populous provinces, with well-developed agriculture along the St Lawrence Seaway and the Great Lakes, with orchards and market gardening as well as animal husbandry and dairy. Quebec,

particularly, with its French heritage has many dairies producing some of the most interesting and diverse cheese styles. While the Prairie provinces are largely given over to grain and cattle production, the West Coast has a mild climate that has encouraged dairy farming and artisan cheesemakers.

Many of the cheeses reflect France, Great Britain and Holland, and are not just faint copies, but true artisan-made forms that highlight the traditional recipes and embrace the *terroir* with the flavours and textures derived from the mineral-rich soil fed by the purest water.

OPPOSITE ABOVE LEFT, TOP CHEESE That Dutchman's Farm, Gouda **BOTTOM CHEESE** Old Growler **FRONT CHEESE** Dragon's Breath Blue

OPPOSITE ABOVE RIGHT Fromagerie du Pied-de-Vent, Pied-de-Vent

OPPOSITE BELOW, LEFT CHEESE, Cow's Creamery, Avonlea Clothbound Cheddar **RIGHT CHEESE** Cow's Creamery Extra Old Block

Cow's Creamery 🐄 NEAR
CHARLOTTETOWN, PRINCE EDWARD
ISLAND

Following a visit to the Orkney
Islands, Scott Linkletter decided
to produce a true artisan-made
cheese with head cheesemaker
Armand Bernard. They tweaked
the recipe with excellent results.
Prince Edward Island has an iron-
rich red soil, from the soft rich
sandstone composition that allows
huge agricultural activity and great
pastures for grazing.

Avonlea Clothbound Cheddar is a 10 kg (22 lb) Cheddar aged
a minimum of one year, using unpasteurized milk and
a vegetarian rennet. The cheeses are cloth-wrapped in
the traditional way, and rubbed with lard or butter to
seal and prevent unwanted moulds growing on the rinds.
You can taste the briny sea and the earthy richness of the
soil mingling with the crumbly texture in the cheese. It is
wonderful matched with a full-bodied dry red Bordeaux
wine or a bold hoppy beer.

Cow's Creamery Extra Old Block is the other side of the coin
for the Creamery, where the block Cheddar, made with
unpasteurized cow's milk is sold as deli-packs at 200 g
(7 oz) or as slicing blocks of 2.25 kg (5 lb). However,
the texture may not be quite as crumbly and intense
as the cloth-bound Cheddar, but it still has a lovely
sweetness with a chewy density making it perfect for cheese
sandwiches, or 'toasties'.

That Dutchman's Farm 🐄 UPPER ECONOMY,
NOVA SCOTIA

Maja and Willem van den Hoek arrived in Canada from
the Netherlands in 1970. This rural community is a
perfect setting to make their Dutch cheese.

Gouda is the heart of their business. A 6 kg (13 lb)
Farmstead Gouda is made following an old recipe using
unpasteurized local milk. It is aged on wooden shelves in
maturing rooms, with the air filtering through naturally.

Old Growler is an aged version of the Gouda, weighing
5.4 kg (12 lb) and is really exceptional. The density of the
texture with the crisp, almost crystalline flavours and that
briny hit of grassy freshness quite takes you by surprise. I
always love blonde beer with Gouda.

Dragon's Breath Blue is a small 300 g (10 oz) black-wax-
coated cheese that is supposed to be a blue; while
definitely pungent like a blue, on opening the cheese it
is quite wet and almost weeping out
of the paste. The texture is soft and
crumbly and the flavours are strong
and persistent; I suggest you eat this
on the young side and accompanied
by a strong beer with a rye bread.

Pied-de-Vent 🐄 FROMAGERIE
DU PIED-DE-VENT, ÎLES-DE-LA-
MADELEINE, QUEBEC

Jérémie Arseneau brought to his
Pied-de-Vent farm the only breed
of cow developed in North America
— the virtually extinct stocky,
hardy Canadienne, a cross between
Norman and Breton stock. His 50
milkers provide enough milk for 90
wheels of cheese per day. The grass-
fed cattle get added hay and fodder
produced on the island, which gives
the milk its unique flavours. The
cheese weighs 1.2 kg (2½ lb) and has
a piquant taste with a chewy texture
and a robust aromatic washed rind.

Fromagerie de L'Abbaye St Benoît 🐄🐐 SAINT-
BENOÎT DU LAC, QUEBEC

Situated on the west shore of Lake Memphremagog, in the
picturesque southernmost part of the Eastern Townships
community in the Chaudière-Appalaches region. The
Benedictine monks work by hand to make several cheeses,
and visits and tours of this architecturally interesting
Abbey are really worthwhile.

Bleu Bénédictin is a pasteurized 1.5 kg (3⅓ lb) cow's milk
blue and is stronger than their other Blue Ermite, but
has a soft almost melting centre and a long lingering
taste. The natural rind with its wild mushroom aroma is
a perfect foil for the mineral intensity and richness of the
cheese. A classic Burgundy would be good with this cheese
or a dessert wine.

Frère Jacques is a pasteurized cow's milk 1.5 kg (3⅓
lb) washed-rind cheese that has a chewy density that
almost 'squeaks' between your teeth. The milky-sweet
hazelnut flavours and aroma are similar to Reblochon,
but the mildness of the cheese is perfect for breakfast.
Alternatively, this Frère Jacques is fantastic for melting
on toast.

Le Moutier is a pasteurized goat's milk cheese weighing
1 kg (2 lb 4 oz) and is similar to their cow's milk version,
St Benoît. But the sweet lightness of the milk, together
with the almost springy open texture of the cheese with
its irregular holes make this a perfect cheese for children
and adults alike. The monks make a wonderful cider that
would partner all these cheeses very well.

Ewenity Dairy Co-Op 🐑 CONN, ONTARIO

Elisabeth and Eric Bzikot formed the co-operative in
2001 with a small group of ewe's milk producers and the
membership has grown, along with Elisabeth's knowledge
of cheesemaking. They are now the largest sheep dairying
co-operative in Canada.

Eweda Cru is an unpasteurized ewe's milk cheese which is
based on a Gouda recipe and aged a minimum of nine
months. Each 3 kg (6½ lb) green waxed-coated cheese has
a marking identifying the farm where the milk came from,
and the rich, savoury flavours mingle with the earthy,
sweet and nutty aroma.

Sheep in the Meadow is a pasteurized fresh (aged for just
two weeks) 280 g (10 oz) cheese with a light bloomy
rind covered with Herbes de Provence
with rosemary and thyme the dominant
aromas. There are hints towards the
Corsican Fleur de Maquis, but the
texture is like Camembert. The young
cheeses taste sweet with the herbs still
green and fresh, while with a little
ripening the texture will become richer
and smoother and the herb coat a little
more earthy.

Brebette is a lovely 250 g (9 oz) bloomy
rind pasteurized milk cheese, again aged
for only two weeks, but it can be further
ripened. It is delicate on first impact,
becoming really sophisticated and
luxurious in flavours and textures, and
is a perfect cheese for a fine red wine or
even Champagne.

Mouton Rouge or 'red sheep' is a delightful
play on words for a cheese. The washed-
rind unpasteurized milk cheese is
ripened for 60 days, and the 1 kg (2 lb
4 oz) to 3 kg (6½ lb) cheeses have a pale
pate with small holes scattered through
the creamy texture. The washing gives a
grassy aroma and contrasts well with the
richness of the sweetly earthy cheese. A
lovely cheese for fresh dry white wines.

LEFT, BACK TOP CHEESE Salt Spring Island Cheese
Company, Montaña, cut RIGHT CHEESES WITH
TOPPINGS Marinated fresh goat's cheeses: truffle,
basil, peppercorns FRONT MIDDLE CHEESE Romelia
LEFT CHEESE Blue Juliette RIGHT CHEESE Marcella

RIGHT, LEFT CHEESE Fromagerie de L'Abbaye St Benoît, Bleu Bénédictin RIGHT CHEESE Frère Jacques FRONT CHEESE Le Moutier

ABOVE LEFT, BACK CHEESE Ewenity Dairy Co-Op, Eweda Cru LEFT CHEESE Sheep in the Meadow RIGHT CHEESE Brebette

ABOVE RIGHT Ewenity Dairy Co-Op, Mouton Rouge

Salt Spring Island Cheese Company 🐐🐑 NEAR

RUCKLE PARK, SALT SPRING ISLAND, BRITISH COLUMBIA
Tucked between Vancouver Island and the mainland of British Columbia, Salt Spring is the largest of the Gulf Islands. The temperate climate all year round enhances its pastoral setting and the quiet, rural life is enjoyed by both the residents and many visiting tourists. When David and Nancy Wood started the cheesemaking in 1994 they concentrated exclusively on ewe's milk, but they now make wonderful goat's cheeses too, in many different styles.
Montaña is a 4 kg (9 lb) semi-hard ewe's milk (with a little goat's milk added) cheese matured for 3–8 months, similar in style to Pecorino or Manchego, but probably more in tune with Pyrénées cheeses. It has a slightly dry crumble to the texture with a fresh nutty lighter taste than the more artisan mountain cheeses partly due to the milk being pasteurized.
Marinated Fresh Goat Cheeses weighing 140 grams (5 oz) these pasteurized goat's milk cheeses have a tangy, light almost frothy texture from the gentle handling of the curds into the moulds. After just two days they are ready, and are either plain, or packed into a clear plastic container with a little olive oil and toppings of truffle paste, basil leaf, peppercorns and even flowers, chilli, and roasted garlic.
Romelia is a delightful 200 g (7 oz) washed-rind pasteurized goat's cheese with high aroma on the orange smear rind. The goat's milk gives a really tangy edge to the flavours. Good with beer.

Blue Juliette is a Camembert pasteurized goat's milk cheese of 200 g (7 oz), but mixed with the white bloomy moulds is a *Penicillimn roqueforti* blue mould. As it is only brushed onto the rind it doesn't penetrate into the cheese. What you get in flavour is a fudgy centre and tangy taste with the edges softer and just starting to melt, giving the flavour of the blue and white moulds a spicier finish.
Marcella is a Crottin cheese weighing just 95 g (3½ oz) with a close white bloomy rind. It has a tartness of the goat's milk, which is quite prominent.

Australia and New Zealand are the most recently settled major landmasses in the south-western Pacific Ocean. The first Europeans known to have landed were the Dutch in 1642 and the British in 1768-71. The influences of these countries are evident in Australia's prolific Cheddar production and very good Gouda. A large proportion of Australia is desert or semi-arid land and not given to fertile soils; however, rainfall has slightly increased over the past century, with the south-east and south-west corners having a temperate climate. New Zealand's climate corresponds closely to that of Italy in the Northern Hemisphere, but its isolation from continental influences and exposure to cold southerly winds and ocean currents give the climate a much milder character.

The New Zealand Food Safety Authorities have been discussing the option of making unpasteurized milk cheese, as well as importing unpasteurized cheeses from Europe. This matter is also under government discussion in Australia. Whilst this is not universally applauded, it is of immense importance to those cheesemakers interested in experimenting with new starters and cultures in their techniques. Agriculture has been and continues to be the main export and hopefully, as Australia and New Zealand work closely together, they can bring a more diverse structure to the cheese industry.

This is especially relevant as cheese cultures emerge in Japan and China. In particular, Kyodo Gakusha Shintoku Farm in Japan, who produce exceptional artisan varieties, and Yellow Valley Cheese Dairy in China's Shanxi province who make a delicious Gouda.

Australia & New Zealand

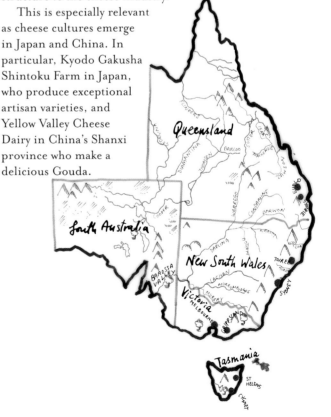

AUSTRALIA

La Luna 🐐 HOLY GOAT, SUTTON GRANGE ORGANIC FARM, CENTRAL VICTORIA
Ann-Marie Monda and Carla Meurs, having gained experience in Australia and Europe, set up their organic goat's cheese dairy in 2000. The land is harsh, being made up of granite and sandy loam, but they supplement the natural grazing with additional grasses and vitamins. La Luna is a 150 g (5½ oz) doughnut-shaped, white mould soft cheese that is fast gaining an iconic status. Accompany with a sharp, dry white wine.

Ironstone 🐄 PIANO HILL FARM, GIPPSLAND, VICTORIA
Cheesemaker Steven Brown has trained in Switzerland, Italy and New Zealand, which has paid dividends in the development of his Ironstone cheese. It is a 5 kg (11 lb) Gouda-style hard cheese, made from the biodynamic milks of his Friesian herd, with a fruity and earthy flavour.

Marrook Farm 🐄 NORTH WEST OF TAREE, NEW SOUTH WALES
Cheesemakers David and Heidi Marks started their biodynamic farm on the Bulga plateau in the mid-1980s.
Brinawa This is a 3 kg (6½ lb) washed and rubbed Swiss-style cheese that is 'hand hooped', pressed and washed before maturing. There is an intensity to the flavours, with a Swiss sweetness and a slightly softer texture.

ABOVE TOP LEFT, TOP CHEESE Marrook Farm, Brinawa
BOTTOM CHEESE Bulga
ABOVE TOP RIGHT Piano Hill Farm, Ironstone
ABOVE Holy Goat, La Luna
RIGHT, TOP CHEESE Woodside Cheese Wrights, Edith
BOTTOM CHEESE Etzy Ketzy

Bulga A 10 kg (22 lb) Gruyère-style cheese that uses a similar hand production and ageing of 8–12 months. It highlights the grazing pasture, which is rich in rye and clover, as grassy elements can be detected in the flavour.

Woodside Cheese Wrights 🐄🐐 ADELAIDE HILLS, SOUTH AUSTRALIA
Cheesemaker Kris Lloyd has given style and modernity to her cow's and goat's milk cheeses.
Edith A 250 g (9 oz) soft goat's cheese with an ash coat and patches of white bloom. It has a rich, tangy flavour.
Etzy Ketzy This 125 g (4½ oz) mixed Friesian and goat's milk cheese is lightly washed. There is a clean, floral yet earthy nuttiness to the flavours.

Annwn 🐄 BALLYCROFT CHEESES, GREENOCK, BAROSSA VALLEY, SOUTH AUSTRALIA

This tiny farm is based in a vineyard and run by two sisters, Tracey Skepper and Sue Evans. Annwn is a 1 kg (2 lb 4 oz) pressed cheese from Jersey and Holstein cow's milk. The rind is rubbed with salt, then placed in the ripening room where it has regular washings with a mixture of Shiraz vine lees over a two-month period.

Cheddar 🐄 PYENGANA CHEESE DAIRY, NEAR ST HELEN'S, TASMANIA

Four generations of Jon Healey's family have farmed in this fertile dairy-farming region since the 1890s making it the oldest speciality cheese producer in Australia. This stirred curd Cheddar made with a traditional rennet has a sweet earthy taste to the layers of herbal, grassy flavours. The cloth-bound cheese comes in various sizes from 1 kg (2 lb 4 oz) up to 14.5 kg (32 lb). Since the laws in Australia prevent the cloth being rubbed in lard, as it is an animal fat, they use an oil.

Tongola Goat Dairy 🐐 NR CYGNET, WATTLE GROVE, TASMANIA

Hans Stutz and Esther Haeusermann migrated from Switzerland to become farmers in the Huon Valley of Tasmania. They raise and hand-milk their 30 hardy long-haired Toggenburg goats on the 6 hectares (15 acres) either on open mixed pasture and brush, or in wooden shelters during cooler months.

Billy At 4–6 weeks, this 150 g (5½ oz) to 250 g (9 oz) cooked curd cheese has been brine-washed to produce a pale golden rind flecked with white moulds, and has an aromatic pungency that is not too strong. The cheese is smooth with a dense and fudgy texture and the rind is also delicious.

Big B This is the 800 g (1 lb 12 oz) larger version of Billy, which is matured between three and six months to become richer, more aromatic and fuller flavoured.

Capris At just 120 g (4½ oz), this cheese is in the Curdly style but with added salt. It is a little like a Camembert with its white bloomy rind, but the texture is a little more tender. This cheese is perfect as part of a cheeseboard.

Curdly A very fresh small cheese with a light, frothy lemony taste. There is no added salt so this cheese is great for both sweet and savoury dishes. It should be eaten very young.

Fromart 🐄 EUDLO, QUEENSLAND

Situated in the foothills of the Glass House Mountains, Christian Nobel started out in 2006 buying Holstein and Guernsey milk from a local farm to make his traditional Swiss-style cheeses. Fromart cheeses include a Gruyère, Tilsit, Magoth (Appenzell style), the traditional melting cheese Raclette and a young 800 g (1 lb 12 oz) sized semi-soft washed-rind cheese they call Mutschli. The richness of the milk certainly gives a unique flavour profile.

ABOVE TOP, FROM TOP CHEESE Fromart cheeses, Gruyere, Tilsit, Raclette, Magoth and Mutschli

ABOVE BOTTOM Ballycroft Cheeses, Annwn

Gympie Chèvre 🐐 GYMPIE FARM CHEESE, GYMPIE, QUEENSLAND

Cheesemaker Camille Mortaud hails originally from the village of Archigny, near Poitiers in West France, a region famous for its goat's cheeses such as Chabichou (see page 64) and Mothais (see page 64). Initially, he made cheese with his mother, before emigrating to Australia and starting his cheese business in 1999. The dairy has now moved to Conondale, approximately 88 km (54 miles) north of Brisbane on the Sunshine Coast.

The Gympie Chèvre, weighing approximately 115 g (4 oz), has the typical coated rind of *Penicillium album* to produce the patchy grey/white mould that is so desirable for goat's cheeses to enhance the flavours and texture. The flaky, rich texture with nutty aftertaste is very good and as Camille reflects would be even better if he was allowed to make his cheese with unpasteurized milk.

ABOVE, LARGE CHEESE
Pyengana Dairy
Cheddar
LEFT CHEESE Tongola
Goat Dairy, Billy
FRONT CHEESE Capris
RIGHT CHEESE Big B
FAR RIGHT CHEESE
Curdly

LEFT Gympie Farm
Cheese, Gympie
Chèvre

NEW ZEALAND

Curio Bay Pecorino 🐑 BLUE RIVER, SOUTHLAND, SOUTH ISLAND

Just to prove a point that big is also beautiful, Blue River are probably the biggest operators in New Zealand. They have a herd of East Friesian sheep, with some cross breeding with tougher breeds to withstand life in the southern climes. They make some of the best Pecorino-style cheeses in the country, as well as a great Feta. Their Head Cheesemaker is Maxi Robertson, and with his 35 years' experience he produces a fine selection of styles. Curio Bay Pecorino is made from pure ewe's milk, and matured for at least 6–8 months. A natural thin rind forms around the pale straw-coloured pate to produce sweet, earthy and floral flavours. This cheese will mature for a further year to give a gamey caramel style that is magnificent.

Gouda 🐄 MERCER CHEESE, NORTH WAIKATO, NORTH ISLAND

Alfred Alfrink makes the cheese and his wife Ineke takes care of their small shop where his 20 tonne annual output sells as fast as it is made. The farm is situated in a large caldera (the shallow ring of alluvial soil from a time of volcanic eruption), which has created a gorge on the land with a waterfall running down to the river Waikato. Often

flooded, the land around the farm is not unlike that of Alfred's Dutch homeland, which perhaps explains the wonder of his cheese. His farm covers 8 hectares (20 acres) of land and production is limited to what he can physically make himself. The milk is from local farms and the cheeses vary in size from 1 kg (2 lb 4 oz) to 12 kg (26½ lb). Although Alfred has to pasteurize his milk, he is hoping that he will be able to use unpasteurized milk in the not too distant future, which will give his cheeses more complex flavours. In addition to the plain Gouda, his cheeses include cumin and fenugreek Gouda and Edam.

Rich Plain & Cumin Gouda 🐐 AROHA ORGANIC GOAT CHEESE, TE AROHA, NORTH ISLAND

This delightful farm is situated at the foot of Mount Te Aroha in the Thames Valley region. The farm is run by John and Jeanne Van Kuyk, who make a selection of cheeses in the Gouda style.

Te Aroha is the centre for dairy farming in this region with its very fertile land and famous thermal springs. The herd of Saanen goats graze freely on open pastures, and there are plenty of shelters dotted around as they are not fond of the rain! The flavours of these simple cheeses are sweet and nutty, with the additions of traditional Dutch spices such as cumin, fenugreek and nettle, as well as a more unconventional chilli and mixed herbs addition.

Cloudy Mountain Cheese 🐄 PIRONGIA, WAIKATO REGION, NORTH ISLAND

Cheesemakers Cathy and Peter Lang have a small farm, situated 10 km (6 miles) to the west of Te Awamutu on the banks of Waipa River near Mount Pirongia. They produce a few very interesting cheeses, each in a different style and with a care and commitment that showcases not only the purity of the milk, but their hands-on approach. Cathy is predominantly self-taught, but her background in microbiology and lab diagnostic skills in her previous career in animal health has proved a useful tool in transforming the milk into cheese.

ABOVE Blue River, Curio Bay Pecorino
LEFT Mercer Cheese, Gouda

Joie A Camembert-style cheese with a smooth and creamy pate and white bloomy rind.

Pirongia Blue This is a dense, rich and soft blue cheese almost bursting out of its thin natural rind.

Kaipaki Gold This cheese has a wonderful rich and melting pate with a washed rind, which gives a pungency to the aroma and a kick to the flavours.

Ricotta CLEVEDON VALLEY BUFFALO COMPANY, NORTH ISLAND

Helen and Richard Dorresteyn have persevered since 2006 in creating and naturalizing their herd, after importing a few animals from Shaw River in Australia. Their hard work has paid off. Not only are they responsible for producing what is considered to be New Zealand's first buffalo milk Mozzarella and Ricotta, but also their cheeses are seen to be as good as anything from Battipaglia in Campania, Italy. The weather conditions and climate are ideal for the Riverine breed (they give a richer milk for cheesemaking) to thrive. The herd grazes on open pasture in this idyllic south-west corner of Auckland, and the silky, mild and delicate cheeses have been a huge hit. The Ricotta has a dewy freshness and lightness that can only be achieved by making and selling the cheese as soon after milking as possible, as the sweetness of the milk is a real pleasure. The cheeses have acquired a cult status and it is hoped that the herd will be increased in order to keep up with the demand.

ABOVE LEFT Aroha Organic Goat Cheese, Rich Plain Gouda
ABOVE MIDDLE Aroha Organic Goat Cheese, Cumin Gouda
ABOVE RIGHT Clevedon Valley Buffalo Company, Ricotta
BELOW LEFT Cloudy Mountain Cheese, Pirongia
BELOW RIGHT Cloudy Mountain Cheese, Joie
BOTTOM Cloudy Mountain Cheese, Kaipaki Gold

Appreciating Cheese

The cheese course is the link between the main course and dessert, although in Britain cheese is often served at the end of the meal with a glass of Port. Regardless of where you place the cheese course in the order of things, the important considerations are the styles and strengths of the cheeses and their ability to add to the overall enjoyment of the whole meal. This course can be thought of as the expression not only of the chosen wine but also of the meal in its entirety.

The cheese course is where the quality of the produce shines rather than the cooking ability of the host or hostess. A thoughtfully chosen, well-balanced cheese course is a delight for your guests and reflects the real sense of care and consideration you have given to your guests' enjoyment. Always try to buy from a shop with a good selection and knowledgeable staff, and taste before buying and also evaluate your own preferences.

BELOW Bringing cheese to room temperature: place a damp cloth over the board after taking the cheese out of the refrigerator

WRAPPING & STORING CHEESE

I always follow the saying 'little and often' when it comes to buying cheese, and even if you have bought vacuum-wrapped supermarket cheeses, you can help keep them looking and tasting better by rewrapping in waxed kitchen paper. Blue cheese does not mind being wrapped in aluminium foil as well as being kept in the coldest part of the fridge, although I prefer to wrap the cheese in wax paper first before covering with foil. If you have splashed out on a chunk of Parmigiano Reggiano or similar hard cheese, then wrapping it in unbleached dampened cotton calico or several layers of muslin will keep the cheese quite fresh in the fridge or larder. You may have to check and refresh the cheese every day and make sure the cloth is damp. Small whole hard cheeses wrapped first in waxed paper are best covered in several layers of newspaper as it is 'pulped' and will hold the moisture very well in a cool environment.

For cut pieces of cheese place the wrapped cheeses in a plastic container with a tightly fitting lid, having first spread a slightly dampened tea towel or cloth on the bottom. Don't put blue cheeses in the box as these should be kept separate from other cheeses to avoid the blue moulds spreading. Before closing the box pop in a few sugar cubes, which will act as a natural preservative, preventing the growth of moulds and holding back oxidization, as well as distributing the humidity in the sealed box and preventing bacteria growing in the confined atmosphere. You will be amazed how fresh the cheese remains; we have tested semi-hard and hard cheeses for up to three weeks successfully, although softer varieties will only last up to one week.

ABOVE Storing cheeses with sugar cubes: a natural preservative
BELOW LEFT Parmigiano Reggiano wrapped in muslin BELOW RIGHT Cheese wrapped in waxed kitchen paper

SERVING CHEESE

To serve cheese it is best to unwrap the pieces and place on a wooden board or platter, then cover with a clean damp cloth and leave to come to room temperature. This takes between half an hour to an hour depending on how warm or cool the room. Some washed-rind cheeses become dry on their rinds, and to restore them simply mix dry white wine or eau de vie in boiled and cooled water (say half a coffee cup of water to a dessertspoon of alcohol) and with your (clean) fingertips massage a little liquid over the rind until it looks dewy and glistening again. Think of the cheese course as a carefully thought through selection and don't be tempted to put too many on the board, as this can be confusing to the palate. You can either go with one stand-alone cheese like a Roquefort with a dessert wine, or up to eight maximum for a varied selection based on the season.

CUTTING CHEESE

Cutting your cheese in the appropriate way will not only look more appetizing at the end of the meal, it will also allow you to enjoy the cheese again at your next meal! Neat slices showing the central tip to the outer edge will allow for complete enjoyment of the cheese as the ripest part (and the strongest-tasting) is the outside and the more mellow flavours are in the centre.

Cutting log-shaped cheeses is easy, but remember if you are offering a selection of five or six cheeses you do not need to cut big chunky rounds since the maximum amount of total cheese per plate should be about 150 g (5½ oz) or five pieces at 30 g (1 oz) each or the equivalent for a smaller selection.

BACK LEFT CHEESE Soft bloomy rind: Brie de Meaux BACK MIDDLE CHEESE Log shape: Sainte-Maure BACK RIGHT CHEESE Pyramid shape: Pouligny-Saint-Pierre MIDDLE LEFT CHEESE Square bloomy rind: Pont l'Évêque MIDDLE CHEESE Soft washed: Ami du Chambertin MIDDLE RIGHT CHEESE Blue cylinder: Fourme d'Ambert FRONT CHEESES Hard cutting: Comté d'Estive, Semi soft rind: Taupinerè

If you are using a simple cheeseboard-knife, then have a couple of small jugs or tumblers of boiled water to dip the knife and clean between each cut of cheese. You don't want to have blue cheese coating a white soft cheese, or goat's cheese smearing onto a hard cheese. Dipping the knife blade in hot water and drying with kitchen paper will ensure lovely clean, neat cuts. Very crumbly cheeses like Roquefort can be cut with a long thin-bladed knife, or the special 'guillotine'-style tool with the metal handle and a fine taut wire.

I do love the right tools for cutting cheese and specialists make knives and cutters specifically for certain styles of cheeses. The large Gruyère and Emmental cheeses have a square-bladed slicer that chops through the rind and pate with ease, and the flat 'tongue'-shaped blade for soft spreadable cheeses or butter is very useful. A Parmesan knife is well worth getting if you like chipping away at the cheese as part of a cheese course. Scandinavian and Dutch cheeses have a simple shaver to slide across the cut piece to create long fine slivers. Taking the trouble at this stage of the presentation will give you immense pleasure in the way the cheese looks plated up and also cut on the board. Lastly, remember to start with the mildest cheese at the top of the plate (at 12 o'clock) and work round clockwise, ending with the blue cheese.

The way to cut is not to attack the whole cheese from all sides! For square-shaped cheeses such as Pont l'Évêque or small round cheeses, cut in half and take portions from just one half in order to be able to wrap the other half and store for another day. For blue cheeses that hold their crumbly texture well such as Fourme d'Ambert, Stilton or Gorgonzola Naturale, if served in rounds (Fourme or Stilton) then again take slices like a cake from each half, or if the piece is a whole or half cheese, then carefully score a 1–1.5 cm (½–¾ in) circle around the top and carefully cut small wedge-shaped pieces (see picture). For blue cheeses cut as a wedge rather than a round, use a long, thin-bladed knife to avoid breaking the cheese and slice end to end rather than in chunks. Clean the blade to ensure the cuts are neat and the soft cheese doesn't stick to the blade. For Brie, you can create a wonderful patchwork pattern (see picture), but this is because you want to try and get the outer and inner parts of the cheese to taste on each piece – and never cut the 'nose' from the pointed end as this is 'bad manners' in the rules of cheese etiquette!

Very soft cheeses once opened should be eaten quickly as they will not taste the same when kept overnight or eaten a few days later. Alternatively, you can cut the cheese in half and immediately return the unused cheese to the fridge.

1 Cheese wire for cutting through large semi-hard to semi-soft cheeses 2 Big rectangular cutting tool for Gruyère-style and Emmental cheeses 3 Flat blade for spreading very soft curd cheese and ricotta 4 Grater for hard cheeses 5 Triangular cutting tool serrated on one side, sharp on other with a slicer in middle – a buffet-style tool 6 Triangular cutting tool with slicer in middle – a buffet tool 7 Thin blade for small soft cheeses and goat's cheeses 8 Metal frame with thin wire stretched across for cutting soft blue cheeses like Roquefort 9 Small fork for chopping off smaller chunks of Parmesan 10 Small trowel for chipping off even smaller pieces of Parmesan 11 Kitchen-style knife for harder cheeses 12 Slightly angled-handle knife for Brie and semi-soft larger cheeses 13 Fancy cheeseboard knife for cutting semi-soft cheeses or harder cheeses in thin slices 14 Larger Parmesan knife/trowel for cutting larger chunks of Parmesan

WHAT TO SERVE WITH CHEESE

The ubiquitous grapes and celery can be put to good use if properly matched with the right cheeses, and nuts, too, have a place. Try raw almonds in their papery skins with Beaufort Chalet d'Alpage cheese, or freshly cracked walnuts with creamy triple cream cheeses or soft goat's cheeses. Spain produces muscatel raisins not only for sweet wine but also to be eaten with all styles of cheeses; it also produces that compact fruit paste Membrillo, made with quince, which is a stylish accompaniment to Manchego or blue cheeses (see page 144).

The French board This is a typical French supper or lunch *en famille* (see above picture) and this platter of Roquefort, Brie and Comté cheeses has all the elements for a varied and convivial meal. Sourdough bread like Pain de Poilâne, rillettes of shredded duck, goose or pork meat mixed with the fat to spread on the bread and accompanied with tart cornichons (gherkins) and a celeriac remoulade of shredded raw celeriac with grain mustard mayonnaise accompany the gritty fruitiness of Comté cheese. The meaty saucisson from the Auvergne is lovely when placed on the bread with a sliver of Brie on top. A little spoonful of wine jelly with the Roquefort provides a delicious savoury-and-sweet taste along with sweet Chasselas Moissac grapes grown in South West France.

The British Ploughman's board The simplicity of a ploughman's lunch (bottom left) is deceiving – the bread should be white, thickly sliced with a good golden crust to accompany a hearty Cheddar like Keen's and slices of crisp Cox's Orange Pippin apples and sticks of celery. The cheese is also served with a hand-raised Pork Pie, and the final flourish is Piccalilli, that mustardy spicy relish perfectly matched to the pork pie and the cheese.

ABOVE The French board BACK ROW, LEFT TO RIGHT Sourdough Pain Poilâne bread, Red grapes, Rillettes d'Oie (goose rillettes), celeriac remoulade, Saucisson d'Auvergne FRONY ROW, LEFT TO RIGHT Roquefort, Brie de Meaux, Comté, white grapes, wine jelly

LEFT The British Ploughman's board RIGHT TO LEFT Keen's Cheddar, hand-raised water crust pork pie, piccalilli relish with crusty bread, apples and celery

OPPOSITE TOP The American Farmstead board LEFT TO RIGHT New York State Cheddar, Fresh goat's log, home-made chutney, cured ham

The American Farmstead board This platter (above) was put together with the help of my wonderful hostess Lynda in Great Barrington, New York. The salad from her little garden plot, her homemade wholemeal loaf and a thick slice of her home-cured, maple-syrup-basted ham. A tangy Rhubarb chutney partnered the fresh goat's milk log coated in herbs perfectly. The local Cheddar-style cheese with the ham and bread are ideal for lunch.

Cured meats board The sheer variety of salame and prosciutto from Italy is mouthwatering, along with their different styles of olives, which are perfect with a cheese-and-cured-meat platter (below left). The bread is a ciabatta and the cheeses range from creamy Piedmontese Robiola delle Langhe, to a Swiss Emmentaler, three-year-aged Parmesan, Cantal Laguiole from South West France and a Picos de Europa blue cheese from Spain. The meats — paper-thin slices of Bresaola from Lombardy, to fresh soft Salami with fennel seeds and truffle-infused Tuscan salame — make this a memorable meal.

Hearty Dutch breakfast board Dutch Gouda cheeses (below right) are delightful in the morning with their chewy density and spicy flavours of mustard seeds, nettles or cumin. They are great partnered with a dark rye bread, simple boiled ham, juicy tomatoes, crisp 'hot' radishes and sticks of celery sprinkled with raw salt crystals. There is also butter for the bread, because I love buttered bread with cheese in fine shards on top. You may think this a dairy overload but a quality butter is one of the most perfect, simple accompaniments for the cheeseboard.

BELOW LEFT Cured meats board BACK ROW, LEFT TO RIGHT Truffle Salame, Cinte Sinese Salame, mixed olives, baby gherkins, SECOND ROW Malencia beef, Bresaola THIRD ROW Fennel salame, Swiss Emmentaler FRONT CHEESES Parmigiano Reggiano, Robiola Delle Langhe, Picos de Europa, Cantal Laguiole FRONT ROW Mostarda di frutta, crusty bread

BELOW RIGHT Hearty Dutch breakfast board BACK, LEFT TO RIGHT Rye bread, boiled ham, butter, radishes, tomatoes, celery FRONT ROW, LEFT TO RIGHT Four year aged Gouda, Mustard and Cumin Gouda, Two year aged Gouda, Nettle Gouda

ULTIMATE CHEESE-BOARDS

The range on a cheeseboard should always start with something light and palate-cleansing like a goat's cheese, followed with a simple crumbly style, then something creamy with a bloomy rind. Next should come a harder fruitier cheese, then a washed-rind cheese with a rich full-bodied flavour and aroma. Then try something with a strong outer coating like herbs or vine leaves and finally a blue cheese. This gives a rounded progression of flavours and textures to make the tasting selection truly memorable. Here are my ultimate cheeseboards for British, American and French cheeses. For more information on the cheeses listed go to the relevant chapter for each country.

LEFT TOP Britain

1 St Tola 2 Ticklemore
3 Berkswell 4 Isle of Mull
5 Montgomery's Cheddar
6 Appleby's Cheshire
7 Stilton 8 Stichelton
9 Beenleigh Blue 10 Cardo
11 Ardrahan 12 Wensleydale
13 Gorwydd 14 Wigmore
15 Tunworth 16 Innes Buttons

LEFT MIDDLE USA

1 Cavatina 2 Twig Farm Tomme
3 Bleu Mont Clothbound
Cheddar 4 & 5 Bayley Hazen
Blue 6 Battenkill Brebis
7 Grayson 8 Tarentais 9 Pondhopper 10 Cadence

LEFT BOTTOM France

1 Selles sur Cher 2 Charolais
3 Ossau 4 Comté d'Estive
5 Beaufort Chalet d'Alpage
6 Fourme d'Ambert 7 Roquefort
8 Ami du Chambertin 9 Camembert 10 Val de Loubières 11 Brie
de Meaux (truffled cream) 12
Anneau du Vic Bihl 13 Banon
14 Morbier 15 Crottin

CHEESE & DRINKS

Wine and cheese are good partners, but matching them does require some consideration. However, once you have thought about how the wine reacts with the cheese and the flavour profiles you want to experience, then it all becomes clear. If in doubt think about the region's wines and cheeses to match.

There are no hard and fast rules when matching drinks with cheese; for instance, fresh white wines partner goat's cheeses, but they can also be good with washed-rind soft cheeses such as Munster or hard Gruyère styles with their sweet nuttiness. Sweet wines are generally great with blue cheeses. You can even match spirits such as whisky or even rum (try a dark rum with a triple cream Brillat or Explorateur cheese). Other alcoholic beverages such as cider, beer and even sparkling wines all have cheese partners.

1 Red wine With a full body and vibrant aroma, these wines require cheeses with good acidity levels coupled with their own earthy, robust flavours. The three cheeses pictured are Camembert, Livarot and Pecorino Sardo to give you an indication of the styles, but some softer red wines can take many other cheeses from rich and creamy to crumbly goat's cheeses. New World wines are big on flavour and sometimes overpower cheeses.

①

② ③
④ ⑤

2 White wine The fresh acidity and clean sharp flavours of these wines partner goat's cheeses perfectly, but also consider Beaufort and other hard cheeses that don't want to be overpowered by red wines. From Riesling to the elegant Jura wines it is surprising how many different cheeses work with white wines. The cheeses here are Sainte-Maure, a minerally goat's cheese, Bachensteiner that matches the Riesling and Beaufort for Chignin wines.

3 Port Served at the end of a meal, I suggest you stick to the classic combination of Cheddar and Stilton when drinking port. Serving a single cheese with a Spanish Picos port ends the meal on a high note. The richness of port, both red or tawny lends itself to cheeses like Serra da Estrela.

4 Champagne The bubbles in this wine work well with Parmesan, which has a gritty, salty 'fizz', as does the Langres. I personally love a mature dry Charolais goat's cheese for its nutty flavour but also the long, lingering finish, which copes well with the wine.

5 Sauternes Sweet wines love Roquefort mainly because of the high minerality coming through from the noble rot on the grape. It is one of life's superb umami pleasures.

6 Beer Whether a dark, monastery style to go with the chewy traditional cheeses such as Abbaye de Trois Vaux or a crumbly territorial-style cheese, or a classic hoppy beer with a yeasty aroma and flavours that partner Cheddar so well, there are many cheeses that work with beer.

7 Cider This is not the overly gassy version, but unfiltered, pressed, gently petillant cider with a real apple coming through and yeasty fermented notes. Pont l'Évêque is the perfect cheese partner.

8 Whisky While it is not the obvious choice you will be amazed when you try cheese with whisky. For the softer styles like Singletons, try with Comté aged for two years. For the single malts, add a splash of water and drink with salty, crumbly cheeses like Parmesan, Isle of Mull Cheddar or even an aged Mahón with its dense, gritty style. A matured Crottin de Chavignol is very elegant with an Islay.

⑥

⑦ ⑧

RECIPES

There are some food aromas that are just too irresistible – for me it is cheese melting and bubbling on a piece of toast under the grill. What is it about hot, melted cheese? As much as I love preparing and creating cheeseboards, the versatility of the product in cooking is also showcased in the La Fromagerie shop and café with dishes reflecting not only the different styles of cheeses, but also the seasons. The recipes in this chapter include many from our repertoire, and reflect the La Fromagerie philosophy and commitment to bringing the cheese into the forefront rather than hiding it or mixing it up too much.
The point is that you should never think that when cooking with cheese you can compromise on quality and taste. The better the cheese, the better the outcome of the dish, and you will also find that you do not use as much because the best cheeses will be packed with flavour.

Making & flavouring cheese

There is a big difference between cheeses that are mixed with other flavours and ingredients while being made and before packaging, and the flavour sensations involved in creating homemade recipes. Making your own fresh cheese is really very simple. It's all about understanding what works and enhancing the cheese as opposed to masking and overpowering it. If you go to a farmer's market look for unpasteurized milk to make your own cheese, or simply enjoy it as a drink or over your breakfast cereal.

Labneh

This strained yoghurt, with its subtle, sour lemony taste, is used in all sorts of sweet and savoury Middle Eastern dishes. Try to use a farmhouse–made yoghurt rather than a commercial brand for the best flavour. You can add labneh to spicy meat dishes or serve on top of salads and roasted vegetables. It is also delicious with honey and toasted hazelnuts or pistachios, as well as with summer berries or winter compote.

Makes 24–30 walnut-sized balls
3 x 500 g (1 lb 2 oz) pots goat's, cow's or sheep's milk yoghurt (or a mixture)
Few good pinches of fine sea salt, to taste
Olive oil, to marinate (use a light-flavoured one)
Large handful of finely chopped fresh mint
Freshly ground black pepper

1 Line a mixing bowl with muslin. In another bowl, mix together the yoghurt and salt, then taste to check the seasoning, adding more salt if necessary. Spoon the yoghurt into the centre of the muslin, pick up the edges of the cloth and tie them together to form a bundle.

2 Hang the bundle over a sink or a large bowl by suspending it from a stick or rolling pin, then leave it to drain (see page 229). If your kitchen is cool enough, there is no problem in leaving it out, but you may prefer to transfer the suspended bundle to the warmest part of the fridge. After 48 hours, most of the liquid will have drained away and it can be served at this stage (see page 229). Alternatively, for an improved taste and texture, leave the yoghurt to hang for an extra day.

3 Remove the labneh from the cloth and place in a sealed container in the fridge. Once thoroughly chilled, preferably after 24 hours, roll the cheese into balls somewhere between the size of an olive and a walnut.

4 In a shallow dish, pour in olive oil until about 2 cm (¾ in) deep. Lay the labneh in the oil, rolling them until coated, then every so often spoon more oil over the cheese balls. Before serving, mix together the mint and ground pepper on a flat dish and roll the labneh balls into the mixture; serve immediately.

Cook's Note
❧ You can store the freshly made labneh balls in the oil in a sealed container or Kilner jar for 5 days.

Fresh Ricotta

The emergence of farmer's markets in towns and cities has meant there is now more choice in how we shop and we have become reacquainted with the seasonality of foods. But the most exciting thing for me is seeing small farms and cheesemakers showing their produce, and especially giving us the chance to taste really fresh milk from single herds — sometimes even unpasteurized. What a joy, and what a revelation.

Dave Paul, who produces Hurdlebrook Guernsey milk also has the richest cream, the silkiest soured cream, and his crème fraîche is almost perfect in its consistency. Such thick fresh milk needs to be drunk straight from the bottle — who can wait to pour it into the glass? Very naughty — but very nice!

Fresh goat's milk is really sweet and delicious, and if it is available locally do try it: the fresher the better when it comes to making Ricotta-style cheeses. This fresh cheese is so simple and easy, and unbelievably takes less than an hour to make. Just follow these steps, but please do make the Ricotta with the freshest milk possible as most supermarket or UHT milk will not work and the taste and texture of the cheese will not be as light and fluffy.

Makes about 500 g (1 lb 2 oz)
2.4 litres (4 pints) full-fat goat's milk
300 ml (10 fl oz) goat's cream
Juice of 1 large unwaxed Amalfi lemon
Pinch of fine Fleur de Sel sea salt (optional)

1 Stir together all the ingredients, except the salt, in a large saucepan; use one with a non-reactive interior or better still a copper pan if you have one. Warm the milk mixture slowly over a low heat (you may want to use a heat diffuser). Do not be tempted to stir the milk, as you do not want to break up the forming curds, but gently lift the curds every now and then using a wooden spoon to monitor the progress. As the milk reaches about 82°C/180°F the 'grains' of curd should be about the size of a lentil.

2 Turn up the heat slightly and cook for another 5–8 minutes until the curds mound on the spoon like soft white custard. When the curds start to 'erupt' like a volcano in slow motion, and the temperature is just above 93°C/200°F turn off the heat and leave to stand for 10 minutes.

3 Carefully turn into a colander lined with damp unbleached muslin and drain for at least 15 minutes; you may want to gently squeeze out some of the liquid, then turn out the Ricotta into a basin and add a little salt, if liked. Refrigerate until needed; the Ricotta will last up to 4 days.

Cook's Notes
❧ This fresh Ricotta can be used in the Stuffed Courgette Flowers with Ricotta recipe, as pictured opposite (see page 284).
❧ The drained-off whey or liquid can be used in muffins, pancakes or, indeed, scones.

1 Beat the fromage blanc until thick. Over a bowl, place a fine mesh colander lined with muslin. Put the thickened fromage blanc in the muslin and tie up the cloth.

2 Allow the watery whey to drain through into the bowl. Pick up the cloth and gently squeeze out any watery residue.

3 When sufficient liquid has been released, place the Fromage Blanc in a bowl. In a second bowl, beat the single cream and the vanilla scented sugar until thickened and airy (it will not go into peaks).

4 Combine the cream with the Fromage Blanc very gently and either use straightaway or store in the fridge by first lining a bowl or several ramekin dishes with muslin and spooning into the muslin. Tie up the ends of the muslin to encase the creamy cheese and place in the coldest part of the fridge.

5 Serve with fresh berries in season and extra vanilla sugar on the side.

Fontainebleau

This recipe takes a little organization and advance preparation: the muslin should be scalded in hot water, then squeezed almost dry before using. The fromage blanc and single cream should not be too cold, room temperature is best. The finished cream will keep for up to 3 days stored in the refrigerator.

Serves 8
350 g (12 oz) full fat fromage blanc
150 ml (5 fl oz) single cream
2 tsp vanilla scented caster sugar
plus extra to serve (see Cook's Notes)

Cook's Notes

❦ Vanilla sugar is such a useful sweetener to have in the storecupboard. To make, put a vanilla pod into the middle of a kilner jar of caster sugar, close the lid and store in a larder or food cupboard to allow the vanilla to infuse the sugar. The sugar will take on a lovely scented sweetness and can be used in baking or whipped cream or simply sprinkled over fresh fruit. The vanilla pod lasts for ages, so keep re-filling the jar with sugar until it loses its potency.

❦ For a cream cheese with a lighter, 'fluffier' texture, whisk a large egg white until it forms soft peaks then gently fold it into the cream mixture.

Camembert au Calvados

Philippe Olivier, whose famous cheese shop in Boulogne is a jewel of beautiful cheeses, especially those from Picardy, Normandy and Pays d'Artois, invented this cheese 'confection'. This region in France all but lost its artisan cheesemakers during the two World Wars, but the Oliviers have single-handedly brought them back to life by encouraging and championing their cheeses. Philippe has now retired and his son Romain has taken up the cause. Their Camembert au Calvados is really the most delicious creation, and I have recreated it here for you to make.

Serves 4–6

3 slices of day-old milk bread or *pain de mie*, crusts removed

2 tbsp Calvados or half Calvados and half Apéritif de Normande
   (sweet wine mixed with Calvados)

1 x 200 g (7 oz) farmhouse Camembert, not too ripe

1 slice of dried apple or walnut half (optional), soaked
   in Calvados

1 Preheat the oven to 180°C/350°F/Gas 4. Dry the slices of bread in the oven until crisp – this will only take about 5 minutes – then crush into very fine crumbs. Put the crumbs on a small plate.

2 In a shallow bowl, pour in the Calvados or a mixture of Calvados and Apéritif de Normande.

3 Using a small sharp knife, carefully remove the bloomy rind from the Camembert and then place the cheese in the bowl of liqueur, turning it until thoroughly coated and very wet.

4 Carefully lift out the cheese and place it in the crumb mixture, turning it over until the cheese is thickly covered. You can, if liked, dip the cheese in the liqueur and crumbs for a second time.

5 Place the apple or walnut on top of the cheese, if using. This cheese is delicious with a lighter style Rhône wine or a Gamay (Beaujolais family).

Gorgonzola Torte with Basil

This layered cheese 'torte' infused with basil is really indulgent but so much better than shop-bought versions. It is important to use a really good farmhouse mascarpone — it's what makes the finished result so special.

Serves 8

500 g (1 lb 2 oz) mascarpone cheese, plus extra for coating (optional)
300 g (10½ oz) Gorgonzola Naturale, cut into 1 cm (½ in) thick slices
Fresh basil leaves
Walnut bread, thinly sliced, to serve

1 Take a medium-sized round mesh sieve and place it over a mixing bowl. Line the sieve with a double layer of muslin, leaving enough cloth hanging over the side of the bowl to allow you to tie it up.
2 Spoon a thin layer of mascarpone into the lined sieve to cover the bottom. Place a layer of Gorgonzola into the sieve, then scatter over a few basil leaves. Repeat with another layer of mascarpone, Gorgonzola and basil leaves until you have filled the sieve.
3 Tie the overhanging muslin to encase the cheese. Place a plate on top and then a weight (not too heavy, just something to weigh it down sufficiently to remove any excess liquid).
4 Place the bowl in the fridge and leave for 1 hour or until any excess liquid stops dripping through the muslin. Untie the cloth and turn out the cheese onto a plate.
5 Cover the dome of cheese with a layer of mascarpone, if you wish, and scatter over a few basil leaves. Serve as a single cheese course with thin slices of walnut bread and chilled Prosecco or Vin Santo.

Savoury Blue Cheese Butter

This flavoured butter is perfect with grilled or pan-fried steak, melted on top of a hamburger, or simply as a filling for baked potatoes.

Serves 6

125 g (4½ oz) Bleu d'Auvergne, Roquefort or Bleu des Causses (or another blue cheese with a rich, buttery texture)
125 g (4½ oz) unsalted butter
A sprig of fresh sage or thyme, stalk removed and finely chopped

1 Using a wooden spoon, beat together the cheese and butter in a bowl or blitz in a blender. Mix in the herbs.
2 Place 2–3 sheets of clingfilm on top of one another on a work surface. Spoon the butter mixture onto the film and roll up like a sausage, twisting both ends to secure. Wrap the roll in foil and freeze: it is easy to cut the frozen butter into rounds as needed.

Triple Cream with Walnuts

This easy but luxurious idea involves steeping a triple cream cheese in a fruit liqueur and then rolling it in coarsely chopped walnuts.

Serves 6

Scrape off the excess rind from a fresh rather than mature Explorateur (see page 54) or Brillat-Savarin (see page 52), or a similar soft triple cream cheese.

Pour about 250 ml (9 fl oz) of your chosen liqueur — try pear, apple or peach — in a bowl and add the cheese, turning to coat well.

Cover, then leave to marinate for 30 minutes in a cool larder. Toast a handful of walnuts in a dry frying pan until starting to brown. Place on a clean tea towel, and coarsely crush with a rolling pin.

Remove the cheese from the liqueur and shake off any excess. Put on a plate, then sprinkle over the walnuts, pressing into the outside of the cheese until covered.

Sauces, dips & soups

Simple to make but glorious to taste, these recipes are a million miles away from shop-bought sauces and dips. I am very fond of soup, whether hot or cold, and a dollop of something creamy on top that you can mix in is a lovely finish.

Seasonal Pesto

Serve these fresh homemade pestos stirred into pasta, rice or pilaff dishes, or place a spoonful on top of roasted or grilled vegetables just before serving. Alternatively, bake slices of bread (as for bruschetta) until crisp and spread with a little pesto before placing slices of Mozzarella or soft goat's cheese on top.

Makes 10–12 servings

AUTUMN PESTO

This autumnal pesto is a combination of fiery Espelette peppers from South West France, together with creamy Marcona almonds and Ossau ewe's milk cheese. Espelette peppers arrive in early autumn, and you can use fresh or hang them up with string to dry. They are very beautiful but deceptively hot. This pesto is lovely served with roasted or barbecued chicken.

Simply take one or two peppers, depending on how hot you want the pesto, and then grind in a pestle and mortar or blitz in a food processor or blender. If you can buy fresh Espelette all the better, otherwise use dried ones and grind everything, including the seeds.

Grind a handful of Marcona almonds (de-skinned) in a food processor until almost smooth and then add 250 g (9oz) Ossau cheese and whizz for a minute or two until combined. Next, add the chopped peppers and blitz again until mixed together. Add sufficient olive oil to make a sauce-like consistency. Spoon into a jar, cover the pesto with olive oil, then store in the fridge.

WINTER PESTO

A spoonful of this winter pesto, made with toasted walnuts blended with fragrant winter herbs, can lift a risotto or pasta dish, and it goes especially well with pork.

Toast or dry-fry a good handful of walnuts until golden and then grind in a pestle and mortar or roughly blitz in a food processor or blender. Finely chop 1-2 sprigs of sage (depending on how strong you want the flavour). Mix the walnuts into the sage and stir in 250 g (9oz) grated Pecorino (one with a good flavour like Sardo or Siciliana).

Take one or two fat garlic cloves and crush slightly with the blade of a knife, then blitz in a food processor until smooth. Add the Pecorino mixture and blitz again. Add sufficient olive oil to make a sauce-like consistency, then taste to check the seasoning and if to your liking – it should have a lovely toasted nut, herb and cheese flavour with a hit of garlic. Spoon into a jar, cover the pesto with olive oil, then store in the fridge.

SPRING PESTO

Bitter rocket leaves mixed with salty anchovies and fruity Manchego cheese work well together, while the addition of almonds give the pesto a delicious creamy texture.

Take a couple of handfuls of rocket leaves and chop roughly. Rinse one or two salted anchovies to remove the salt, take out the backbone and then carefully take off the flesh and mash with the back of a fork.

Blitz a good handful of Marcona almonds (de-skinned) until almost smooth, then add 250 g (9 oz) grated Manchego, the rocket and anchovies to the processor. Blend again, then add sufficient olive oil to make a sauce-like consistency; taste to check the seasoning. Spoon into a jar, cover the pesto with olive oil, then store in the fridge.

WILD GARLIC PESTO

Try foraging for wild garlic from late March for a few weeks and use the leaves to make a rather wonderful-tasting pesto. The long, wide leaves are delicate and very pungent, and towards the end of the season the white frilly flowers are simply beautiful.

To make the pesto, take a handful of wild garlic leaves and blitz in a food processor or blender with 200 g (7 oz) of pine nuts. Add 2 big bunches of fresh basil and 200 g (7 oz) finely grated Parmesan, or a mixture of Parmesan and Pecorino, or Parmesan and a hard goat's cheese. Blitz again until finely chopped and then, with the motor running, drizzle in a fruity-tasting, single-estate Tuscan olive oil until it reaches a sauce-like consistency.

SUMMER PESTO

The sweet and savoury flavours of high summer make the perfect pesto. Serve this seasonal pesto stirred into pasta with Mascarpone and a grinding of black pepper.

Cook 200 g (7 oz) fresh shelled peas (or you could use frozen) briefly in boiling water until just tender. Drain and crush into a coarse mixture and set aside. Blitz 2 fat garlic cloves and 100 g (3½ oz) pine nuts in a food processor or blender until almost smooth. Add a handful of chopped mint and process again. Remove from the processor or blender and set aside.

Add 150 g (5½ oz) medium grated Grana and Tuscan Pecorino (either half and half, or to your taste) to the processor or blender and whizz until still slightly gritty. Add the herb and nut mixture and blend until stiff.

With the machine still running, slowly pour in extra-virgin olive oil until it reaches a sauce-like consistency. Taste and if liked, add the zest of a lemon. Transfer to a bowl and fold in the peas. Spoon into a jar, cover the pesto with more olive oil, then store in the fridge.

Liptauer

This easy cheese spread or dip will keep in the fridge for up to a week. It is delicious served with crudités or salad and crusty bread.

Serves 8–10
150 g (5½ oz) full-fat cream cheese, softened
100 g (3½ oz) quark or low-fat soft cheese, softened
100 g (3½ oz) unsalted butter, softened
1 tsp English mustard powder
1 tsp sweet paprika (preferably Hungarian), plus extra to serve
1 tsp baby capers, not in brine, rinsed
2 anchovy fillets, rinsed, patted dry and very finely chopped
1 shallot, very finely chopped
½ tsp caraway seeds
Coarse sea salt and freshly ground black pepper
To serve:
Vegetable crudités
Thin crisp crackers

1 In a bowl, cream together the cream cheese and quark or soft cheese, then beat in the butter until smooth. Beat in the mustard powder, paprika, capers, anchovies, shallot and caraway seeds, then season with salt and pepper to taste.
2 Cover the bowl with clingfilm and chill for a day to let the flavours develop. Serve the cheese dip with vegetable crudités and/or thin crispy crackers.

Cook's Notes
❦ Instead of vegetable crudités, serve the liptauer with a ramekin dish of baby cornichons and a platter of various rye breads.
❦ An alternative way to prepare the cheese is to wrap it in clingfilm to make a round, then leave for a day to allow the flavours to meld. Before serving, unwrap the mound of cheese. Mix together a little paprika with groundnut or sunflower oil, then brush the surface of the cheese with the mixture to give it a light gloss.

Cervelle de Canut

This cheese is also known by the name Claqueret Lyonnais, which refers to the wooden spoon used to mix herbs, shallots, soft herbs and garlic into the silky-smooth cheese curd.

Serves 6–8 as a starter
500 g (1 lb 2 oz) fresh curd cheese, or strained Fromage Blanc
1 tbsp crème fraîche
1 shallot, very finely chopped
1 garlic clove, very finely chopped
1 tbsp very finely chopped herbs such as parsley, chervil, thyme, dill, fennel fronds or chives, or any combination
2–4 tbsp verjuice or light white wine vinegar
1–2 tbsp extra-virgin olive oil
Course sea salt and freshly ground black pepper
To serve:
Crusty sourdough or rye bread
Cornichons or pickled cucumbers

1 In a mixing bowl, beat the curd cheese or fromage blanc with the crème fraîche until smooth. Add the shallot, garlic and herbs. Season with salt and pepper, then taste and add more if necessary.
2 Cover the bowl with clingfilm and chill for 2 days to allow the flavours to meld. Add the verjuice or white wine vinegar and olive oil – add the smaller quantity first, adding more if liked. Store in the fridge.
3 Serve with sourdough or rye bread and cornichons or pickled cucumbers.

Sweetcorn Soup with Crème Fleurette

As soon as we see the early autumn sweetcorn appear in our local farmer's market this soup appears on the menu in La Fromagerie. The corn ears fold back to expose plump kernels that when squeezed between your fingers ooze out their milky sweetness. The sweetness of this soup is absolutely from the corn and no other sugar is added.

Serves 4–6
125 g (4½ oz) unsalted butter
2 large white onions, finely chopped
1 large leek, finely chopped (I like to include some of the green top)
2 celery sticks, finely chopped
6–8 fresh corn cobs, kernels removed
2 litres (3½ pints) boiling water, or half stock/half water, if preferred
Coarse sea salt and freshly ground black pepper
To serve:
Crème fleurette or crème fraîche, drained to remove some of the 'watery' residue
Cornbread, sliced or cubed (see page 294)

1 In a large, heavy-based saucepan, melt the butter until foaming, then sauté the onions, leek and celery for 10 minutes or until softened and just turning golden. Season with a little salt. Mix the corn kernels into the softened vegetables, then cook for 2–3 minutes.
2 Add the water/stock to cover the vegetables completely, then bring to the boil. Turn down the heat to barely a simmer and cook for 5–7 minutes (depending on the size of the corn kernels) until tender. Press the soup through a fine mesh sieve, or purée in small batches in a blender, or use a hand-held blender.
3 Adjust the seasoning to taste and top each serving with a spoonful of crème fleurette or crème fraîche. Serve with the cornbread.

Pumpkin Soup with Gorgonzola Walnut Toast

This is a favourite soup, simply because it has such a satisfying and honest flavour. The colour is beautiful, the texture creamy and silky, and the addition of a blue cheese and the walnut bread makes such a lovely meal.

Serves 4–6
150 g (5½ oz) unsalted butter
2 large onions, finely chopped
2 large leeks, finely chopped
4 garlic cloves, roughly chopped
2 medium pumpkins (firm orange flesh or Potimarron pumpkin), skinned, seeded and cut into small cubes
2 litres (3½ pints) Chicken Stock (see below) or vegetable stock
Few sprigs of fresh thyme and 1 bay leaf, tied into a bundle
Coarse sea salt and freshly ground black pepper
To serve:
Walnut bread, sliced
100 g (3½ oz) Gorgonzola Dolce, thinly sliced

1 In a large, heavy-based saucepan, melt half of the butter until foaming and then sauté the onions, leeks and garlic for 10 minutes or until softened and just turning golden. Add the pumpkin and cook for 5 minutes.
2 Add the stock with the herb bundle and then bring to the boil, taste and season lightly. Turn down the heat to a simmer and cook until the pumpkin is very tender. Take out the vegetables with a slotted spoon and purée in batches in a food processor or blender. Return the purée to the pan with the stock, stir, taste and season. Stir in the remaining butter to give the soup a lovely gloss.
3 Meanwhile, preheat the oven to 180°C/350°F/Gas 4. Put the walnut bread on a baking sheet and bake for about 10 minutes until just crisp. Top with slivers of Gorgonzola Dolce, then leave until melted on top of the warm toast; serve alongside the soup.

Chicken Stock

This flavoursome homemade stock makes 3 litres (5¼ pints).

In a large, heavy-based saucepan, melt 50 g (1¾ oz) butter with 2 tbsp olive oil until foaming but not brown. Sauté 2 large, finely chopped red onions until softened, then stir in 2 large finely chopped carrots. After a couple of minutes, add 2 finely chopped celery sticks and leeks, then sauté the vegetables until softened.

Add 1 rinsed chicken carcass and cover with 3 litres (5¼ pints) water. Create a herb bunch with a few sprigs of flat-leaf parsley and thyme and 1 bay leaf tied into a bundle with string, add to the pan and bring to the boil.

Carefully scoop out any 'scum' that rises to the surface with a slotted spoon and turn the heat to a gentle simmer. Add a pinch of salt and a few white peppercorns.

Turn the heat down to a bare simmer, cover the pan with a lid, then cook for at least 2 hours. You can add a little more boiled water if the liquid appears to be reducing too quickly. Strain the stock, discarding the solids, to make a wonderful broth.

Leave to cool, then store in an airtight container in the fridge or freezer for up to 3 months. To defrost the stock, leave in the fridge overnight, skim off any fat, then use as desired.

Beetroot Soup with Labneh Balls

The sweet, earthy flavour of beetroot lends such a different taste to the usual root vegetable soups. The colour alone is exotic, and the addition of the fresh cheese balls really is delicious. You may think that the amount of butter used here is rather excessive, but it gives flavour as well as a silky texture.

Serves 4–6
800 g (1 lb 12 oz) raw beetroot, trimmed and scrubbed
125 g (4½ oz) unsalted butter, plus extra to serve
1 onion, coarsely grated
1 carrot, coarsely grated
1 fennel bulb, coarsely grated
Juice of 2 large lemons
1–2 tbsp caster sugar (you may need a little more or less, according to taste)
1.5 litres (2¾ pints) Chicken Stock (see page 238) or vegetable stock, or use salt-free stock cubes, if necessary
Coarse sea salt and freshly ground black pepper
Labneh Balls (see page 227), to serve

1 Preheat the oven to 200°C/400°F/Gas 6. Put the beetroot in a deep roasting tin. Pour in about 7.5 cm (3 in) water, then cover with tin foil, fitting it tightly around the rim of the tin. Bake for 45–60 minutes, depending on the size of the beetroot, until tender all the way through when pierced with a skewer.

2 Rub off the outer skins of the beetroot using your thumbs (wear kitchen gloves otherwise you will stain your hands) and then cut into bite-sized pieces.

3 In a large, heavy-based saucepan, melt the butter until foaming and then sauté the vegetables for 10 minutes or until softened and just turning golden. Stir in the beetroot, the juice of 1 lemon and half of the sugar, then pour in the stock and bring the mixture to the boil. Taste and add more lemon or sugar, if necessary.

4 Season with salt, then add a few twists of black pepper; taste again to make sure you are happy with the seasoning. Cover the pan with a tight-fitting lid. Turn the heat down to barely a simmer and cook for 25 minutes or so, until the beetroot is completely soft and crushable (try this with the back of a fork like mashing potatoes).

5 Remove from the heat and blitz in a blender or food processor to a coarse or fine purée, depending on taste. Return to the saucepan and, over the lowest heat, whisk in a good knob of butter to give the soup a lovely gloss. Check the seasoning and serve warm in summer and hot in winter. Pop in one or two labneh balls just before serving.

Fresh Pea Soup with Herb Fromage de Cervelle

This is a summer soup when fresh peas are in abundance but if you are in a hurry you can use frozen peas, although this really does spoil the fun of the shelling. If you are making a vegetable stock you can use the pea pods in the stockpot and any pea shoots attached to the pea pods make a delicious addition to a salad. If you must use frozen peas then 1 large bag will suffice.

Serves 4
1.5 kg (3 lb 5 oz) fresh peas (just under 1 kg (2 lb 4 oz) shelled weight)
2 Little Gem lettuces, sliced
1 medium-thick slice of cooked ham
2 Cipolotti onions or large spring onions, finely chopped
2 litres (3½ pints) water, or half stock/half water, if preferred
Scant 1 tsp caster sugar, or to taste
50 g (1¾ oz) unsalted butter
Coarse sea salt and freshly ground black pepper
Herb Fromage de Cervelle:
350 g (12 oz) full-fat fromage frais, drained, or Petit Suisse
1 tbsp finely chopped fresh herbs, such as chervil, chives, flat-leaf parsley, thyme or mint, or a mixture of herbs

1 Put the shelled peas in a saucepan with the lettuce, ham and onions. Cover with the water/stock, bring to the boil, then reduce the heat. Cover with a lid and simmer gently for about 15 minutes until the peas are quite soft.

2 Press the soup through a fine mesh sieve, or purée in small batches in a blender, or use a hand-held blender. Return to the pan and adjust the seasoning (be careful with the sugar as the amount you use depends on how sweet the peas are). Bring back to the boil, then whisk in the butter.

3 To make the Herb Fromage de Cervelle, drain the cheese in a sieve to remove as much liquid as possible, place in a bowl, then add the herbs. Season with salt and pepper and mix together. Pour the soup into bowls and top with a spoonful of the herb mixture.

Light meals

Cheese is the perfect food and ingredient element for lighter meals, since it is a whole food in itself and with just a few added elements becomes a meal. The combinations are thoughtful rather than a mish-mash of ideas, and remember that the better the quality, the better the finished result.

Cheese Club Sandwiches

Club sandwiches aren't usually made with cheese, but try experimenting with different types of cheese and breads, using all the knowledge you have gained from this book!

WHITE BREAD
· Cheddar, cut into rough shards, Branston pickle and crisp salad leaves
· Cheddar, cut into rough shards, Marmite and watercress

BAGUETTE
· Emmental, sliced ham, Brie, sliced salame and rocket
· Fresh goat's cheese, roasted sliced beetroot, finely chopped thyme and rocket

WALNUT BREAD
· Comté, sliced cooked Morteau sausage, sliced white chicory and celeriac remoulade mixed with crème fraîche and grainy mustard
· Garrotxa goat's cheese, cut into slices, peppers roasted in garlic, olive oil and peppery salad leaves

DARK RYE BREAD
· Triple cream cheese, melon and grapes in a vinaigrette, and watercress
· Rove des Garrigues fresh goat's cheese, smoked salmon (lox), cucumber salad tossed in a sweet dill vinaigrette and trevise
· Tilsiter, grilled crisp smoked bacon, cream cheese or quark and pickled cucumber

Croque Monsieur

I never usually advocate freezing, but you can do this successfully with this recipe, and therefore make a few at a time and then they're ready whenever the urge takes you.

Makes 10
20 medium-thick slices of *pain de mie* or milk bread (this can be day-old bread)
20 medium-thick slices of cooked ham, from your local butcher or deli-counter
300 g (10½ oz) each Emmental and Gruyère, grated and mixed
Béchamel Sauce:
125 g (4½ oz) unsalted butter
125g (4½ oz) unbleached plain flour
500 ml (18 fl oz) full-fat milk, plus extra just in case
1 tbsp wholegrain mustard
Few gratings of fresh nutmeg
Coarse sea salt and freshly ground black pepper

1 To make the béchamel, melt the butter in a heavy-based saucepan over a medium heat until foaming. Sift in the flour and cook the roux mixture over a medium-low heat, stirring constantly, for 3–4 minutes to remove the raw taste of the flour and until it turns a very pale biscuit colour and smells toasty; this is important.

2 Meanwhile, warm the milk in a pan. Pour the milk into the roux in a steady stream, beating continuously to form a smooth, very thick paste similar to the texture of soft cream cheese. Stir in the mustard and nutmeg, then season. Pour the béchamel into a bowl and leave to cool.

3 Spread a slick of béchamel over a slice of bread, follow with a slice of ham and a sprinkling of grated cheese and top with a slice of bread and thick sprinkling of cheese. If storing, wrap in clingfilm and aluminium foil. Repeat to make more croque and freeze them, uncooked, for future use if wished (see below).

4 Preheat the oven to 180°C/350°F/Gas 4. Place the croque on a baking sheet and bake for 10–15 minutes until the top is golden and the cheese bubbling.

Welsh Rarebit

Welsh rarebit was once considered a 'poor man's' dish. However, it has become a rather posh snack, with many variations.

Preheat the grill to medium high. Toast one side of a slice of bread – this can be white, brown or Granary, or even sourdough. Butter the untoasted side lightly and spread over a thin layer or either Dijon, grainy or English mustard, then top with thick shards of aged Lincolnshire Poacher cheese, which is rather like Cheddar but with its own savoury bite. Place under the grill until the cheese is bubbling and golden.

Pagnotta Toasts with Lardo, Porcini & Truffle Pecorino

Pagnotta is a very large round loaf traditionally baked in a wood-burning oven. Its crust is hard and crisp, and the texture of the bread is chewy and open. If you can't get hold of it, then a sourdough, rustic-style bread, or even a crusty baguette will work.

Fresh porcini mushrooms arrive in the shop in early autumn, and sometimes even in late August. If you want an alternative then girolle or chanterelles are fine, or even brown cap, but it is really the meaty flavour of the porcini that makes this recipe so special.

Lardo is the thick layer of fat found immediately below the skin of a pig. It is cured in herbs and spices in marble baths or 'conche' as they are called in Italy. The most famous area for this delicacy is Carrara in the north west of Italy although Aosta in the Italian Alps is another region known for this delicacy.

Serves 2 as a starter

In a frying pan, heat 2–3 tbsp of good olive oil then add a small handful of sliced fresh porcini or other mushrooms and allow to sizzle for a minute or two over a high heat. As soon as the sizzling stops the mushrooms are ready; if you cook them for too long water oozes out and they toughen.

On a piece of hot toasted bread, lay slices of wafer-thin lardo until entirely covered, spoon over some porcini and then crumble a young Truffle Pecorino over the top.

Season with freshly ground black pepper, and then serve the toasts with a side salad of mixed hot peppery salad leaves dressed in extra-virgin olive oil and a drizzle of balsamic vinegar.

Cook's Note
❧ Instead of the Truffle Pecorino try a fresh goat's cheese or a young Parmesan, or even a young Wensleydale, but it is the delicious truffle taste in the Pecorino that partners both the porcini and lardo so well.

Michon Franche-Comté

This is a take on toasted cheese and is a speciality of the Bouchoux plateau area at the southern end of the Franche-Comté region of France. Serve warm, cut into wedges with a glass of Jura wine made with Chardonnay, or a German Spätlese using the same grape style. This is a lovely snack or aperitif, and certainly one of the oldest recipes I have come across.

Serves 6–8

Mix together 300 g (10½ oz) unbleached plain flour and sufficient water to make a soft, floppy paste, season sparingly with salt, especially if using an aged Comté. Stir in 350 g (12 oz) thinly sliced Comté.

Brush a knob of butter over the base of a hot frying pan and place the doughy cheese paste in the pan, spreading it out like a thick pancake. Fry the paste as you would a crêpe until the cheese bubbles and the base is light golden. If you feel confident enough flip it over, otherwise flash the top under a hot grill to brown.

Serve the Michon Franche-Comté cut into 4–6 wedges.

Cook's Note
❧ The Comté region utilizes its cheeses in many recipes from classic chicken with a creamy cheese and morel (*morille*) mushroom sauce to Morbiflette, which is a traditional potato dish with melted Morbier, and Raclette using Bleu de Gex (a blue cheese with a distinct but not too strong a taste). The region's tarte au fromage is probably the best version of a cheese flan using Comté, eggs and cream for the custard filling.

Flambéed Banon de Chèvre

Provence in South East France is famous for its small medallions of goat's cheese, and Banon is one that is covered in chestnut leaves. Before wrapping, the cheesemaker brushes over a little eau de vie to heighten the flavour of the cheese. This dish makes an end-of-meal 'savoury' treat. When choosing the Banon, you want one that is neither too ripe as it may split, nor too hard, so be careful to choose one that is just right! This is served with a salad of bitter leaves with toasted crushed hazelnuts.

Serves 2 to share

Remove the outer chestnut leaves of the Banon and leave the cheese to reach room temperature.

In a small pan, brush the tiniest amount of groundnut or other flavourless oil over the base and heat. Add the cheese and gently cook on both sides being careful not to split the tender skin of the cheese.

Pour about 1 tablespoon eau de vie into a metal ladle, and then hold the ladle over the bare flame of a gas cooker and before you know it the alcohol will alight. Taking great care, very slowly pour the flaming liquid over the cheese in the pan and let the flames 'lick' the cheese. When the flames die down, lift out the cheese and pop it on top of some salad leaves. Sprinkle with toasted crushed hazelnuts and serve immediately.

Cook's Note

🐾 When making the bitter leaf salad be careful not to use a strong-tasting vinegar because it will not agree with the cheese – or to be more blunt with your digestive system, which sometimes starts gurgling when a mixture of soft creamy cheese and vinegar meld together. Dress the salad in a light olive oil with lemon, verjuice or a light white wine vinegar.

Baked Vacherin

There are a few simple but necessary rules when baking a whole Vacherin. One is that the cheese has to be at room temperature; if it isn't, then you will be waiting hours for it to cook. Secondly, keep it simple as it's really all about the cheese mingling with a little wine, and not about garlic or herbs.

The loveliest accompaniments are steamed whole new potatoes (Charlotte are good), steamed broccoli, toasted slices of baguette, cooked or cured (or both) smoked ham and a green salad, which has been simply dressed in walnut oil and a squeeze of lemon juice.

The small boxed cheeses can serve 2 people for a light meal or one if it is a main course; this is just such a warming and friendly way of eating, especially in the winter.

Serves 2 to share

Preheat the oven to 220°C/425°F/Gas 7. For each baby-boxed Vacherin take off the lid and rub the rind with dry white wine, massaging it in well. Pop the lid back on and then cover the whole box with foil.

Place the box on a baking sheet and bake in the preheated oven for at least 25–30 minutes. Check after about 20 minutes by carefully opening up the foil, lifting off the lid and prodding the rind to check how hot and soft it is – when ready the cheese should almost be erupting out of its rind. If not ready, replace the lid and foil and return to the oven.

When cooked, unwrap the foil and remove the box lid, push back the top 'skin' of the cheese, which should slide off very easily. Pour in a little more white wine, season with pepper and then serve immediately with your choice of accompaniments.

1. Preheat the oven to 180°C/350°F/Gas 4. Cut the top off each garlic bulb, and maybe a little from the base so it will stand upright in a baking tin. Stand the bulbs snugly in the tin, spoon over the chicken stock or water and pour over the wine, verjuice or white wine vinegar. Season liberally with salt and pepper, and then top with the bay leaves or myrtille and thyme.

2. Cover the tin with foil and place on the middle shelf of the oven. Cook for 30 minutes, then remove the foil and cook until the garlic becomes golden and the liquid reduces slightly. Test with a skewer (the garlic should be tender) and then remove from the oven; leave to cool to room temperature.

3. To serve, drizzle olive oil over a slice of crusty sourdough or lightly toasted white bread and place on a plate with a couple of tablespoons of fresh curd per person, then lightly season with salt and a grinding of black pepper. Next, place a garlic bulb on each plate and spoon over a little of the syrupy juices.

Cook's Note

❧ You can also use new season fennel available in early summer to make this recipe. Cut the fennel into chunky quarters if large, or halve if smaller, put it in a roasting tin and spoon over the wine or verjuice. Next, sprinkle with 1 chopped red chilli and herbs such as thyme, marjoram, oregano or coriander. Roast for 30 minutes until tender and golden.

Slow-roast Garlic with Fresh Curd Toasts

New season Italian garlic arrives at the beginning of March. They are quite unlike the bulbs found normally in the shops, as they look similar to large, thick-stemmed spring onions. However, they are pungently sweet and wonderful to slow roast in olive oil, or alternatively in a glass of white wine or stock, and then served warm with toasted sourdough and a light, frothy goat's milk or ewe's milk curd — this really does herald a new season with its fresh yet robust flavours.

Serves 6
6 whole heads of new season garlic
250 ml (9 fl oz) Chicken Stock (see page 238) or water
200 ml (7 fl oz) dry white wine or verjuice, or light white wine vinegar
3–4 fresh bay leaves or myrtille, which is a smaller version with a sweeter flavour
3–4 sprigs of fresh thyme
Coarse sea salt and freshly ground black pepper
To serve:
Good-quality extra-virgin olive oil
Sliced crusty sourdough or white bread
250 g (9 oz) fresh curd (goat's, cow's, ewe's or buffalo's), at room temperature

Gravadlax and Petit Suisses

Homemade Gravadlax does take time, but if you make it a couple of times it really is easy and a great centrepiece for a party or as a starter for the Christmas meal — it is always served at my table on festive occasions.

Serves 10–12

2.25 kg (5 lb) whole salmon, gutted, filleted and pin-boned, head and tail discarded

2 tbsp coarse sea salt, plus extra to taste

2 tbsp granulated sugar

2 tbsp white peppercorns, lightly crushed

2 tbsp coriander seeds, roasted in a dry frying pan, then crushed

Grated zest of 2 large lemons

At least 3 handfuls of fresh herbs, including dill, coriander and chervil

125 ml (4 fl oz) vodka

125 ml (4 fl oz) white wine

To serve:

Petit Suisse pistols, serve 1 per person

Freshly ground black pepper

Lemon wedges

1 Lay a long sheet of clingfilm across a large serving dish. Place one half of the salmon, skin-side down, on the clingfilm. Place the second side of salmon on a separate dish, skin-side down.

2 Mix together the salt, sugar, white pepper, coriander seeds and lemon zest and then spread it evenly across each piece of salmon. Divide the mixed herbs between the salmon and press them into each fillet. Combine the vodka and wine and pour over the salmon.

3 Carefully place the salmon, not on the clingfilm, on top of the other piece, flesh-side down, so the fillets are sandwiched together; pour over any excess liquid.

4 Wrap the fillets tightly in clingfilm. Press down and place a plate large enough to cover the salmon on top, followed by weights such as cans or kitchen weights. Store the salmon overnight in the fridge. After 12 hours, unwrap and turn over each side of salmon. Spoon over any excess juices and then re-wrap and weigh down again. Repeat this procedure every 24 hours for the next 3 days.

5 On the fourth day, unwrap the salmon and remove most of the herb and pepper topping, although you can leave a little as this is rather tasty, and drain off any excess liquid. Using a very sharp kitchen knife, slice the salmon very thinly at a slight angle taking care to remove the skin (you don't want to slice through the skin).

6 Serve each portion with a Petit Suisse and wedge of lemon. Season the Petit Suisse with salt and pepper.

Main meals

A main meal with cheese as a component really does not need a big starter or indeed a heavy pudding to follow. The cheese is in itself filling, so lighten up the rest of the menu with a simple salad starter and to finish stewed fruits with shortbread biscuits.

Fondue

Try experimenting with your own favourite cheese combinations when making this fondue. Many of the cheeses mentioned in this book, especially those in the Alpine chapter, are suitable. Even Irish and British cheeses work beautifully.

When making a fondue there are a few important points to remember: use a good-quality cheese and ensure it is at room temerature; grate the cheese before starting to cook using a heavy-based saucepan and stir the fondue in a figure of eight to ensure it is evenly mixed.

To calculate the amount of cheese required, reckon on about 350 g (12 oz) per person, with rind removed. My favourite cheese combination, include: Comté aged at least 2½ years (see page 84) or aged Gruyère (see page 95); aged Beaufort Chalet d'Alpage (see page 86); Emmenthaler (see page 97) and Reblochon (see page 89).

1 Grate the Comté or Gruyère, Beaufort Chalet d'Alpage, Emmenthaler and Reblochon and mix together in a bowl. I always start the fondue on the kitchen stove as this is quicker and you can control the melting process much better. Rub the inside of a large heavy-based saucepan with a large garlic clove, crushing it against the inner surface. Discard any large chunks of garlic but leave the smaller pieces in the pan.

2 Turn on the heat to medium and pour in a couple of large glasses of dry white wine, about 400 ml (14 fl oz), for 6 people. Heat until the wine starts to bubble and then mix in the cheese, a handful at a time, stirring it in with a wooden spoon using a figure-of-eight motion (see above). Once the cheese has melted, add another handful, until all the cheese is used and the sauce is thick enough to coat the back of the spoon – pour in more wine if the mixture looks too thick.

3 Finally, add the Reblochon, which you can scoop out with a spoon after removing the rind on top of the cheese. This final addition will add a lovely gloss to the fondue and lend an even more velvety texture. Season with salt and freshly ground black pepper to taste and then pour into the fondue pot that you have warmed through in the oven in readiness. At the table, place the fondue pot on its little stove and then stir in a slug or two of Kirsch liqueur. To serve, dip cubes of day-old baguette, bite-sized steamed potatoes, with skin on, and steamed broccoli florets into the fondue.

Raclette

Raclette is not only the name of a cheese, but also a dish that began as a peasant-style meal and then somehow turned into a gourmet offering, especially at ski resorts. Raclette is a derivative of the word 'racler', which means 'to scrape', and traditionally a whole cheese was cut in half and placed in front of an open hearth and the melting cheese was scraped off onto thick wedges of bread or potatoes.

Here are a few tips when serving Raclette:

1 If using ready-sliced cheese, brush over a little white wine before placing under the grill section of your cooker, or if you have an electric table-top Raclette grill, place slices in the little pans and brush with a little wine before placing under the heating element. If you are using a traditional machine, prepare the quarter or half cheese by rubbing the outside rind with white wine – massage it well into the rind so that it is a little sticky but not soaking. Cook for a few minutes until bubbling.

2 Have ready all the bits and pieces that go well with Raclette: slices of Bayonne or other cured ham; speck, a smoked cured ham; different types of salame; thin slices of crusty bread; steamed vegetables such as broccoli florets and new potatoes; small gherkins called cornichons are also good; as well as small pickling onions, roasted in olive oil and balsamic vinegar. Another serving idea is to pour the melted Raclette over a baked potato.

3 If using a quarter or half cheese, you must use it all, as otherwise you will be left with rather a sorry-looking molten mess that will harden as it cools and be inedible.

Tartiflette

This hearty winter dish is perfect for a family lunch with a green salad on the side.

Serves 4–6
2 kg (4 lb 8 oz) Desiree potatoes, scrubbed and skins left on
1 tbsp olive oil
2 large onions, finely sliced
500 g (1 lb 2 oz) thickly sliced pancetta, cut into small cubes
1 small glass white Savoie wine or similar dry fruity white wine
1 large garlic clove, peeled
8 tbsp crème fraîche
1 x 1 kg (2 lb 4 oz) Abbaye de Tamié cheese, or 2 Reblochon, rind removed if dry and cut into long slices
50 g (1¾ oz) unsalted butter
125 g (4½ oz) Comté, grated
125 g (4½ oz)Parmesan, grated

1 Steam or boil the potatoes for 15–20 minutes until cooked all the way through but not falling apart. Drain the potatoes, then peel them and cut into 1 cm (½ in) thick slices. The potatoes should not crumble, but don't worry if some do; set to one side.

2 Heat the oil and sauté the onions for 5 minutes until golden. Remove from the pan with a slotted spoon and set to one side. Add the pancetta to the frying pan – there is no need for any extra oil – and sauté over a medium-high heat until golden but not too brown. Remove with a slotted spoon, place on kitchen paper to remove any excess oil and set aside.

3 Put the potatoes and onions back in the frying pan and cook for about 2 minutes, gently shaking the pan, then pour over the white wine; cook over a medium-low heat for a minute or two.

4 Select a square casserole or ovenproof dish, rub well with garlic, squeezing the clove to crush it. Spoon a slick of crème fraîche over the base of the dish until lightly coated and then add a layer of the potato and onion mixture, a sprinkling of pancetta and slices of the Abbaye de Tamié or Reblochon. Then repeat the layers finishing with a top layer of sliced potatoes and onions. There should be no need to add salt and pepper to this dish as the cheese and the pancetta should provide enough flavour – but if you want to add extra then do so but judiciously.

5 Dot the butter over the top and add blobs of crème fraîche and finally a layer of grated Comté and Parmesan. Bake in an oven preheated to 200°C/400°F/ Gas 6 for 25 minutes until the cheese is beautifully golden and bubbling.

Pasta Carbonara

This warming winter dish makes a great supper with a green salad, or it can be served as an accompaniment to roasted meats.

Serves 2
2 tbsp extra-virgin olive oil
250 g (9 oz) smoked pancetta, cut into small cubes
1 large garlic clove, crushed
Handful of chopped fresh flat-leaf parsley
2 organic free-range eggs, plus 2 extra yolks
4 heaped tbsp Pecorino Romano, Pecorino Siciliano or Sardo Canestrato, finely grated, plus extra to serve
150 ml (5 fl oz) double cream
Coarse sea salt and freshly ground black pepper
250 g (9 oz) pasta (spaghetti, tagliatelle or penne), to serve

1 Heat the olive oil in a frying pan and fry the pancetta for 5 minutes until golden; remove and place on a dish. Add the garlic and parsley and cook for 1 minute, then remove and set aside.

2 Whisk the eggs, extra yolks, cheese and cream in a bowl and season well with freshly ground black pepper.

3 Cook the pasta and drain. Immediately return the pasta to the hot saucepan and over a low heat, add the cooked pancetta, garlic and parsley, then turn off the flame.

4 Add the egg and cream mixture, stirring thoroughly, until the pasta is coated in sauce. The liquid egg will cook as it comes into contact with the hot pasta, but it must not get too hot otherwise it will scramble. If the sauce is not cooking, return the pan to a very low heat for a short while. Serve sprinkled with grated cheese.

Cauliflower Cheese

I couldn't contemplate a Sunday roast without cauliflower cheese. Cauliflower is in season during the winter months and this is the perfect time for warming dishes like this, as well as layered gratins with cabbage and potatoes.

Serves 4–6

1 large cauliflower, cut into large florets
100 g (3½ oz) unsalted butter, plus extra for greasing
2 tbsp plain flour, sifted
600 ml (1 pint) full-fat milk, plus extra just in case
1 onion, peeled and studded with 6–8 cloves
1 bay leaf, torn
350 g (12 oz) Montgomery's Cheddar or other well-flavoured farmhouse Cheddar, coarsely grated
150 ml (5 fl oz) crème fraîche
1 tbsp Dijon mustard
Freshly grated nutmeg, to taste
50 g (1¾ oz) Parmesan, finely grated
Coarse sea salt and freshly ground black pepper

1 Cook the cauliflower in boiling salted water for a few minutes until al dente. Strain, return the cauliflower to the pan and shake gently over a medium heat until any liquid evaporates, then place in a buttered baking dish.

2 To make a roux, melt the butter over a medium heat. Turn down the heat slightly and add the flour, then cook, stirring the mixture continuously to 'cook' out the flour taste.

3 Meanwhile, warm the milk with the onion and bay leaf. Strain the milk into a jug. Off the heat, pour a little of the milk into the roux and mix to a creamy consistency. Place the pan back on the heat and, in a steady stream, pour in the rest of the milk, stirring until thick.

4 Sprinkle in the Cheddar, a small handful at a time, and mix thoroughly reserving a handful for the top. Taste and season with salt and pepper then add, off the heat, the crème fraîche and Dijon mustard, mixing thoroughly before grating over a little nutmeg.

5 Pour the sauce over the cauliflower florets in the dish. Sprinkle with the rest of the Cheddar and the Parmesan. Finish with extra grated nutmeg and bake in an oven preheated to 220°C/425°F/Gas 7 for about 10 minutes or until the top is bubbling and golden brown.

Mac 'n Cheese

This American midweek staple is real comfort food. Given a little thought, you can turn a rather mundane dish into something really delicious.

Serves 4

450 g (1 lb) macaroni or 'elbow-shape' pasta
4 tbsp unsalted butter, beef dripping or bacon fat, plus extra as required
4 tbsp flour
1.2 litres (2 pints) full-fat milk, warmed
½ tsp salt
½ tsp freshly ground black pepper
1 heaped tsp English mustard powder
450 g (1 lb) strong farmhouse Cheddar such as Lincolnshire Poacher or a mixture of Parmesan and Cheddar, grated
Dry breadcrumbs (1–2 day-old bread, dried – not toasted), tossed in a little melted butter, for sprinkling
8 rashers of streaky bacon, grilled until crisp, to serve (optional)

1 Cook the macaroni until al dente, drain, toss in a little butter and place in a casserole dish. To make a roux, melt the butter over a medium heat. Turn down the heat slightly and add the flour, then cook, stirring continuously, for 2 minutes.

2 Off the heat, pour a little of the milk into the roux and mix to a creamy consistency. Place the pan back on the heat and, in a steady stream pour in the rest of the milk, stirring until thick.

3 Take the pan off the heat and stir in the salt, pepper, mustard and grated cheese, mixing well. Return to the heat and stir continuously until the cheese has melted. Pour the sauce over the macaroni in the casserole and stir to ensure the pasta is coated.

4 Sprinkle the top with the breadcrumbs and bake in an oven preheated to 200°C/400°F/Gas 6 for 15 minutes. Before serving top with the bacon rashers, if liked.

Lasagne with Bologna Sausage and Fontina Sauce

We are lucky enough at La Fromagerie to have fresh sausages direct from Bologna, Italy, with their rich, almost fruity taste, but many butchers now make their own version of this pure meat sausage. I have not used garlic because the other ingredients provide more than enough flavour. Enjoy this dish with a simple bitter leaf salad.

Serves 4–6
2–3 tbsp olive oil, plus extra for greasing
2 red onions, finely sliced
5 or 6, about 500 g (1 lb 2 oz), fresh chunky Italian sausages
    made with pure meat, sliced into small rounds
200 g (7 oz) pancetta, cut into small cubes
250 ml (9 fl oz) red wine (something fruity!)
500 g (1 lb 2 oz) dried lasagne sheets
250 g (9 oz) Fontina, coarsely grated, plus extra for topping
250 g (9 oz) Parmesan, grated, plus extra for topping
Tomato sauce:
50 g (1¾ oz) unsalted butter
1 tbsp olive oil
1 large onion, finely diced
1 large carrot, finely diced
1 celery stick, finely diced
1 kg (2 lb 4 oz) San Marzano tomatoes, chopped, or canned
1 tbsp finely chopped fresh marjoram, sage or thyme
Béchamel sauce:
100 g (3½ oz) unsalted butter
4 tbsp unbleached plain flour
850 ml (1½ pints) full-fat milk, warmed
Freshly grated nutmeg, to taste
1 torn bay leaf
Coarse sea salt and freshly ground black pepper

1 Heat the oil in a frying pan and add the red onions, then sauté for 5 minutes until softened. Add the sausages and pancetta and cook until they begin to caramelize, then add the wine. Let the wine gently bubble and reduce until syrupy – around 5 minutes. Take the pan off the heat and set aside.

2 Cook the lasagne in plenty of boiling salted water until al dente or not totally soft. Put a few sheets in at a time so they don't stick together; I sometimes add a splash of oil to the water to avoid this happening. Remove with a slotted spoon and set aside, then repeat with the remaining sheets. After cooking, do not pile the lasagne on top of one another as it will stick together.

3 To make the tomato sauce, heat the butter and olive oil in a saucepan over a medium heat until foaming. Add the onion, carrot and celery and sauté until softened and just starting to turn golden. Add the tomatoes and, once bubbling, turn the heat right down. Season with salt and pepper, add the herbs and cook very slowly for at least 30 minutes until a rich, thick sauce – you want to achieve a thick purée. Set to one side.

4 To make the béchamel sauce, melt the butter in a heavy-based saucepan, then stir in the flour and let this cook, stirring continuously, for 2–3 minutes but do not let it brown. Gradually pour the warm milk into the roux in a steady stream, stirring all the time, until it reaches a lovely thick, creamy consistency. Season with salt, pepper and a little nutmeg. Add the bay leaf and cook the sauce over a very low heat for 15 minutes, stirring regularly.

5 To assemble, lightly oil a 20–30 x 25 cm (8–12 x 10 in) deep ovenproof dish, either glass or terracotta. Spoon a little of the béchamel over the base of the dish, add a layer of lasagne, then spoon over half of the sausage mixture, followed by half of the tomato sauce, another layer of pasta, then béchamel, sprinkle with half of the Fontina and Parmesan. Repeat this again and finally top with a slick of béchamel and the remaining Fontina and Parmesan.

6 Place the lasagne on the middle shelf of an oven preheated to 190°C/375°C/Gas 5 and bake for 40–45 minutes until golden on top and bubbling.

Shepherd's (and Cottage) Pie with Potato and Lancashire Mash

I do prefer a shepherd's pie to have minced beef as well as lamb, hence the combined names in the title. This family-style meal can be tweaked and changed to your taste but this is how my family prefer it!

Serves 6–8

2–3 tbsp olive oil
2 large onions, finely sliced
2 large carrots, chopped or grated
600 g (1 lb 5 oz) beef mince
400 g (14 oz) lamb mince
1 tbsp tomato purée
Small knob of unsalted butter
5 cremini or 4 portobello mushrooms, sliced
2 tbsp Worcestershire sauce
1 tbsp mushroom ketchup
Freshly grated nutmeg, to taste
1 tbsp finely chopped fresh thyme
Salt and freshly ground black pepper

Mash:

1.5 kg (3 lb 5 oz) Desiree potatoes, peeled and cut into chunks
1 large celeriac, peeled and cut into chunks
250 ml (9 fl oz) full-fat milk
150 g (5½ oz) unsalted butter
500 g (1 lb 2 oz) Lancashire cheese, grated, plus 4 heaped tbsp
150 ml (5 fl oz) double cream

1 In a large frying pan, heat the olive oil, then sauté the onions and carrots over a medium heat until softened. Add the beef and lamb mince and cook until browned, breaking the meat down with the back of a spoon. Add the tomato purée and cook, stirring for a few minutes.

2 In a separate pan, heat a knob of butter until foaming and add the mushrooms. Cook for a few minutes over a high heat until water starts to seep out of the mushrooms, then take off the heat. Using a slotted spoon, take the mushrooms out of the pan, shaking off as much liquid as possible.

3 Add the mushrooms to the mince, then stir in the Worcestershire sauce and mushroom ketchup. Finely grate over some nutmeg, being careful at first, then taste before adding any more. Add the thyme and then season with salt and pepper, to taste. Turn the heat right down and, cover the pan, and cook gently for a further 8 minutes.

4 While the mince is cooking, steam the potatoes and celeriac (rather than boiling them in water) until tender; test they are done by piercing with a skewer. Take off the heat, pour away the water and return the vegetables to the empty pan to 'dry' them over a low flame for a minute or two – take off the heat.

5 In a small pan, heat the milk with the butter and when hot, but not boiling, start pouring it slowly onto the potatoes, beating as you go. Continue until the milk and butter are incorporated and the mixture is smooth. Stir in the cheese, reserving 4 heaped tablespoons, before adding the cream, then season with salt and pepper to taste.

6 Spoon the meat mixture into a 30 x 5 cm (12 x 2 in) deep ovenproof dish, then top with the creamy mash. Using a fork, make little peaks in the potato, then scatter over the remaining cheese. Bake in an oven preheated to 200°C/400°F/Gas 6 for 25–30 minutes until the top is golden and the meat bubbling beneath.

Veal Escalope with Taleggio and Sage

Rose veal has a delicate flavour and is not to be confused with baby white veal, which in the past had put off many people from buying because of the way the animals were reared. This is veal with a good conscience. It has an affinity with cheeses such as Taleggio with its salty, creamy taste, but you could easily use a goat's cheese.

Serves 1

Flatten the escalope with a wooden flat paddle or wooden spatula. Place thin slices of cooked ham, or prosciutto di Parma on top to cover, followed by thin slices of Taleggio (a young one would be best for this dish) and finally a leaf or two of sage.

Roll up the veal and secure with one or two cocktail sticks to hold the filling in place. Dust the roll in seasoned flour, coating all sides and ends, then dip in beaten egg. Lift out and shake off any excess egg, then dust again in flour to coat well.

In a frying pan, heat 2–3 tablespoons olive or sunflower oil and 50 g (1¾ oz) unsalted butter until melted. Over a medium heat, fry the escalope roll, carefully turning to cook all sides, for about 5–8 minutes until golden and cooked through.

Drain on kitchen paper and serve with sauté potatoes and green beans, or a rich and densely fruity tomato sauce. This is for one serving, but if you are cooking for more people, increase the quantity of ingredients accordingly.

Alpine Sautéed Brown Trout

The monastery of La Grande Chartreuse is hidden away in the mountains of the national park of Chartreuse. It was here that the wonderfully aromatic green liqueur, Chartreuse, was invented by the monks. This protected area of natural beauty is a magnet for tourists at all times of the year. The rushing streams are home to trout, and a day can be very pleasantly spent fishing and picnicking. Here is a recipe of stark simplicity that says a lot about its origins.

Serves 1

1 brown trout, gutted and de-scaled
100 g (3½ oz) unsalted butter
1 slice of lemon
Small handful of fresh herbs such as parsley, bay leaf, marjoram or thyme
1 garlic clove
1 thick slice of brioche or other sweet milk bread, cut into croutons
Sunflower oil, for frying (optional)
1 thick slice, about 85 g (3 oz), of ventrèche (French unsmoked bacon), streaky bacon or pancetta, cut into small cubes
Flour, for dusting
50 g (1¾ oz) Beaufort Chalet d'Alpage cheese at room temperature, cut into small cubes
Coarse sea salt and freshly ground black pepper

1 Rinse the trout under cold running water and pat dry. Salt the inside of the fish and place a little butter, slice of lemon and a few herbs into the cavity.
2 Crush the garlic slightly with a knife. Put the garlic in a frying pan with a largeish knob of butter and heat until it starts to foam. Throw in the croutons and fry until golden and crisp. Take out with a slotted spoon, drain on kitchen paper and put to one side.
3 There should be enough butter still in the pan but if not, add a splash of sunflower oil and heat up. Now, add the cubes of ventrèche, or if you can't find this streaky bacon or pancetta, and cook until nicely golden with crispy edges. Take out with a slotted spoon and drain on kitchen paper and set aside.
4 Add a good-size knob of butter to the pan with the juices from the bacon and let it foam over a medium heat. Lightly dust the trout with flour, place in the pan, then cook for about 2 minutes each side, depending on the size of your fish; spoon over the melted butter as you cook.
5 Lift out the fish with a spatula and drain off any excess fat. Place on a plate and carefully remove the herb and lemon stuffing. Spoon a small amount of the buttery juices from the pan over the fish.
6 Transfer the bacon and croutons to the pan and quickly heat through, then using a slotted spoon place them around the trout. Finally, add the cubes of Beaufort and serve with a chilled glass of Chignin Bergeron.

Seasonal Risottos

Risotto and cheese work so well together, and there are numerous ways of incorporating the latter into this classic Italian dish. I have given a few variations, all with a seasonal slant, but what you won't see is the addition of mascarpone, which I feel is far too rich for risotto. If you use a good-quality cheese, you will not need to add mascarpone.

Spring Risotto

Around Easter, or perhaps a little later if it falls at the beginning of April, asparagus starts appearing in the shops. Also making a welcome appearance are spring herbs, and peas and fave (broad) beans from the Continent. Follow the method closely for this green risotto and you will have the most wonderfully aromatic and tasty dish. Do also remember that the rice will continue to cook in hot liquid even if you think it is not quite ready at step 4. Have faith!

Serves 6–8

3 kg (6 lb 8 oz) fresh peas, shelled, or cheat with 900 g (2 lb) frozen petit pois

2 large handfuls of fresh broad beans, shelled and squeezed out of their hard skins

2 bundles, about 600 g (1 lb 5 oz) of fresh asparagus, trimmed and sliced diagonally into 3 pieces

2 tbsp finely chopped fresh mint

250 g (9oz) unsalted butter

500 g (1 lb 2 oz) cipolotti onions or large spring onions, roughly chopped

2 large garlic cloves, finely chopped

450 g (1 lb) Carnaroli rice

1.5 litres (2¾ pints) hot Chicken Stock (see page 238), or 1 bouillon cube

Small handful of fresh basil leaves

150 ml (5 fl oz) dry white wine or vermouth

100 g (3½ oz) Seirass ewe's Ricotta or buffalo Ricotta, or fresh cow's milk Ricotta, crumbled (see page 228)

Finely grated zest of 2 large lemons

Large handful of coarsely grated Tuscan or Sardinian Pecorino

Coarse sea salt and freshly ground black pepper

1 Cook the peas, broad beans and asparagus with half of the mint in simmering salted water for a couple of minutes until al dente but not soft. Drain the vegetables and mint, reserving 100 ml (3½ fl oz) of the cooking water. Return the drained vegetables and mint to the reserved water and set aside.

2 In a large heavy-based saucepan, melt half of the butter, then add the onions, stir and sauté for about 8 minutes until softened. Add the garlic, then pour in the rice. Mix with a wooden spoon for a few minutes until the rice is coated in the buttery onions.

3 Now start to add the hot stock, one ladleful at a time, stirring as you go. When the rice has absorbed the liquid, add another ladleful of stock; this will take around 8–10 minutes. (The rice will continue to cook in the heat of the pan.)

4 Return the peas, broad beans and asparagus with the reserved liquid to the pan. Tear the basil leaves and add them to the pan with the wine or vermouth.

5 Crumble in half of the Ricotta and stir in the remaining butter, then continue to cook for a few minutes, stirring, until the butter has melted into the rice. Taste the rice; it should now be tender with the centre of each grain still al dente. Fold in the rest of the fresh mint.

6 To serve, divide the risotto between the plates and top with the remaining Ricotta, then sprinkle over the lemon zest and Pecorino. Add a final seasoning of salt and black pepper and it's ready.

Cook's Note

❧ The mint can be replaced with nettles but blanch them first to remove most of the 'sting'. Their sharp, vibrant flavour will complement the vegetables. Also around at this time of year is wild garlic, found growing prolifically by streams and in meadows. It tastes very strong but can be used in small quantities in risottos, especially when served alongside a roast chicken.

Summer Risotto

This version uses baby artichokes available from late summer, which are so tender and need hardly any preparation or trimming, combined with sweet, salty, crumbly Pecorino.

Serves 6–8

Make the risotto with 3 large white onions, which you have first finely chopped and sautéed in butter and olive oil until softened, then add the rice and stock, and continue as for the Spring Risotto. Just before serving, add pan-fried sliced baby artichokes or artichoke hearts with a large handful of grated Pecorino Vilanetto from Tuscany with its flaky texture and rich, creamy taste.

Cook's Note

❦ Ricotta Salata made with buffalo milk is an excellent alternative to the pecorino. This useful hard cheese has a delicious salty yet creamy taste and can be grated into the risotto. It also goes well in a tomato risotto with lots of lovely fresh basil.

Autumn Risotto

This is such a beautifully textured dish — intensely creamy with a deep golden colour. The strength of the cheese makes a great foil to the sweetness of the pumpkin, and the topping of aromatic crisp sage leaves really does finish off the dish.

Serves 6–8

Roast chunks of pumpkin in the oven with a little oil, lemon zest and finely chopped chilli. Follow the instructions for the Spring Risotto, then just before serving, stir in the roasted pumpkin as well as crumbled Gorgonzola Naturale for a strong flavour or Gorgonzola Dolce for a creamier taste. Stir the cheese into the rice, gently heating it until melted, and then serve sprinkled with crisp sage leaves (fried in a little olive oil until toasted).

Cook's Note

❦ Wild mushrooms are available in abundance in early autumn and their bosky, earthy flavour and aroma work well in risotto. Porcini, or cep, have a unique flavour but are expensive, so use in combination with girolles and chestnut mushrooms. Stir the mushrooms into the risotto along with a soft primo-sale or fresh cow's milk Ricotta and 1 tablespoon finely chopped fresh thyme. Sprinkle with an aged Grana instead of Parmesan before serving.

Winter Risotto

I love Cavolo Nero, Italian black cabbage, with its dark greeny-black leaves. It is a great vegetable with both meat and fish dishes, but follow the original risotto recipe above and then carry on as below and you will have a really lovely fragrant yet savoury dish.

Serves 6–8

Braise thinly sliced Cavolo Nero in a large pan with olive oil, a splash of water, thinly sliced garlic, finely chopped fresh rosemary and salt and pepper. This will only take a minute or two (you know when the Cavolo is ready as it will stop sizzling and hissing in the pan). Work this through the risotto, adding copious amounts of finely shaved Parmigiano Reggiano before serving.

Cook's Note

❦ January and February can be bleak months, but there are still herbs around, and Trevisana (Italian red chicory) and Castelfranco (looks like a lettuce but is a beautiful speckled green and red chicory) are delicious with finely chopped fresh thyme and flat-leaf parsley, diced pancetta and lots of tangy Pecorino Toscano from the last of the November cheesemaking before the winter sets in.

Tarts

If there is one thing that the kitchen at La Fromagerie does well, it's savoury tarts. Every single day several come up for lunch at 12.30 pm adorned with different cheeses, and I can safely say that even though the word 'quiche' seems kitsch, for me, the savoury tart lives on forever. I suggest you go with the seasons for the vegetable fillings and embrace the wonderful offerings.

Savoury Tarts

There are endless permutations on the savoury tart, but the important thing to remember when making a flan is that the cheese used in the filling is not so strong that it dominates the flavour of the other ingredients. There are a few variations given here and on page 269, but all use the same basic recipe for the shortcrust pastry case and savoury custard filling.

Serves 6
Shortcrust Pastry:
85 g (3 oz) cold unsalted butter, cut into small pieces, plus extra
    for greasing
175 g (6 oz) plain flour, sifted, plus extra for dusting
Good pinch of salt, sifted
1 organic free-range egg, plus 1 egg white, lightly beaten
Splash or two of water
Savoury Custard Filling:
300 ml (10 fl oz) double cream
2 large organic free-range eggs, lightly beaten
¼ tsp coarse sea salt
¼ tsp freshly ground black pepper

1 To make the pastry, rub the butter into the flour until the consistency of fine breadcrumb, then stir in the salt, whole egg and a splash or two of water and bring together with your fingers. Knead lightly to form into a ball of dough, then wrap in clingfilm and leave to rest for 10-15 minutes in the fridge. (Alternatively, make the dough in a food processor.)
2 Preheat the oven to 200°C/400°F/Gas 6. Lightly grease a 25 cm (10 in) loose-bottomed flan tin, then dust with flour, tipping out any excess. Roll out the dough on a lightly floured surface and line the prepared tin, making sure you don't have any cracks or splits in the pastry. Trim the top of the pastry case and line the base with greaseproof paper, then pour in baking beans to cover.
3 Bake on the middle shelf of the oven for 10 minutes, then remove the baking beans and greaseproof paper. Lightly brush with the egg white (this helps to seal the pastry shell) and return the pastry case to the oven to bake for another 3–5 minutes or until a pale golden colour. Remove from the oven and leave to cool before filling with the savoury custard.
4 To make the filling, mix together the ingredients for the savoury custard filling in a jug. To flavour the tart, choose one of the options either below or on page 269.

Selles sur Cher and Tomato

I love the oval-shaped San Marzano tomato as it is superb used for simple tomato sauces or roasted in the oven with herbs and olive oil and served warm alongside steak and chips. The flavour is really fruity and the flesh does not disintegrate; there is also no need to remove the skin — just use them whole and enjoy their wonderful taste.

5 large San Marzano tomatoes, halved
Olive oil (not a strongly flavoured one), for drizzling
2 Selles sur Cher, about 175 g (6 oz) each, or other fresh crumbly
    goat's cheese, cut into wedges
100 g (3½ oz) unsalted butter
2 large onions, finely sliced
Small handful of fresh basil leaves, roughly torn
1 tbsp finely chopped fresh thyme
Coarse sea salt and freshly ground black pepper, to taste

1 Follow the instructions for the pastry case above. Preheat the oven to 180°C/350°F/Gas 4. Place the tomatoes on a baking sheet, drizzle over a little olive oil and sprinkle with salt, then cook in the oven for 10 minutes until softened and slightly caramelized around the edges; set aside.
2 Mash a quarter of the Selles sur Cher, then stir into the savoury custard (see above) mixture.
3 In a frying pan, melt the butter until foaming then sauté the onions until softened. Leave to cool a little before spooning into the pastry case. Put the tart on a baking sheet (this makes it easier to transfer to the oven).
4 Pour half of the savoury custard into the case then arrange the tomatoes and Selles sur Cher on top. Scatter over the basil and thyme, and season with salt and pepper to taste. Pour in the remaining savoury custard.
5 Put the baking sheet on the centre shelf of the oven and cook for about 30 minutes or until golden on top.

Broccoli and Bleu des Causses

100 g (3½ oz) unsalted butter
500 g (1 lb 2 oz) shallots, finely sliced
250 g (9 oz) smoked pancetta, cut into small cubes
300 g (10½ oz) broccoli florets, cut into bite-sized pieces
300 g (10½ oz) Bleu des Causses or other strong blue cheese, crumbled
1 tbsp chopped fresh sage leaves
Coarse sea salt and freshly ground black pepper, to taste

1   Follow the instructions for the pastry case on page 265. Preheat the oven to 200°C/400°F/Gas 6. In a frying pan, melt the butter until foaming, then sauté the shallots until just turning golden, add the pancetta and sauté until the bacon is starting to crisp. Add the broccoli and sauté for a few minutes until al dente. Leave to cool to room temperature.
2   Place the broccoli mixture into the pastry case. Put the tart on a baking sheet (this makes it easier to transfer to the oven). Pour in the savoury custard (see page 265), then sprinkle with the blue cheese and sage leaves. Season with salt and pepper, to taste. Bake for 20–25 minutes until golden on top.

Pumpkin and Goat's Cheese

500 g (1 lb 2 oz) butternut squash or pumpkin seeded and cut into bite-sized chunks
2 tbsp extra-virgin olive oil
1 tbsp finely chopped fresh marjoram, plus extra for sprinkling
1 chilli, seeded and finely chopped
500 g (1 lb 2 oz) spinach
250 g (9 oz) rindless fresh Caprini or Ryefield goat's cheese, crumbled
Coarse sea salt and freshly ground black pepper, to taste

1   Follow the instructions for the pastry case on page 265. Preheat the oven to 200°C/400°F/Gas 6. Put the pumpkin in a roasting tray, drizzle over the olive oil, then sprinkle with the marjoram and chilli. Season with salt and pepper. Roast for 25–30 minutes until the pumpkin tender and slightly caramelized, remove from baking dish and leave to cool to room temperature.
2   Heat a little olive oil in a large frying pan and cook the spinach until wilted. Leave the spinach to cool to room temperature before spooning it into the pastry case. Top the spinach with the pumpkin.
3   Put the tart on a baking sheet (this makes it easier to transfer to the oven). Pour in the savoury custard (see page 265) then sprinkle with the goat's cheese and a little marjoram. Finally, season with salt and pepper, to taste. Bake for 20–25 minutes until golden on top.

Red Pepper and Ricotta

3 large red peppers, seeded and thickly sliced
100 g (3½ oz) unsalted butter
2 large onions, finely sliced
300 g (10½ oz) Seirass ewe's milk Ricotta or buffalo, or cow's milk Ricotta, crumbled
Handful of fresh basil leaves, roughly torn
Coarse sea salt and freshly ground black pepper, to taste

1   Follow the instructions for the pastry case on page 265. Preheat the oven to 200°C/400°F/Gas 6. To prepare the red peppers, place them on a baking sheet and roast for 15 minutes, until the skin is blackened. Place them in a bowl and cover with clingfilm. Once cool enough to handle, rub off the blackened skin.
2   In a large frying pan, melt the butter until foaming, then add the onions and sauté until softened. Leave to cool to room temperature before spooning into the pastry case. Put the tart on a baking sheet.
3   Arrange the roast peppers on top of the onions. Pour in the savoury custard (see page 265), then sprinkle with the crumbled Ricotta and basil. Season with salt and pepper, to taste. Bake for 20–25 minutes until golden on top.

Leek and Beaufort

2 large leeks, trimmed of most of the green part, washed and finely sliced
100 g (3½ oz) unsalted butter
4 large shallots, finely sliced
300 g (10½ oz) Beaufort Chalet d'Alpage cheese, coarsely grated
Freshly grated nutmeg
1 tsp finely chopped fresh thyme
Coarse sea salt and freshly ground black pepper

1   Follow the instructions for the pastry case on page 265. Preheat the oven to 200°C/400°F/Gas 6 and pat dry the washed leeks. In a large frying pan, melt the butter until foaming, then add the shallots and sauté until softened. Next, add the leeks and continue to sauté until soft and starting to turn golden.
2   Leave the onions and leeks to cool to room temperature before spooning into the cooled pastry case. Put the tart on a baking sheet (this makes it easier to transfer to the oven).
3   Pour over the savoury custard (see page 265), then scatter over the Beaufort. Finally grate over about ¼ teaspoon nutmeg or to taste, sprinkle with the thyme, then season with salt and pepper to taste. Bake for 20–25 minutes until golden on top.

Twice-baked Soufflés with Mimolette

You can prepare the soufflés in advance and freeze or chill until required, then in a matter of minutes you've prepared an impressive light supper or appetizer. I've used Mimolette, which is a hard cheese from Flandres, because its lovely orange colour lends a warmth to the soufflés.

Makes 6 individual soufflés
50 g (1¾ oz) unsalted butter, plus extra for greasing
280 g (10 oz) aged Mimolette
225 ml (8 fl oz) full-fat milk
1 small shallot, peeled and studded with 2 cloves
1 bay leaf
6 whole black peppercorns
40 g (1½ oz) unbleached plain flour
4 large organic free-range eggs, separated
85 g (3 oz) Parmesan finely grated
Fine sea salt and freshly ground black pepper

1 Brush the insides of 6 x 7.5 cm x 4 cm (3 x 1½ in) deep ramekins with softened butter, using even upward strokes, then chill and repeat again. Finely grate 85 g (3 oz) of the Mimolette, then use to coat the insides of the ramekins. Chill the ramekins again while preparing the soufflé mixture.

2 Heat the milk, shallot, bay leaf and peppercorns in a medium-sized saucepan until it reaches simmering point, then strain the milk into a jug, throwing away the solid ingredients. Rinse out the saucepan.

3 Melt the butter in the saucepan and add the flour, then cook over a medium-low heat for about 3 minutes, stirring continuously, until it forms a smooth pale-golden paste. Gradually add the strained milk, whisking (use a small balloon whisk) until the sauce has thickened and starts to leave the sides of the pan. Season lightly and cook the sauce over the lowest heat possible for 2 minutes, stirring now and then. If you find the paste is too stiff, add a little more warm milk (take care not to make the mixture too soft as there are the other ingredients to add).

4 Preheat the oven to 180°C/350°F/Gas 4. Remove the pan from the heat and let it cool slightly, before starting to beat in the egg yolks, one at a time. Coarsely grate the remaining Mimolette and add 115 g (4 oz) of the cheese to the soufflé mixture; stir until almost melted.

5 In a large metal bowl, whisk the egg whites to soft peaks, then gently fold in a spoonful of the stiffened egg white into the soufflé mixture to loosen it a little. Now gently add the rest of the mixture into the egg whites using a large metal spoon in a cutting and folding motion.

6 Divide the mixture equally between the ramekins. Put them in a roasting tin placed on the centre shelf of the preheated oven, then pour boiling water into the tin until it reaches half way up the sides of the ramekins.

Bake the soufflés for 20 minutes, then remove them from the bain-marie to a wire rack. (It is not a problem if they sink a little while cooling as they will rise again during the second cooking.)

7 When they are almost cold, run a small palette knife around the edge of each ramekin and carefully turn the soufflés out onto the palm of your hand, then place them the right way up on a lightly greased baking sheet. They can now be kept in the fridge for up to 24 hours, lightly covered with double wax paper and with clingfilm loosely placed over the top.

8 To reheat the soufflés, preheat the oven to 350°F/ 180°C/Gas 4. Take the soufflés out of the fridge and wait until they reach room temperature. Mix the Parmesan with the remaining Mimolette and sprinkle over the top of the soufflés, then place them in the oven, on the shelf above the centre, for 30 minutes until risen and golden.

Cook's Notes
There are a few tricks when making a soufflé to ensure perfect results every time:

- Use a large balloon whisk when whisking egg whites. Alternatively, start off with an electric whisk, then finish off whisking by hand – it does make all the difference.
- If possible, use a metal bowl when whisking egg whites and make sure it is absolutely clean and there are no traces of grease. If necessary, rub half a lemon over the inside to neutralize the surface.
- Preparation is key if you want your soufflé to rise. Brush softened butter using even upward strokes over the inside of the ramekins or dish. Do this once, then chill the ramekins and repeat again. Then coat the insides of the ramekins with finely grated cheese such as Parmesan, or with this particular recipe, a mature Mimolette. Chill the ramekins again before filling with the soufflé mixture.
- Always preheat the oven in readiness for the soufflé, since the correct temperature is essential before cooking.
- To help the soufflés cook evenly, sit the ramekins in a baking tin and place on the middle shelf of the oven. Carefully pour hot water from the kettle into the tin until it reaches half way up the sides of the ramekins to make a water bath or bain-marie.

Tatin of Caramelized Shallots and Persillé du Marais

We make dozens of versions of this tatin simply because they are so easy and quick to prepare. Tiny tatins make great canapés or appetizers, while larger ones — the size of a side plate — can be served as a lunchtime dish or first course; they're rather like a posh pizza!

Serves 2–4
200 g (7 oz) ready-made puff pastry
Flour, for dusting
100 g (3½ oz) unsalted butter
500 g (1 lb 2 oz) medium shallots, halved
1 tsp balsamic vinegar
1 tbsp chopped fresh thyme
175 g (6 oz) Persillé du Marais or Roquefort

1 Preheat the oven to 200°C/400°F/Gas 6. Roll out the pastry on a lightly floured work surface to fit snugly into a 15 cm (6 in) ovenproof frying pan or skillet; set aside in a cool place.
2 Melt the butter in the pan and when foaming add the shallots, then cook over a medium heat, turning and coating them in the butter until they start to caramelize.
3 Pour over the balsamic vinegar and shake the pan until the shallots are coated, then sprinkle with thyme.

4 Place the sheet of puff pastry neatly over the onions as you would if making an apple tarte tatin and press down the edges. Put the pan in the oven on the middle shelf and bake for 15 minutes or until the pastry is golden. Carefully turn out onto a serving plate and crumble over chunks of Persillé du Marais or Roquefort before serving.

Pissaladière

Typical street food in the South of France, Pissaladière is simple to make and you can vary the topping depending on the season, although traditionally it is caramelized onion, anchovies and small black Niçoise olives. When ready to serve, slice into squares or triangles but be quite generous — no dainty little portions!

Makes 9 portions
Roll out 250 g (9 oz) ready-made puff pastry (try and get one that is made with butter) into a thin square and place on a lightly oiled baking sheet. Score the pastry 1 cm (½ in) from the inside edge to form a ridge.

In a frying pan, heat a good knob, say 55 g (2 oz), of butter and 1 tablespoon olive oil until foaming. Fry 3–4 finely sliced onions until golden and almost caramelized, then leave to cool. Arrange the onions in a thick layer over the pastry; you want to be generous with the onions.

Shave thin shards of Comté, about 300 g (10½ oz) over the onions — again being very generous — and bake for 15 minutes until the pastry is golden and the topping bubbling and brown. Leave to cool to room temperature, then cut into wedges.

Cook's Note
❦ You can vary this recipe by crumbling a fresh young goat's cheese over the caramelized onions with perhaps roasted baby tomatoes and stoned black olives. Or try Fontina or Manchego.

Salads & Sides

The most important part of cooking is understanding ingredients and being able to mix them in a cohesive way. When it comes to salads, you may not be actually doing a lot of 'cooking' but you are putting together a selection of items that not only work together, but have textures and tastes that surprise and delight the palate and look beautiful on the plate.

Castelfranco Salad with Cashel Blue and Pears

Castelfranco salad leaves are grown in and around Venice, and in the past would be seen growing wild. The delicate pale green and cream leaves have red flecks, which almost look like they've been painted on, and taste a cross between chicory and trevise (which is similar to radicchio) with a bitter, nutty flavour, and are delicious when partnered with sweet fruit such as pears. The Italians love 'agro dolce' (sweet/savoury) flavours, and this is a perfect salad to serve as an appetizer to a main dish of fish or chicken.

Serves 2

12–16 hazelnuts or fresh cobnuts, shelled
1 head of Castelfranco lettuce
2 tbsp Ligurian or Provencal extra-virgin olive oil
2 tbsp verjuice or light white wine vinegar
1 bay leaf, torn
1 dessert pear such as Comice or 2 Martin Sec (a small dessert pear from Piedmont), quartered, cored and sliced with skin on
60 g (2¼ oz) Cashel Blue cheese, or Bavarian Blue, or other mild blue cheese
Coarse sea salt and freshly ground black pepper

1 Put the hazelnuts or fresh cobnuts in a dry frying pan and toast for a couple of minutes until light golden. Rub off the brown papery skin if necessary and then roughly crush.
2 Tear the Castelfranco leaves rather than cut or chop them – this looks so much better and tastes better too as they retain more of their crunch.
3 To prepare the dressing, mix together the olive oil, verjuice or white wine vinegar and bay leaf in a small bowl then season with salt and pepper. Dip the slices of pear in the dressing and arrange them on the leaves.
4 Crumble over the Cashel Blue and sprinkle with the nuts. Spoon over a tablespoon or so of the dressing (discarding the bay leaf) until all the leaves are lightly coated but not swamped and serve immediately.

Winter Leaf Salad with Orange

Just the thought of actually being able to serve a seasonal salad in the middle of December fills me with joy, and this is the sort of dish I like to serve as an appetizer or starter for our family Christmas lunch.

Serves 4–6

1 large handful of wild watercress

1 large handful of Barbe de Capucin

2 medium-sized trevise leaves

1 large head of Castelfranco

2–3 Tarocco oranges, depending on their size, as they are not a
   traditionally large fruit

Small handful of shelled hazelnuts (optional)

200–250 g (7–9 oz) Capretta semi-hard goat's cheese, shaved

Dressing:

4 tbsp new season Tuscan extra-virgin olive oil – new season
   single-estate oils are available from the start of December

2 tbsp verjuice or light white wine vinegar

1 Trim the watercress and Barbe de Capucin of any tough stalks and wash the leaves under a running tap, then shake off excess water and pat dry with kitchen paper.

Cut the trevise into long boat-shaped wedges and roughly tear the Castelfranco leaves. Place the salad leaves in a shallow serving bowl.

2 Using a sharp small knife, remove the peel and any pith from the oranges and then cut into segments by scoring in between the membrane of the orange. Place the segments in a separate bowl and squeeze out any remaining juice in the membrane.

3 If using the hazelnuts, toast them whole in a dry frying pan, shaking the nuts occasionally, until light golden. Remove the hazelnuts from the pan and wrap in a clean tea towel, then bash them with the end of a rolling pin until roughly broken – don't be too harsh, as you want the nuts to be quite chunky. Set the nuts aside in a bowl.

4 Sprinkle over the olive oil and verjuice or white wine vinegar – enough to coat the leaves without drowning them – then turn the leaves to amalgamate them. Place the orange segments between the leaves, with the excess juices squeezed from the membrane of the fruit poured on top. Using a vegetable peeler or cheese 'shaver', shave thin slices of goat's cheese on top and as a final flourish scatter over the toasted hazelnuts, if using.

Cobb Salad

There are many variations on this famous salad, a signature dish in the Brown Derby restaurant in Hollywood, Los Angeles, named after its creator Robert H. Cobb. Here is my version, which is particularly useful after Christmas when there are plenty of leftovers to add to it! I like the salad to be in layers rather than mixed up together.

Serves 4

Roughly tear spinach and crisp salad leaves, then place in a shallow glass salad bowl or white serving dish. Top with slices of avocado (tossed in lemon juice to prevent the flesh turning brown) and cooked roast chicken or turkey.

Skin some tomatoes by placing them in a bowl of just boiled water for a minute or two, then scoop out of the water. Gently press the skins and they should come away very easily. Slice the tomatoes in half and take out the seeds, then cut into large chunks. Place them on top of the rest of the salad ingredients.

Make up a vinaigrette in a small mixing bowl, with 6 tablespoons extra-virgin olive oil, 1 teaspoon Dijon mustard, 3 tablespoons white wine vinegar, a splash or two of balsamic vinegar and the grated zest of a lemon. Add some chopped marjoram and thyme and season with salt and freshly ground black pepper. Mix thoroughly and drizzle over the salad.

Finally, roughly crumble 150 g (5½ oz) soft blue cheese (Rogue River would be great, or Bayley Hazen Blue from Jasper Hill Farm, Vermont) over the top and lay 6–8 thin slices of speck, baked to a crisp, across the salad.

Spring Salad of Asparagus, Proscuitto and Fava

The first of the English asparagus arrives around Easter, or just after depending on the weather, and then there are Italian fava (broad) beans, fresh peas and purple basil all heralding the new season. What a relief, after the long dark winter and all those delicious filling stews, to have a crisp fresh salad again. I have to tell you I enjoy this with a glass of Prosecco, as the fizz works so well with the salty and fresh flavours.

So get shelling those fresh peas and fava (broad) beans and blanch them briefly for a minute or two. Squeeze the fava out of their thick outer shells to reveal shiny green morsels within. Blanch the asparagus for a matter of minutes to retain its crisp bite; after all this is freshly picked stuff and is equally delicious uncooked, I can assure you.

Serves 4

Toss a handful of fresh peas, fava beans and asparagus in extra-virgin olive oil, which could be a Tuscan or Provencal one according to your preference. Next, add some chopped mint, purple basil and delicately scented chervil, which tastes of sweet aniseed, followed by grated lemon zest and a good squeeze of fresh lemon juice; stir until combined.

Crisp up a few slices of prosciutto in the oven (the smell is almost too much to bear – it's so delicious as it wafts into the kitchen and beyond), then place the hot prosciutto slices on top of the salad before finally shaving over a crumbly Pecorino from Tuscany.

Marinated Feta with Watermelon, Fennel and Mint

Barrel-aged Feta, which is matured for at least six months, is far removed from the plastic-wrapped versions, and is a perfect example of how slow, traditional methods of cheesemaking actually make a great difference to the taste and texture of a cheese.

Serves 6–8

800 g (1 lb 12 oz) barrel-aged Feta, in one piece, drained of any watery residue

Splash of sunflower oil

2 tbsp unsalted shelled pistachio nuts

1 tsp nigella seeds

2 handfuls of fresh flat-leaf parsley, tough stalks removed and leaves left whole

2 fennel bulbs, thinly shaved on a mandolin or with a vegetable peeler

1 tbsp fresh mint finely chopped

1 small watermelon, about 1 kg (2 lb 4 oz), skinned, seeded and cut into 4 cm (1½ in) cubes

Dressing:

6–8 tbsp fruity single estate-olive oil

2 tbsp verjuice or light white wine vinegar

Coarse sea salt and freshly ground black pepper

Marinade:

About 1 tbsp each fresh herbs, including coriander, mint, thyme and oregano, finely chopped

1 small red chilli, seeded and finely chopped

Juice and zest of 2 lemons

6 tbsp fruity single-estate olive oil

2 tbsp verjuice or light white wine vinegar

Freshly ground black pepper

1 Place the cheese in a shallow bowl. Mix together the ingredients for the marinade, season with pepper, then pour it over the cheese. Turn the cheese in the marinade until well coated. Cover the bowl with clingfilm and marinate in the fridge for an hour or two.

2 Brush a little sunflower oil over a frying pan and cook the pistachios for a few minutes until lightly toasted. Remove from the pan and repeat this with the nigella seeds. Coarsely crush the pistachios with the end of a rolling pin and mix with the nigella seeds. Set aside.

3 In a large shallow salad dish, place the flat-leaf parsley, fennel, mint and watermelon. To make the dressing, mix together the olive oil, verjuice or white wine vinegar and season with salt and pepper, to taste.

4 Pour the dressing over the salad and, using your hands, gently turn the ingredients until coated. Remove the Feta from the marinade and break into large rough chunks, then scatter over the salad, followed by the pistachios and nigella seeds.

Truffade d'Auvergne

This is a traditional loose potato galette from the French Auvergne, where thin slices of Cantal cheese (a cross between Cheshire and a dry Lancashire) are placed on top of cooked potatoes before being flipped over. Don't worry if it looks a bit messy, as it's all part of the charm of the dish!

Serves 4

1 kg (2 lb 4 oz) peeled potatoes, thinly sliced using a mandolin or vegetable peeler

100 g (3½ oz) unsalted butter

3 tbsp olive oil

100 g (3½ oz) pancetta or streaky bacon, finely diced

1 fat garlic clove, finely chopped

175 g (6 oz) young Cantal Laguiole, or a young Tomme de Savoie, Cheshire or aged Lancashire, thinly sliced

Coarse sea salt and freshly ground black pepper

1 Wash the slices of potato in copious amounts of water to remove the starch, and then drain and pat dry with kitchen paper.

2 Heat the butter and oil in a heavy-based frying pan and when foaming fry the pancetta or bacon and garlic for a minute or two. Remove with a slotted spoon and place to one side. Add a little more butter and oil to the pan if you think there is insufficient to fry the potatoes.

3 In the frying pan, arrange the sliced potatoes to form a galette (a round pancake). Cook over a medium heat for about 5 minutes before turning the potatoes with a spatula to bring the golden slices to the top and the pale slices to the bottom. Add the pancetta or bacon and garlic and put a lid on the pan. After 5 minutes, turn the potatoes again and put the lid back on for another 5 minutes. By now, all the potatoes should be tender, and some should be golden brown.

4 Spread the cheese slices out over the potatoes, season with the salt and pepper, put the lid back on and cook for another 5–10 minutes until all the potatoes are soft. Turn off the heat, turn the potatoes again to mix in the cheese, and put the lid back on. Leave for 5 minutes until the cheese is all melted.

5 Serve with roasted meats or baked sausages.

Winter Roast Vegetable Salad with Ricotta Salata

Warm winter salads are really delicious, especially when made with naturally sweet vegetables as they roast so well. Many farmer's markets sell heritage carrots, which come in a range of different colours such as purple or pink. Ricotta Salata is a favourite cheese as it also serves as a condiment due to its salty flavour. It is either made from buffalo's or ewe's milk and is a hard cheese with a light crumbly texture, meaning it's especially good sprinkled over roasted vegetables. If you find it difficult to buy locally then substitute Feta, or a semi-hard goat's cheese.

Serves 4–6
4–5 tbsp fruity olive oil from Puglia or Tuscany
2–3 kg (4 lb 8 oz–6 lb 8 oz) selection of vegetables, including orange-fleshed pumpkin, cut into boat-shaped wedges, seeded but with the skin on; heritage carrots, cut into long wedges; parsnips, scraped but not peeled and cut into long wedges; and red onions, peeled and cut into quarters
1 tbsp finely chopped fresh thyme
200 g (7 oz) Ricotta Salata, or Feta, well drained
Coarse sea salt (be careful, you may not need much as the cheese is already salty) and freshly ground black pepper

1 Preheat the oven to 180°C/350°F/Gas 5. Brush a baking sheet with a little of the olive oil and add the prepared vegetables, spreading them out so they are in a single layer. Drizzle over the olive oil to coat all of the vegetables but not drown them.
2 Season the vegetables with salt and pepper, and top with the thyme. Place the sheet on the middle shelf of the oven and cook for about 20 minutes – you may need to cook the vegetables for a further 10–15 minutes depending on their size – until they are tender and caramelized at the edges; test with a skewer to make sure they are not too hard.
3 Take out of the oven and leave to cool to room temperature or until just warm but not hot. Arrange on a shallow serving plate and top with shavings of Ricotta or crumbled Feta. Serve as a side course with roasted meat or as a first course with toasted crusty bread brushed with a fruity olive oil.

Roast Beetroot Salad

If you are using red beetroot as well as the other coloured varieties, it may be prudent to put them in a separate bowl after cooking to prevent their colour bleeding into the others, and then amalgamate just before serving.

I like to use wine vinegars from Volpaia, a Tuscan vineyard that makes its own vinegars from wine pressings. Another alternative is verjuice, which is a delicious condiment made from the unfermented juice of wine grapes, both red and white, which are picked when not fully ripe, then pressed. It lends a fresh, fruity acidity and is not as sharp as vinegar.

4–6 servings
500 g (1 lb 2 oz) mixed coloured beetroot, including red, yellow, white or candy (look out for different coloured varieties from farmer's markets), scrubbed and green part trimmed, if necessary
6 tbsp light white wine vinegar or verjuice
6 tbsp extra-virgin olive oil
1 garlic clove, very finely chopped
3 tbsp chopped fresh herbs such as thyme, marjoram or coriander, or use a mixture
Splash of sunflower oil
Handful of halved walnuts
200 g (7 oz) fresh rindless goat's cheese such as Ryefield, crumbled
Coarse sea salt and freshly ground black pepper

1 Preheat the oven to 180°C/350°F/Gas 4. Place the beetroot in a baking dish with enough water to cover the bottom of the dish, then season with salt.
2 Tightly cover the dish with foil and bake for around 40–45 minutes or until cooked through; test with a skewer to make sure they are tender. Leave until cool enough to handle.
3 Cut off the tops and roots of the beetroot, then peel away the skin with your fingers. Cut the beetroot into wedges or halve, or keep whole if small enough. Sprinkle over a few slugs of white wine vinegar or verjuice, then add the olive oil, garlic and herbs. Season with salt and pepper to taste.
4 Brush the merest hint of sunflower oil over a frying pan and cook the walnuts for a few minutes until lightly toasted, then roughly chop. Scatter the walnuts over the beetroot, then top with the crumbled goat's cheese before serving.

Cook's Notes
❧ Instead of scattering the goat's cheese over the beetroot salad, serve with a crostini of goat's cheese. Simply slice a baguette on the diagonal, rub with a garlic clove and bake in the oven until crisp. Roughly mash the goat's cheese, season with salt and pepper and pile onto the crostini.
❧ Serve the beetroot with bitter salad leaves, dressed in olive oil and white wine vinegar.

Balsamic Roasted Carrots, Red Onions and Trevise with Beenleigh Blue

Slow-roasting really enhances the natural sweetness of carrots and onions, and served as a warm salad with the addition of a sharp tangy blue cheese, such as Beenleigh, makes a lovely first course, light meal or a side dish to roasted or barbecued meats. In spring, when the small carrots appear in bunches you can roast them whole.

Serves 4–6

4 large carrots, cut into long wedges, or 8–10 baby carrots, left whole

3 large onions, cut into quarters or sixths if very large

4 trevise leaves, sliced into 2, or 4 if very large

extra-virgin olive oil

1–2 tbsp balsamic vinegar, to taste

2 fat garlic cloves, lightly crushed

Few fresh sage leaves and sprigs of thyme

1 red chilli, seeded and finely chopped

Grated zest of 1 lemon

300 g (10½ oz) Beenleigh Blue, or other strong blue cheese, roughly chopped

1 tbsp finely chopped flat-leaf parsley

Coarse sea salt, optional

1 Preheat the oven to 220°C/425°F/Gas 7. Place the carrots, onions and trevise in a large mixing bowl. Sprinkle over the olive oil and balsamic vinegar until the vegetables are coated but not drowned. Add salt to taste and turn the vegetables with your hands to amalgamate the ingredients.

2 Spread onto a large baking sheet or shallow baking tin (a deep one will be troublesome as you need to be able to turn the vegetables). Scatter the garlic, herbs, chilli and lemon over the vegetables.

3 Roast for about 10–15 minutes, then turn the vegetables and return to the oven. They should be cooked in a matter of 30 minutes but check every so often by piercing with a skewer to see if they are tender. It is important that the vegetables are roasted at a relatively high heat to avoid them becoming leathery. Remove from the oven and leave to cool to room temperature.

4 Place the vegetables and any residual juices in a shallow serving dish and scatter over the Beenleigh Blue or other blue cheese, and then sprinkle with parsley and a little salt, if using.

Cima di Rapa with Garlic and Pecorino Peperoncino

Cima di Rapa is a type of broccoli (sometimes called broccoli rabe) with long slender leaves and clusters of florets that arrive in the shop from Italy in late winter or early spring. Also grown in the UK, and all over the world really now that seeds are available to buy online, it makes a welcome 'green' relief after winter's root vegetable overload, and can be used either as a side vegetable to roast meats or fish, but also transformed into a lovely warm salad. If you see purple sprouting broccoli in the market or greengrocer then this is just as good.

Serves 4–6

Wash and trim 1 kg (2 lb 4 oz) cima di rapa or purple sprouting broccoli and put into a large saucepan with a splash of water; this amount will serve 4–6. Cover the pan with a lid and cook over a high heat, shaking the pan from time to time; it will sizzle at first, and then will settle down. Cook the vegetables until al dente, or until still crisp. Remove and shake off as much water as possible.

In a large frying pan, heat a tablespoon or two of olive oil (doesn't have to be your best one) and gently sauté 1–2 very thinly sliced garlic cloves until slightly softened and turning light golden. Add the greens and toss well in the garlicky oil until coated. Remove from the heat and pile onto a serving dish.

Drizzle over 2–3 tablespoons extra-virgin fruity olive oil (your best one as this is the dressing). Using a vegetable peeler or cheese 'shaver', shave over shards of Tuscan Pecorino studded with chilli, or if you want a stronger flavoured cheese, use the Sardinian or Sicilian hard version with chilli.

Asparagus with Parmesan Butter Breadcrumbs

Although the British asparagus season starts around April, Italian asparagus appears in March and the French a couple of weeks later. The season is short, but by the time the continental asparagus is finishing the British is in full swing so it is lovely to enjoy the vegetable from early spring until the beginning of summer. Serving with buttery breadcrumbs respects the flavour of the vegetable, while the addition of sharp Parmesan finishes the dish perfectly.

Serves 2

Preheat the oven to 180°C/350°F/Gas 4. Crumble a few slices of day-old bread, either pane Toscana or another simple white bread, into breadcrumbs. For every cup of breadcrumbs, add ½ cup of finely grated Parmesan. Mix together the crumbs and Parmesan, then spread out onto a baking sheet. Place in the preheated oven for a few minutes until the crumbs just begin to change colour and are slightly crisp.

Spoon the cheese and breadcrumbs into a saucepan and add a knob of butter, then cook over a medium heat until the crumbs start to darken. Add another knob of butter and stir until the crumbs are completely coated in the buttery juices.

Blanch 2–3 bundles asparagus briefly until al dente. Pile the asparagus onto a serving plate and spoon the buttery crumbs over the tips — eat with your fingers.

Cook's Note

☙ After blanching, drain the asparagus and pat dry with kitchen paper, then fry in a little olive oil until slightly golden.

Stuffed Courgette Flowers with Ricotta

From early summer until autumn, the flower attached to the tip of a courgette — resembling a marigold-orange 'lantern' — is much prized. It is perfect for stuffing, albeit a bit fiddly, but well worth the effort. Serve as a first course with a little salad made with soft leaves and maybe fronds of chervil and fennel. Dress the leaves in a light olive oil and white wine vinegar or verjuice; you want it all to be fragrant and light.

Makes 12–16

First, if the courgette is large, cut away the flower, leaving a little stalk, or if the courgette is small, leave the flower attached.

Finely chop fresh marjoram (or another soft-leaf aromatic herb, say chervil, thyme, tarragon or a mixture), about 2 tablespoons, and I small seeded red chilli. Put them in a bowl with the zest of a lemon and 300 g (10½ oz) drained and sieved fresh Ricotta; this can be cow's, buffalo's, or ewe's. If you find it difficult to get really fresh Ricotta then use a very fresh goat's cheese without any rind or a really light cream cheese. Season with salt and freshly ground pepper and mix. Spoon the mixture into a piping bag with a medium-sized nozzle.

Carefully open the petals of the courgette flower (if you can remove the stamen all the better, but if the flower is small you can leave it intact) and pipe in the filling mixture until about half or three-quarters full and then gently close the flower, twisting the top to stop the filling oozing out during cooking.

Lay the courgette flowers, about 12–16 depending on their size, on a baking sheet, lined with greaseproof paper, and drizzle a little Provencal extra-virgin olive oil (or one that is not too overtly spiky in flavour) over the top. Bake in an oven preheated to 180°C/350°F/Gas 4 for 5–8 minutes; you want the courgette, if still attached, to still have a little crunch.

Aligot

This is an ancient recipe created for the pilgrims in South West France. Ideally, you should use Tomme fraîche, which is a Cantal cheese that is freshly made so does not have a rind or crust. A specialist cheesemonger will be able to order some for you.

Serves 4

100 g (3½ oz) unsalted butter
2 fat garlic cloves (new season fresh garlic is particularly good)
1 kg (2 lb 4 oz) Desiree potatoes or others suitable for mashing
150 ml (5 fl oz) small pot thick cream (double or a single, if preferred), preferably unpasteurized Jersey milk
400 g (14 oz) Tomme fraîche or a young Lancashire, Cheshire, Wensleydale or Cantal, grated
Coarse sea salt

1 Melt the butter with the garlic in a saucepan and leave to infuse – the garlic should become very soft. Mash the garlic into the butter, then set aside while you cook the potatoes.

2 Steam the potatoes in their skins until cooked through (pierce with a skewer to make sure they are very soft). Peel off the potato skins and put the potatoes, back into the saucepan, which should have been rinsed and dried first. Over a very low heat dry the potatoes, then mash them by either passing through a potato ricer or mashing with a fork until they are almost smooth. Beat in the garlic butter.

3 Pour in the cream and over a low heat beat the mash with a large wooden spoon, preferably with a flat round end (it may be difficult to find this sort of spoon but otherwise just use a usual one). Use the same technique as you would for fondue, stirring in a figure of eight with a loose wrist action until the texture changes and becomes creamy.

4 Continue to stir the mixture in a figure-of-eight motion while you gradually add the cheese, then start to lift the mixture to stretch it – it should snap back into the pan. When all the cheese has been added, taste and then add salt if necessary. Serve with roasted meats or cured ham.

a skewer to make sure it is not hard in the centre but nicely cooked all the way through. Take out of the oven and leave until cool enough to handle.

3 In a frying pan, heat the butter with a tablespoon or two of olive oil until foaming and then fry the girolles. (You can tell when the mushrooms are cooked as the hissing sound suddenly subsides.) Remove from the pan with a slotted spoon and set aside.

4 Grate 50 g (1¾ oz) of the Parmesan. Heat the cream with the grated Parmesan, the garlic and the remaining sage until the cheese has melted and the cream is warmed through but not too hot. Season with pepper, to taste.

5 Arrange the pumpkin on individual serving plates with the girolle mushrooms, then spoon over a little of the cream sauce. Using a vegetable peeler or cheese 'shaver', shave the remaining Parmesan over the vegetables. Serve immediately with an accompaniment of bitter salad leaves and toasted bread, such as a country-style pagnotta or ciabatta with a little olive oil drizzled on top.

Roasted Pumpkin with Girolles and Parmesan Cream

The autumn colours of this warm salad make it picture perfect. The marriage of the sweet pumpkin, earthy girolle mushrooms and the salty/savoury Parmesan give it great appeal. It makes a lovely lunch dish in its own right, or an accompaniment to roast veal.

Serves 4

1.5 kg (3 lb 5 oz) orange-fleshed pumpkin, skin intact, seeded and cut into wedges

1–2 tbsp olive oil, plus extra for drizzling

2 tbsp finely chopped fresh sage leaves

50 g (1¾ oz) unsalted butter

300 g (10½ oz) girolle mushrooms, or other wild mushroom of your choice

150 g (5½ oz) aged Parmesan

300 ml (10 fl oz) unpasteurized (if available) double Jersey cream

1 garlic clove, very finely chopped

Coarse sea salt and freshly ground black pepper

1 Preheat the oven to 180°C/350°F/Gas 4. Place the pumpkin in a baking tin and drizzle over some olive oil, then place half of the sage leaves over the top and season with salt and pepper.

2 Bake for around 35–40 minutes or until the pumpkin is tender and is caramelized around the edges – test with

Desserts, Breads & Biscuits

I love rich creamy desserts, but I do urge you to buy the best-quality cream or mascarpone, which has if possible not been treated in any way. Simple savoury bread and biscuits really are easy.

Tiramesù

This dessert is traditionally a combination of zabaglione (a Venetian warm egg custard made with Marsala wine), pastry cream, mascarpone cream and savoiardi biscuits, drizzled with strong espresso coffee. However, I think we can go slightly off-piste and create something a little simpler, although just as rich. This dessert should be made a day ahead in order for all the flavours to meld.

Serves 8
1 tsp caster sugar, plus extra to serve
2 small cups very strong espresso coffee, left to cool
Splash or two of brandy
Savoiardi or ladyfingers (up to 24 if large or 36 if small)
Good-quality cocoa powder (Valrhona, for preference), to serve
Zabaglione:
4 large organic free-range egg yolks
4 tbsp caster sugar
Small wine glass Marsala wine (or Amaretto, if preferred)
½ tsp vanilla extract
Grated zest of 2 lemons
Mascarpone cream:
750 g (1 lb 10 oz) fresh mascarpone
1 heaped tbsp caster sugar
A little vanilla extract or a scraping of fresh vanilla seeds
425 ml (15 fl oz) double cream

1 Using a double boiler (or a saucepan of simmering water with a mixing bowl resting on top but not touching the water), add the ingredients for the zabaglione. Whisk continuously over a low heat for 3–5 minutes until the custard has thickened and coats the back of a spoon. Take off the heat and leave to cool (it can be left overnight in the fridge).

2 For the mascarpone cream, put all the ingredients, except the double cream, in a mixing bowl and then beat together until smooth. Whisk the double cream into soft peaks and gently fold into the mascarpone mixture, then set to one side.

3 To assemble: either make in small individual bowls or a large serving dish. In a shallow dish, mix I teaspoon caster sugar into the coffee and brandy. Briefly dip the sponge fingers (one at a time) into the coffee mixture until barely coated – you don't want a soggy sponge base. Line the bowls or dish with the fingers, placing them very close together.

4 Spoon over the zabaglione in a thick layer, then arrange more fingers on top. Next, add the mascarpone cream in an even layer and smooth the top. Chill for a few hours or overnight. Before serving, sift over a dusting of cocoa powder and sprinkle with a smattering of sugar, if liked.

Cook's Note
❦ Simple desserts like this one do require the best possible ingredients. If you can find a farm-made mascarpone, and you have a coffee machine at home to brew espresso, this tiramesù will surpass all expectations.

Autumn Berry Tartelettes with Quark

Make the most of autumn berries as their season is short and once the frosts appear the bounty is finished. Berries in autumn are not only fruity but also acidic and juicy. They make excellent jams and jellies, but also work well in pies and tarts. If you have time, pre-bake the pastry tart shells and freeze them, then all you need to do is fill with soft cheese and fruit before serving.

Makes 6

100 g (3½ oz) unsalted butter, plus extra for greasing
90 g (3¼ oz) caster sugar
¼ tsp salt
¼ tsp vanilla extract
1 organic free-range egg yolk
125 g (4½ oz) unbleached plain flour, sifted, plus extra for dusting

Filling:

200 g (7 oz) quark (choose the drier version, which is similar to a dry curd, or a low- to medium-fat cream cheese, drained)
Icing sugar, to taste
300 g (10½ oz) blackberries, rinsed and hulled
2 tbsp caster sugar

1 Cream together the butter and sugar in a mixing bowl. Stir in the salt, vanilla extract and egg yolk, then fold in the flour to make a smooth dough. (You can do this by hand or in a food processor.) Form the dough into a ball, wrap in clingfilm and leave to rest for 2 hours or overnight in the bottom of the fridge.

2 Preheat the oven to 200°C/400°F/Gas 6. Lightly grease 6 x 8 cm (3¼ in) loose-bottomed shell cases or a 20 cm (8 in) loose-bottomed tart tin.

3 On a lightly floured surface, roll out the dough and use to line the tart tin(s), prick the base(s) and bake blind (place a circle of greaseproof paper inside the pastry shell and fill with dried beans) for around 10 minutes until the sides of the pastry shell are golden. Take out of the oven and remove the beans and greaseproof and put the tart(s) back into the oven for a few minutes until the base is light golden. Leave to cool.

4 Put the quark in a mixing bowl and sweeten with icing sugar to your taste; set aside. Place the blackberries in a saucepan with the caster sugar and cook for a few minutes until the sugar has melted and the fruit has softened a little; leave to cool.

5 Spoon the quark into the pastry shells and spoon over the blackberries (without the syrup). Put the syrup from the blackberries in a pan and heat until reduced and thickened. Leave to cool before drizzling over the tarts.

Plums with Quark

When I found a handmade version of quark made by Mrs Wild's dairy in Isny, in the beautiful Alpine region of Bavaria, I was both delighted and relieved to know that a traditional version of this cheese still exists.

Quark is delicious on its own or with the addition of puréed fruits or minced nuts. Preserved or baked fruit, like plums, are superb accompaniments as the sharp yet sweet taste of the fruit is perfect alongside the smooth, silky texture of the soft fresh cheese.

This is no ordinary plum recipe. I have discovered that a sweet fruit wine called Visciolata made with small cherries, (similar to Morellos in look and taste) from the Marche region in Italy, is the perfect dessert wine to macerate the dark plums of late summer.

Fill a large clip-top preserving jar or Kilner jar with plums that are in perfect condition, with no bruises or splits in the skin; choose fruits that are not too large as you don't want to squash them in the jar. Pour over the Visciolata wine to just cover and insert a cinnamon stick and star anise into the middle of the jar. Close the jar and place it in a dark, cool cupboard.

The following day top up with more wine, as some will have been soaked up by the fruit, then repeat this for the next 2 days. On the final day, after filling with more wine, close the jar, make sure the rubber seal is tightly in place and set aside for 2 weeks in a dark cupboard.

Serve the fruit with a good spoonful of cold, soft, velvety quark for a simple dessert.

Brillat-Savarin Cheesecake

This triple cream cheese has a nutty flavour and a rich, buttery texture, and is really rather a luxurious way of making a cheesecake. Obviously, you have to close your eyes to the number of calories, but you really do not need to have a huge slice of this rich confection. The cheese is really at its best in spring or late summer, although it is available all through the year, and is simply delicious served really cold with berries or fruit compote.

Serves 8–10
Butter, for greasing
Flour, for dusting
250 g (9 oz) Brillat-Savarin
100 g (3½ oz) farmhouse mascarpone
½ vanilla pod, split in half lengthways and seeds scraped out
Grated zest of ½ lemon
2 organic free-range egg yolks
50 g (1¾ oz) caster sugar
1 organic free-range egg white, whisked to soft peaks
Stewed winter rhubarb or fruit compote, or fresh berries, to
  serve
Cheesecake base:
200 g (7 oz) biscuits, digestives or crackers, crushed
100 g (3½ oz) unsalted butter, melted
1 tsp runny honey

1 Grease and flour the base of a loose-bottomed, spring-form 20 cm (8 in) cake tin. To make the cheesecake base, combine the crushed biscuits, butter and honey in a bowl, then press the mixture in an even layer into the prepared tin. Put the tin in the freezer for 1 hour or overnight, if preferred.
2 Preheat the oven to its lowest possible setting. To make the filling, blend the Brillat-Savarin, mascarpone, vanilla seeds and lemon zest in a blender for a few minutes or until smooth, or beat by hand.
3 Whisk the egg yolks with the sugar, add to the blender and blitz for a few minutes, or beat by hand. Pour the mixture into a bowl and leave for a minute to settle and then gently fold in the whisked egg white.
4 Remove the cake tin from the freezer and place on a baking sheet. Pour the filling mixture into the tin and bake for 30–40 minutes until set, then leave in the oven with the door slightly ajar until cooled to room temperature before chilling in the fridge.
5 To serve, place the cake tin on a cup or bowl and gently slide down the rim of the tin to release the cheesecake. With a palette knife slide the cake off the base onto a serving plate. Serve with stewed winter rhubarb or another sharp-tasting fruit compote, or fresh berries.

Baked Cheesecake

I could include a dozen or so different kinds of cheesecakes, but prefer to offer you this one, which is really lovely and light and different to the rather posh, indulgent one made with Brillat-Savarin, a triple cream cheese from Normandy (see opposite).

I do like cheesecakes with a crushed biscuit base, but if I have a preference then it is for the pre-baked pastry shell, which holds the cheese mixture perfectly. The secret to a good cheesecake is to mix the filling well so there are no lumps, and also to bake it at a low temperature, then leave the cake in the turned-off oven to cool completely — your patience will be rewarded.

Serves 8
115 g (4 oz) unsalted butter, cut into cubes, plus extra for
  greasing
200 g (7 oz) unbleached plain flour, plus extra for dusting
1 rounded tbsp caster sugar
½ tsp grated lemon zest
½ tsp vanilla extract
1 tbsp iced water
Pinch of salt
Crème fraîche and fresh strawberries, to serve (optional)
Filling:
400 g (14 oz) mild fresh goat's cheese, such as Ryefield, rind
  removed, or a fresh goat's curd
200 g (7 oz) mascarpone
85 g (3 oz) caster sugar, plus 2 tbsp
60 g (2¼ oz) butter, melted
Zest and juice of ½ large lemon
2 tbsp ground almonds
¼ tsp vanilla extract
2 large organic free-range eggs, separated

1 Grease and flour a 23 cm (9 in) loose-bottomed or spring-form cake tin. Put the flour, butter, sugar, lemon zest, vanilla extract, iced water and a pinch of salt into a food processor and whizz briefly until the mixture resembles fine breadcrumbs.
2 Empty the mixture into a bowl and bring it together with your hands to form a smooth ball of pastry. Roll out the pastry on a lightly floured surface and use to line the prepared cake tin. If preferred, you can slice the pastry thinly, then press the slices into the tin with the palm of your hand to make a case. Put the cake tin in the freezer for 30 minutes.

3 Preheat the oven to 200°C/400°F/Gas 6. Bake the pastry case for about 12 minutes until it is pale biscuit in colour and dry to the touch, then remove from the oven and leave to cool. (Don't put the cream cheese mixture straight into the hot pastry shell.)

4 Meanwhile, to make the filling, crumble the goat's cheese into a mixing bowl, then add the mascarpone, 85 g (3 oz) caster sugar, melted butter, lemon zest and juice, ground almonds, vanilla extract and egg yolks, then beat until smooth.

5 Turn down the oven to 180°C/350°F/Gas 4. In a clean, grease-free bowl, whisk the egg whites until they form stiff peaks, then gently fold in the remaining caster sugar. Fold the egg whites into the cheese mixture and pour into the part-baked pastry shell, then bake for 45 minutes or until the top is pale gold.

6 Turn off the oven and leave the cheesecake for 15 minutes, then open the door slightly and leave until completely cool. Spread crème fraîche over the top and decorate with fresh strawberries, if liked.

Cheese Sables

These cheese biscuits are simple to make, but all the more tasty if you use the best-quality Parmesan or other hard tangy cheese.

Makes 10–15
200 g (7 oz) unbleached plain flour, plus extra for dusting
125 g (4½ oz) Parmesan or other hard tasty cheese, finely grated
Large pinch of cayenne pepper
115 g (4 oz) unsalted butter, cubed and softened
1 large organic free-range egg yolk

1 Preheat the oven to 200°C/400°F/Gas 6. Grease and flour a baking sheet. In a mixing bowl, combine the flour, Parmesan and cayenne. Add the butter and with your fingertips lift and work the mixture until you have a breadcrumb consistency.
2 Mix in the egg yolk to form a stiff dough. Wrap in clingfilm and leave to rest in the bottom of a fridge for at least 30 minutes.
3 On a lightly floured surface, roll out the dough to 1 cm (¼ in) thick. Cut into rounds using a wineglass or a 5 cm (2 in) cookie-cutter and place on the baking sheet. Re-roll when necessary, pressing out more rounds. Place the baking sheet in the middle of the oven and bake for 15 minutes or until the sables are golden.

Parmesan Crisps

These thin, lacy crisps can be made in moments, so if you run out just have some finely grated Parmesan in the freezer at the ready. As an aperitif they are hard to beat, especially when served with chilled Prosecco or white wine. The important thing to remember is that you do need to use a well-matured Parmesan as young cheeses do not taste as fruity or have as crisp a texture.

Preheat the oven to 230°C/450°F/Gas 8. Line a baking sheet with greaseproof paper. Finely grate 250 g (9 oz) Parmigiano Reggiano. Place little mounds of the grated cheese on baking sheets or sprinkle a layer of Parmesan into a 5 cm (2 in) cookie ring for more even rounds; make sure you leave sufficient space between the cheese rounds as they spread during cooking. This amount of cheese will make around 12–15.

You can also add a little chopped fresh chilli or paprika to the cheese to give a spicier taste to the crisps, but if you use an aged Parmesan they should be sufficiently flavourful. Bake for just a few minutes until golden and lacy. Leave to cool on the baking sheets and when sufficiently easy to handle, use a palette knife to transfer to a serving plate.

Cheese Straws

No need to write out a laborious ingredient's list for this recipe. You just need a pack of puff pastry, the best quality you can find, and then roll it out to an oblong. Grate some Parmesan or Cheddar, or other similar hard crumbly cheese (or you could use a mixture), into a bowl. Sprinkle the cheese over the rolled-out pastry in a thick layer and press it down. Season with sea salt and freshly ground black pepper, to taste.

In another bowl, mix together a dessertspoon of cayenne and a dessertspoon of English mustard powder,

then sift over the cheese and press down with the back of a spoon. Preheat the oven to 200°C/400°F/Gas 6. Cut the pastry into 20 x 2.5 cm (8 x 1 in) strips and then twist each strip into a spiral, before placing on a buttered baking sheet. Bake for approximately 5 minutes until golden and crisp. Transfer to a wire rack to cool.

Cook's Note
☙ Place a very thin length of Parma or Bayonne ham on each strip of cheese-covered pastry and then twist as before. Alternatively, sprinkle poppy seeds and caraway seeds over the cheese strips and press them down before twisting.

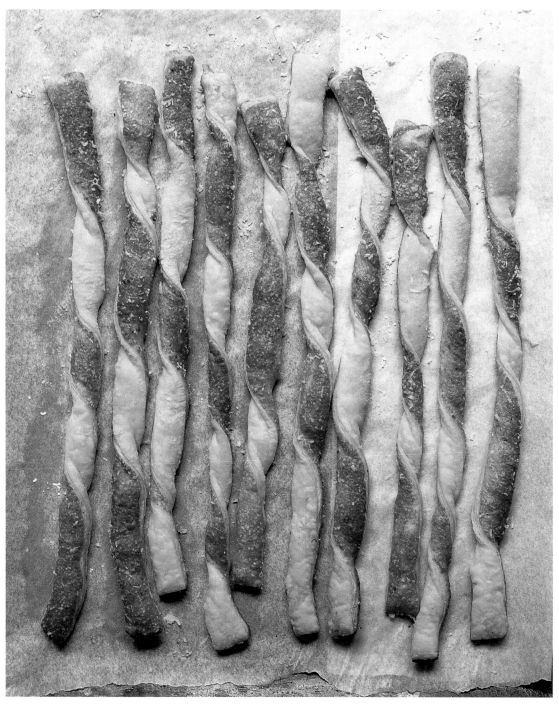

Gougères

These make a great dinner party appetizer or party canapé and they are also a good way of using up odd bits of strongly flavoured hard cheese.

Makes about 24
125 ml (4 fl oz) plain water, filtered for preference
125 ml (4 fl oz) full-fat organic milk
50 g (1¾ oz) unsalted butter
200 g (7 oz) unbleached plain flour, plus extra in reserve
4 large organic free-range eggs
100 g (3½ oz) Emmental Francais or a lighter style Gruyère, grated, plus extra for sprinkling
Good pinch of ground nutmeg
Coarse sea salt and freshly ground black pepper

1 Preheat the oven to 200°C/400°F/Gas 6. Line two baking sheets with baking paper. In a medium-sized, heavy-based saucepan add the water, milk, butter and a pinch of salt, then slowly bring to the boil.

2 Remove from the heat, add the flour and beat with a wooden spoon. Return to the heat beating continuously over a medium-low heat until the mixture forms a smooth dough. Turn down the heat to low and cook the dough mixture until it starts to come away from the sides of the pan – this will only take a minute or two.

3 Spoon the dough into a bowl and leave to cool for a minute. Now beat in the eggs, one at a time, making sure you beat in each one thoroughly; this is important, and don't be afraid if the dough looks like it is going to separate, just keep beating and it will come together, I promise. Stir in the grated cheese, reserving 55 g (2 oz), plus a good pinch of pepper and nutmeg.

4 Place the dough into a piping bag fitted with a 1 cm (½ in) plain round nozzle, or a larger one if you prefer bigger puffs, and pipe little mounds onto the baking

sheets, about 5 cm (2 in) apart. Sprinkle over the reserved cheese and bake for 15–20 minutes, or until the puffs are golden brown.

5 Serve hot straight from the oven, although you can leave them to cool before storing, covered, in the fridge; warm through before serving.

Cook's Note

❦ You can make these in advance: pipe them onto baking sheets, then 'open-freeze'. Once totally frozen, put them in a freezer bag as they won't stick together. To defrost, remove from the bag and place on the prepared baking sheet, then bring to room temperature. Sprinkle with cheese, then bake as above.

Cornbread with Fresh Goat's Cheese

I love to use polenta with the husk intact to give a coarser texture to the bread. This is a lovely accompaniment to pumpkin soup or to serve with a simple side salad.

Makes about 10–12 pieces
50 g (1¾ oz) unsalted butter, melted, plus extra for greasing
225 ml (8 fl oz) full-fat milk
1 organic free-range egg
100 g (3½ oz) unbleached plain flour
1 tbsp baking powder
Scant 1 tsp salt
100 g (3½ oz) yellow coarse polenta flour or cornmeal
1–2 red chillies, seeded and finely chopped
Small handful of fresh basil or coriander, finely chopped
100–125 g (3½-4½ oz) Caprini or other soft fresh goat's cheese, roughly chopped

1 Preheat the oven to 220°C/425°F/Gas 7. Grease and line the base of a 25 cm (10 in) square baking tin. Pour the milk into a jug and whisk in the egg; set aside.

2 In a mixing bowl, sift in the flour, baking powder, salt and polenta, then make a well in the centre. Pour in the milk mixture and stir until mixed together and smooth. Next, stir in the melted butter, chillies and herbs, then gently fold in the goat's cheese.

3 Pour the mixture into the baking tin and bake for 20 minutes or until the top is golden and a metal skewer inserted into the centre comes out clean; if not quite ready, return to the oven for a few extra minutes. Leave to cool slightly in the tin, then turn out onto a wire rack and leave to cool. Serve cut into slices or chunky cubes.

Parmesan Cheese Scones

Savoury scones are really easy to make and are delicious served warm for breakfast, lunch, tea or supper. They are perfect for picnics too, although my favourite way of serving them is with a filling of herb goat's cheese topped with the salty sweet crisp shards of speck.

Makes about 10

250 g (9 oz) self-raising flour, plus extra for dusting

½ tsp baking powder

Large pinch of sea salt

50 g (1¾ oz) Parmesan, finely grated

Good pinch of cayenne pepper (optional)

1 tsp English mustard powder (optional)

60 g (2¼ oz) unsalted butter, cold but not too hard, cut into small cubes

5 tbsp full-fat milk

5 tbsp plain yoghurt

2 large organic free-range eggs, lightly beaten

Filling:

8 slices of speck or other smoked cured ham

250 g (9 oz) fresh rindless goat's cheese or goat's milk curd

1 tsp baby capers, rinsed and dried

1 tbsp finely chopped herbs such as chives, chervil, basil or parsley

1 tsp grated lemon zest

1 Preheat the oven to 180°C/350°F/Gas 4. Place the speck or ham on a baking sheet and cook until crisp, then set aside.

2 Sift the flour, baking powder and salt together in a large mixing bowl. Add the Parmesan, cayenne and mustard powder, if using. Rub in the butter until the mixture resembles fine breadcrumbs, then make a well in the centre.

3 Mix together the milk, yoghurt and lightly beaten eggs (keeping back a little to coat the tops before baking), then trickle it into the flour mixture stirring as you go to form a sticky dough. Line a baking sheet with baking paper and warm it in the oven for a few minutes, then set aside.

4 Meanwhile, lift the dough out of the bowl and knead lightly on a floured surface until smooth. Sift over a little flour and roll out using a floured rolling pin until the dough is around 2 cm (¾ in) thick. Dip the rim of a 7 cm (2¾ in) pastry cutter or glass into flour and then press out about 10 scones, re-rolling the dough when necessary. Place them on the warmed baking sheet. (Alternatively you can form the dough into a large round and score into triangles.)

5 Brush the tops of the scones with the reserved beaten egg and bake for around 8 minutes or until risen and golden. Leave to cool slightly on a wire rack; they are best served warm.

6 To make the filling, mix together the goat's cheese, capers, herbs and lemon zest with a pinch of salt until smooth. Split the scones and place a spoonful of filling on one half then place a few shards of crisp ham on top, followed by the other half of scone.

Directory of cheeses

THE UK

Alderwood 🐄
Cranbourne Chase Cheese, Ashmore, Dorset
W2kg F45% P19

Appleby's Cheshire 🐄
Appleby's Farm, Weston-under-Redcastle, Shropshire
W2–8kg F45% P26

Beenleigh Blue 🐑
Ticklemore Cheese, Totnes, Devon
W3kg F50% P16

Berkswell 🐑
Ram Hall Farm, Berkswell, West Midlands
W3kg F48% P24

Caboc 🐄
Highland Fine Cheeses, Tain, Ross & Cromarty
W1.1kg F69% P36

Cardo 🐐
Sleights Farm, Timsbury, Somerset
W1.2kg F45% P19

Colston Bassett Stilton 🐄
Colston Bassett Dairy, Colston Bassett, Nottinghamshire
W7.5kg F45–48% P28

Cornish Yarg 🐄
Lynher Dairy, Liskeard, Cornwall
W3kg F45% P19

Devon Blue 🐄
Ticklemore Cheese, Totnes, Devon
W3kg F48% P16

Doddington 🐄
North Doddington Farm, Wooler, Northumberland
W5–15kg F45% P33

Dunsyre Blue 🐄
Walston Braehead Farm, Carnwath, Lanarkshire
W3kg F45–48% P34

Gorwydd Caerphilly 🐄
Gorwydd Farm, Tregaron Ceredigion
W2kg F45% P30

Harbourne Blue 🐐
Ticklemore Cheese, Totnes, Devon
W3kg F50% P16

Hurdlebrook 🐄
Olive Farm, Babcary, Somerset
W3kg F45%
Two cheeses produced: a crumbly Caerphilly-style cheese, and the other a softer version of Cheddar with a tactile crust.

Innes Button 🐐
Innes Cheeses at Highfields Farm Dairy, Tamworth, Staffordshire
W80g F45% P25

Isle of Mull 🐄
Sgriob-ruadh Farm, Tobermory, Isle of Mull
W25kg F45% P36

Keen's Farmhouse Cheddar 🐄
Moorhayes Farm, Wincanton, Somerset
W28–30kg F45% P20

Kirkham's Lancashire 🐄
Kirkham's Farm, Goosnargh, near Preston, Lancashire
W11kg F45% P34

Lincolnshire Poacher 🐄
Ulceby Grange Farm, Alford, Lincolnshire
W6–7kg F45% P31

Montgomery's Cheddar 🐄
Manor Farm, North Cadbury, Somerset
W26kg F45% P20

Richard III Wensleydale 🐄
Fortmayne Farm, Bedale, North Yorkshire
W2.5kg F45% P33

Shropshire Blue 🐄
Colston Bassett Dairy & Long Clawson Dairy, Nottinghamshire & Leicestershire
W8kg F45% P26

Single Gloucester 🐄
Smarts Farm, Churcham, Gloucester
W3.4kg F45% P23

Stichelton 🐄
Stitchelton Dairy, Wellbeck Estate, Nottinghamshire
W7kg F45% P29

Stinking Bishop 🐄
Laurel Farm, Dymock, Gloucester
W1.8kg F45% P23

Ticklemore 🐐
Sharpham Creamery, Totnes, Devon
W1.8kg F45% P19

Tunworth 🐄
Hampshire Cheeses at Hyde Farm, Herriard, Hampshire
W250g F45% P22

Waterloo 🐄
Wigmore Dairy, Riseley, Berkshire
W400–500g F45% P22

Wigmore 🐑
Wigmore Dairy, Riseley, Berkshire
W400–500g F45% P22

IRELAND

Ardrahan 🐄
Ardrahan Farmhouse Cheese, Kanturk, Co. Cork
W200g / 1.5kg F45% P42

Cashel Blue 🐄
J&L Grubb ltd., Fethard, Co. Tipperary
W2kg F48% P39

Coolea 🐄
Coolea Farmhouse Cheese, Macroom, Co. Cork
W1–10kg F45% P40

Crozier Blue 🐑
J&L Grubb ltd., Fethard, Co. Tipperary
W2kg F48–50% P40

Dilliskus 🐄
Maja Binder, Castlegregory, Co. Kerry
W1kg F45% P41

Durrus 🐄
Durrus Farmhouse Cheese, Coomkeen, Durrus, Co.Cork
W1.5kg. F45% P43

Gabriel & Desmond 🐄
West Cork Natural Cheese Company, Schull, Co. Cork
W6–8kg F45–48% P41

Gubbeen 🐄
Gubben Cheese, Schull, Co. Cork
W1.3kg F45% P43

Kilcummin 🐄
Maja Binder, Castlegregory, Co. Kerry
W1kg F45% P41

Ryefield 🐐
Fivemiletown Creamery Cooperative, Bailieboro,Co.Cavan
W1kg F45% P39

St Gall 🐄
Fermoy Natural Cheese Company, Fermoy, Co. Cork
W4kg F45% P40

St Tola 🐐
Inagh Farmhouse Cheese, Inagh, Co. Clare
W1kg F45% P39

FRANCE

Abbaye de Trois Vaux 🐄
Abbaye de Trois Vaux, Haut Artois
W1.2kg F45% P54

Ami du Chambertin 🐄
Fromagerie Gaugry, Burgundy
W200g F45% P61

Anneau du Vic Bilh 🐐
Fromage de zone de Montagne, Pyrénées
W180–200g F45% P75

Ardi Gasna 🐑
Fromage de zone de Montagne, Pyrénées Atlantique
W2–2.5kg F45–48%
Similar in style to hard Spanish cheeses like Manchego, but more brittle and gamey in flavour.

Banon Feuille 🐐
Romain Ripert, Provence
W60g F45% P73

Bethmale 🐄
Jean Faup, Ariège
W4–5kg F45–48% P74

Bethmale 🐐
Jean Faup, Ariège
W4kg F45–48% P74

Bleu d'Auvergne 🐄
Morin, Auvergne
W2.5kg F50% P68

Bleu des Causses 🐄
Fromagerie des Causses et Auvergne, Aveyron/Auvergene
W2.5–3kg F45% P68

Bonde de Gâtine 🐐
Fromagerie Bonde de Gâtine, Poitou
W180–200g F45% P64

Boulette d'Avesnes 🐄
Via Philippe Olivier, Boulogne or Fauquet Thiérache
W150g–200g F45% P49

Bouton d'Oc 🐐
Pic, Tarn
W30g F45% P80

Brie de Meaux 🐄
Donge, Île de France
W3kg F45% P56

Brie de Melun 🐄
Rouzaire, Île de France
W1.5kg F45% P57

Brillat-Savarin 🐄
Ferme Lepetit, Normandy
W550g F70% P52

Brin d'Amour 🐑
Pierucci, Corsica (Haut)
W600g F45–48% P81

Brique du Larzac 🐐
Bergers du Larzac, Tarn
W180–200g F45% P78

Buchette de Banon 🐐
Ripert, Provence
W150g F45% P73

Cabécou du Rocamadour 🐐
SAS Les Fermiers du Rocamadour, Lot
W45g F45% P78

Camembert Fermier Durand 🐄
Ferme de la Héronnière, Normandy
W250g F45% P52

Cantel Laguiole 🐄
Plateau of Aubrac, Auvergne
W35kg F45% P70

Casinca 🐐
Pierucci, Corsica (Haut)
W350g F45%
Washed-rind semi-soft goat's cheese which is delicate and fruity when young, ripening to a full-bodied robust goaty style.

Cathare 🐐
Local central market, Lauregais, Carcassonne
W180–200g F45% P79

Cendré de Niort 🐐
Fromagerie Bonde de Gatine, Poitou
W200g F45% P64

Chabichou 🐐
Fromagerie Bonde de Gatine, Poitou
W180g F45% P64

Chaource 🐄
Fromagerie Lincet, Champagne
W250g / 450g F50% P59

Charolais 🐐
Domaine de Saulnieres, Burgundy
W180g F45% P59

Chenette 🐐
Local central market, Montastruc-la-Conseillere
W180g F45%
Small brick shape goat's cheese with natural rind and topped with an oak leaf (Chene). Fudgy texture and good flavour.

Coeur de Neufchâtel 🐄
Gaec Brianchon, Normandy
W200g F45% P52

Coulommiers 🐄
Donge, Île de France
W500g F45% P57

Crayeux de Roncq 🐄
Via Philippe Olivier, Boulogne, Haut Artois/Ferrain Weppes
W550g F45% P49

Crottin de Chavignol 🐐
Dubois-Boulay, Sancerre
W60–70g F45% P63

Crottin Maubourguet 🐐
Fromage zone de Montagne Pyrénées
W80g F45%
Tubby goat's milk Crottin with

a fuller flavour than the Loire version. Good with Pays d'Oc style red wines.

Crottin Pic de Bigorre 🐐
Fromage zone de Montagne, Ariège
W100g F45%
High mountain goat's milk Crottin, with a lovely crumbly sweet flavour and texture. Good lingering finish too, and will partner red wines.

Epoisses 🐄
Fromagerie Gaugry, Burgundy
W250g F45–48% P60

Estibere 🐑
Via Gabriel Bachelet, Bearn
W750g F45%
Washed-rind ewe's milk cheese with a wonderful rich and silky texture and sweetly earthy taste.

Explorateur 🐄
Fromagerie Le Petit Morin, Île de France
W250g F75% P54

Fleur de Chèvre 🐐
Fromagerie Bonde de Gatine, Poitou
W200g F45% P64

Fougeru 🐄
Rouzaire, Île de France
W500g F45% P55

Fourme d'Ambert 🐄
Morin, Auvergne
W1.8kg F50% P68

Gaperon á l'ail 🐄
Patricia Ribier, Montgacon, Auvergne
W250g F45–48% P67

Haut Barry 🐄
Bergers Larzac, Larzac
W3kg F45% P74

Langres 🐄
Schertenleib Saulxures, Champagne
W150–180g F50% P61

Le Gabiétout 🐐 🐄
Via Gabriel Bachelet, Pyrénées
W2kg F45% P74

Lingot Saint Nicolas de la Monastère 🐐
Monastery at La Dalmerie, La Dalmerie, Hérault
W100g F45% P78

Livarot 🐄
Graindorge, Normandy
W500g F45% P52

Lou Bren 🐐
Bergers Larzac, Aveyron
W2kg F45% P78

Louvie 🐐
Via Gabriel Bachelet, Pyrénées
W300g F45% P79

Maroilles 🐄
Philippe Olivier/Syndicat des Fabricants de Maroilles, Thiérache
W700–800g F45% P48

Mascares 🐐 🐑
Ripert, Provence
W150g F45%
A pave (square) shaped soft cheese with a natural rind. The flavours are creamy with a flaky texture and as the cheese ripens it becomes more nutty.

Mimolette 🐄
Maison Losfeld, Flandres
W3kg F40% P50

Mothais 🐐
Fromagerie Bonde de Gatine, Poitou
W250g F45% P64

Munster 🐄
Siffert Freres or Haxaire, Alsace
W500g or 250g F45% P47

Napoleon Montréjeau 🐑
Bouchat, Hautes Pyrénées
W4kg F48–48% P74

Olivet 🐄
Fromagerie d'Onzain, Orleannais
W200g F45% P55

Ossau 🐑
Fromage zone de Montagne, Pyrénées
W5.5kg F48% P75

Pechegos 🐐
Pic, Tarn
W300g F45% P80

Pelardon 🐐
Co-operative de Pelardon les Cévennes, Cévennes
W60g–100g F45% P69

Pérail 🐐
Bergers Larzac, Languedoc
W150g F48% P78

Persillé du Marais 🐐
Charente-Poitou cheese association, Vendée and Poitou
W1.5kg F48%P66

Picodon 🐐
Co-operative de Picodon de la Drôme, Drôme
W80–100g F45% P69

Pont l'Évêque 🐄
Pere Eugene/Graindorge, Normandy
W250g F45% P52

Pouligny-Saint-Pierre 🐐
Syndicat des Producteurs de Fromages de Pouligny-Saint-Pierre, Berry
W250g F45% P62

Rollot 🐄
Via Philippe Olivier, Picardy
W230g F45% P47

Roquefort Carles 🐑
Carles, Rouergue
W1.3kg F48% P77

Roquefort Papillon 🐑
Papillon, Rouergue
W1.3kg F45–48% P77

Rouelle 🐐
Fromagerie Pic, Tarn
W200g F45% P78

Rove des Garrigues 🐐
Compagnons Bergers de Languedoc, Lot, Midi Pyrénées
W100g F45% P78

Saint Félicien 🐄
L'Etoile de Vercours, Dauphiné/Isère
W180g F40% P69

Saint Marcellin 🐄
L'Etoile de Vercours, Dauphiné/Isère
W80–100g F35% P69

Sainte-Maure 🐐
Fromagerie Hardy, Touraine
W250g F45% P62

Saint-Nectaire 🐄
Morin, Auvergne
W1.5–1.7kg F45% P67

Salers d'Estive 🐄
Plateau of Aubrac, Auvergne
W35kg F45% P70

Selles sur Cher 🐐
Ets Jacquin, Loire/Cher
W140–160g F45% P62

Soumaintrain 🐄
Ferme Lorne, Burgundy
W250–280g F45% P61

Soum d'Aspe 🐐
Fromage zone de Montagne, Pyrénées
W100g F45%
Tubby cylinder goat's cheese with a definite goaty flavour, natural thin rind and crumbly texture. Made high in the hills in isolated farms.

Tomme d'Aydius 🐐
Hillside cabins in Valle d'Aspe, Béarn
W3kg F45% P75

Tomme de Cabrioulet 🐐
Fromagerie col de Fach, Ariège
W3kg F45–48% P75

Tomme de Cléon 🐐
Via Gabriel Bachelet, Pays Nantais, Pays de la Loire
W3–4kg F45–48% P66

Tomme Corse 🐄
Pierucci, Corsica
W3kg F45% P81

Tomme Fraîche 🐄
Morin, Auvergne/Aubrac
W300g / 1kg F45% P67

Val de Loubières (Resineux de Loubieres) 🐐
Fromagerie col de Fach, Ariège
W400g F48% P75

Valençay 🐐
Moreau, Berry/Indre
W200g F45% P62

Vieux Boulogne 🐄
Via Philippe Olivier, Pas-de-Calais
W350g F45% P49

Zelu Koloria 🐐
Fromage zone de Montagne, Pays Basque
W6kg F48% P75

ALPINE

FRENCH ALPINE

Abbaye de Tamié 🐄
Abbaye de Tamié, Haut-Savoie
W500g–1.3kg F35% P89

Abondance 🐄
La Cooperative de Vacheresse, Haute-Savoie
W10kg F48% P92

Beaufort Chalet d'Alpage 🐄
Caves Cooperatives du Beaufort de Haute Montagne, Savoie
W28–30kg F55% P86

Besace 🐐
Savoie
W200g F45% P92

Bleu de Gex 🐄
Syndicat Interprofessionnel du Bleu de Gex-Haut-Jura-Septmoncel, Haut Jura
W5.4kg F50% P89

Bleu de Termignon 🐄
Chalets in Parc de la Vanoise, Haut-Savoie
W7–10kg F40% P90

Chevrotin des Aravis 🐐
Cooperative Thones, Haut Savoie
W300g F35% P89

Comté d'Estive 🐄
Comite Interprofessionelle de Gruyere de Comté, Comté
W4kg F50% P84

Emmental de Savoie Surchoix 🐄
Syndicat des fabricants et affineurs d'Emmentals Traditionnels, Savoie
W80kg F45% P89

Grand Colombiers de Aillon 🐐 🐄
Chalet huts and Ecole and Chatelard markets, Savoie
W1.5kg F35% P93

Grataron d'Arêches 🐄 or 🐐
Le Groupement Pastoral du Cormet d'Areches, Savoie
W200g F35% P92

Morbier 🐄
Association des Fabricants de Veritable Morbier au lait cru de Franche-Comté, Franche-Comté
W3–9kg F45% P89

Persillé de Tignes 🐐 🐄
Mountain chalets, Savoie
W1.5kg F35% P93

Reblochon 🐄
La Cooperative Agricole des Producteurs de Reblochon, Savoie
W500g F45% P89

Tarentais 🐐
Mountain chalets, Savoie
W200g F30% P92

Tomme de Savoie 🐄
Fromagerie Cooperative Thones, Savoie
W1.2kg F33–40% P89

Vacherin 🐄
Syndicat Interprofessionnel de Defense du Fromage Mont d'Or ou Vacherin de Haut-Doubs, Haut-Doubs
W500g–3kg F50% P90

SWISS ALPINE

Alp Bergkäse 🐄
Mountain Collective, Canton Graubünden, Chur
W23–33kg F50% P96

Alp Kohschlag 🐄
Mountain chale, Canton St Gallen
W7kg F48% P97

Alpkäse Luven 🐄
Dani Duerr, Canton Graubünden
W5kg F48% P95

Château d'Erguel 🐄
Fromagerie, Courtelary, Bernese Jura, Canton Bern
W7kg F48% P96

Emmentaler 🐄
Mountain collective, Canton Bern
W100kg F45% P97

Etivaz Gruyère 🐄
Farm collectives, Canton Vaud
W18kg F48% P96

Fleurettes des Rougemont (Tomme Fleurette) 🐄
Michel Beroud, Canton Vaud
W170g F45% P97

Gruyère 🐄
Jean Marie Dunand, Le Crêt sur Semsales, Canton Fribourg
W32–40kg F45–48% P95

Le Sous-Bois 🐄
Henchoz Farm, Canton Vaud
W150g F45% P96

Raclette 🐄
Alp Luser-Schlössli mountain dairies, Canton Glarus
W4–5kg F45% P97

Stillsiter Steinsalz 🐄
Stefan Bühler, Gähwil, Toggenburg
W4kg F48% P97

Unterwasser 🐄
The Stadelmann family, Canton St Gallen
W8kg F50% P97

ITALIAN ALPINE

Asiago Pressato 🐄
Consorzio Tutela Formaggio Asiago, Vicenza/Trento
W12kg F45% P100

Bastardo del Grappa/ Morlacco del Grappa 🐄
Alpine and valley dairies, Monte Grappa Massif
W6–7kg F45% P102

Branzi 🐄
Cooperativa Agricola Saint'Antonio in Valtaleggio, Lombardy
W12kg F45% P99

Carnia Altobut Vecchio 🐄
Mountain and valley dairies, Padola
W6kg F45% P100

Fontina 🐄
Cooperativa Produttori Latte e Fontina, Aosta
W8–12kg F45% P104

Formai de Mut 🐄
Cooperativa Agricola Saint'Antonio in Valtaleggio, Lombardy
W8–12kg F45% P99

Franzedas Alpeggio 🐄
Mountain huts, Vicenza/Trento
W2kg F45% P100

Grana Val di Non (Trentingrana) 🐄
Consorzio per la tutela del Formaggio Grana Padano, Trentino
W35–40kg F35–40% P100

Grasso d'Alpe Buscagna 🐄
Mountain Huts, Parco Veglia Devero
W5–7kg F45% P102

Monte Veronese Grasso 🐄
Latteria in and around Verona, Verona
W6–9kg F45% P102

Scimudin 🐄 🐐
Latteria Agricola Cooperativa Livignesi, Sondrio
W1kg F70% P99

Stanghe di Lagundo 🐄
Mountain dairies, Treviso
W2kg F45% P103

Toma Ossolana Alpeggio 🐄
Mountain Huts, Parco Veglia Devero
W5–7kg F45% P102

Toma Ossolana Rodolfo 🐄
Mountain Huts, Parco Veglia Devero
W5–7kg F45% P102

GERMAN & AUSTRIAN ALPINE

Adelegger Urberger 🐄
Isny Cheeses Dairy, Bavaria
W7kg F45% P107

Alp-Bergkäse 🐄
Sennalpe Spicherhalde Dairy, Balderschwang
W23–28kg F50% P107

Bavarian Blue 🐄
Obere Muehle Co-operative, Bad Oberdorf
W2.5kg F48% P107

Butterkäse 🐄
Co-operative Bremenried, south west Bavaria
W6–8kg F50% P107

Emmentaler 🐄
Käserei Bremenried Co-operative, Allgäu
W90kg F35–40% P108

Rasskass 🐄
Dorfsennerei Langenegg Co-operative, Vorarlberg/ Bregenz Forez
W6.5kg F45% P109

Romadur 🐄
Käserei Bremenried Co-operative, Allgäu
W650g F40–45% P107

Tilsiter 🐄
Sibratsgfäll Co-operative, Bregenz
W3.5–5kg F30–60% P109

Weisslacker 🐄
Sibrtsgfäll Co-operative, Wangen im Allgäu
W280g F40–45% P108

Zigorome 🐐
Ziegenhof Leiner Far, Allgäu
W150g F40% P108

ITALY

Blu di Langa 🐄 🐐 🐑
Alta Langa, Piedmont
W1kg F50% P112

Burrata 🐄
Nuzzi, Molise/Puglia
W300–500g F60% P125

Capretta di Toscano 🐐
Azienda Agricole La Querchette, Tuscany
W2.5kg F45% P125

Caprini Freschi 🐐
La Bottera, Piedmont
W100g F45% P116

Caprini Tartufo 🐐
La Bottera, Piedmont
W100g F45% P116

Caprino delle Langhe 🐐
Alta Langa, Piedmont
W90g F45% P116

Caprino Sardo al Caprone 🐐
Associazione Regionale Allevatori della Sardegna, Sardinia
W2kg F45% P133

Casciotta Etrusca 🐐
Latteria in and around Sienna, Tuscany
W1.5kg F45% P125

Castagnolo 🐐
Latteria, Tuscany
W1kg F45% P125

Castelmagno 🐄
Marco Arneodo, Cuneo, Piedmont
W2–7kg F35–40% P114

Castelrosso 🐄
Luigi Rosso Farm, Biella, Piedmont
W5–6kg F40% P114

Fiore di Langhe 🐐
Alta Langa, Piedmont
W180g F45% P116

Formaggio di Fossa 🐄
Latteria in hills, Umbria
W3kg F40% P129

Formaggio Piacentinu Ennese 🐑
Casalgismondo Farm, Sicily
W4kg F45% P132

Gorgonzola Dolce 🐄
Consorzio per total formaggio di Gorgonzola, Lombardy
W8kg F48% P119

Gorgonzola Naturale 🐄
Consorzio per total formaggio di Gorgonzola, Lombardy
W12kg F48% P119

Grana Padano 🐄
No. 205 Dairy, Lombardy
W35kg F32% P117

Maccagnette alle Erbe 🐄
Melo Grand Renato, Bielle, Piedmont
W500g–1kg F45% P114

Mozzarella di Bufala 🐃
Cooperativa Allevatori Bufalini Salernitani, Campania
W250g F45% P130

Parmigiano Reggiano 🐄
Consorzio di Parmigiano Reggiano, Emilia-Romagna
W35kg F32–35% P122

Pecorino Affinato in Vinaccia in Visciola 🐑
Hillside dairies, Apennine Hills, Umbria
W500g F45% P129

Pecorino Marzolino Rosso 🐑
Caseificio Sociale Manciano, Tuscany
W1.2kg F45% P125

Pecorino Montefalco 🐑
Montefalco farm, Umbria
W1.2kg F45% P129

Pecorino Muffa Bianca 🐑
Hillside farms, Appenine Hills, Umbria
W1.8kg F45% P129

Pecorino Peperoncino 🐑
Tuscany
W500g F45% P126

Pecorino Saraceno 🐑
Associazione Regionale Allevatori della Sardegna, Sardinia
W3–6kg F48% P133

Pecorino Siciliano 🐑
Casalgismondo Farm, Sicily
W10–12kg F45–48% P132

Pecorino Siciliano Fresco 🐑
Casalgismondo Farm, Sicily
W10–12kg F45–48% P132

Pecorino Siciliano Peperoncino 🐑
Casalgismondo Farm, Sicily
W10–12kg F45–48% P132

Pecorino Tartufo 🐑
Latteria in and around Siena, Tuscany
W500g F45% P126

Pecorino Tinaio Moresco 🐑
Hillside farms, Sardinia
W3kg F45–48% P133

Pecorino Vilanetto Rosso 🐑
Caseificio Sociale Cooperativo, Tuscany
W3kg F40–45% P126

Pecorino Vinaccia 🐑
Small dairies, Perugia, Umbria
W4kg F48% P126

Pecorino Ubriaco 🐄
Tuscany (Finished in Treviso)
W1kg F45% P120

Provola di Bufala Affumicate 🐃
Cooperativa Allevatori Bufalini Salernitani, Campania
W300g F45% P130

Provolone del Monaco 🐄
Vico Equense, Campania
W3kg F45% P130

Puzzone di Moena 🐄
Caseificio Sociale di Predazzo e Moena, Trento
W9kg F45% P120

Ragusano 🐄
Rosario Floridia, Sicily
W10–16kg F45% P132

Ricotta Carena 🐄
Angelo Carena, Piacenza, Lombardy
W1kg F35–40% P117

Ricotta Salata 🐑 🐐 🐄
Latteria, Puglia, Sicily, Sardinia
W300g F30–35% P130

Robiola delle Langhe 🐄 🐐 🐑
Alta Langa, Piedmont
W300g F45% P116

Seirass del Fieno 🐑
Mountain communities, Piedmont
W2–5kg F45% P114

Seirass Fresca
Fratelli Giraudi, Piedmont
W350g F45% P113

Sottocenere al Tartufo Veneto 🐄
La Casearia, Treviso
W3kg F45% P120

Strachitund 🐄
Communita Montana Valle Brembana, Lombardy
W4kg F48% P120

Taleggio 🐄
Communita Montana Valle Brembana, Lombardy
W1.7kg F48% P120

Toma Maccagno 🐄
Luigi Rosso, Biella, Piedmont
W3kg F45% P114

Truffle Cheese (Tuma Trifulera) 🐄 🐐 🐑
La Bottera, Piedmont
W500g F45% P116

Vezzena Vecchio 🐄
Caseificio Sociale di Lavarone, Trentino/Venezia
W8–10kg F45–48%
A beautifully ripened hard Asiago style cheese with robust fruity flavours complemented by a crumbly, chewy texture.

SPAIN

Arzúa Ulloa Arquesan 🐄
Quesería Agro Despensa, Galicia
W500g–2.5kg F45% P139

Bauma Madurat 🐐
Bauma Farm, Catalonia
W1kg F45% P138

Cabrales 🐄 🐐 🐑
Small Dairies, Penamellera Alta Township, Asturias
W2.5kg F48% P140

Garrotxa 🐐
Bauma Farm, Catalonia
W1kg F45% P136

Idiazábal 🐑
J. Aranburu Elkartea, S.A.T.Caserío Ondramuino, Basque/Navarre
W1.4kg F45% P139

Mahón 🐄 🐐 🐑
Via Ardai cheese specialists, Menorca
W2.5kg F45% P143

Manchego 🐑
Dehesa de los Llanos, La Mancha
W1.5kg F57% P144

Montsec 🐐
Via Ardai cheese specialists, Catalonia
W300g F45% P138

Murcia al Vino 🐐
Via Ardai cheese specialists, Murcia
W2.5kg F45% P143

Perazola Azul 🐑
Via Ardai cheese specialists, Asturias
W2kg F48% P140

Picos de Europa (Valdeón) 🐄 🐐 🐑
Via Ardai cheese specialists, Cantabria
W2.5kg F48% P140

Roncal 🐑
Queso Larra SL, Navarre
W1–3kg F45–50% P138

San Simón 🐑
Via Ardai cheese specialists, Galicia
W375g–1.5kg F45% P139

Tetilla 🐄
Via Ardai cheese specialists, Galicia
W375g–1.5kg F45% P139

Turo del Convent 🐐
Formatges Monber, Catalonia
W400g F45% P138

Vall de Meranges Cremos 🐄
Via Ardai cheese specialists, Catalonia
W480g F48% P138

PORTUGAL

Azeitão 🐑
Small Dairies, Azeitão
W250g F48% P148

Barrão 🐑
Small Dairies, Alto do Chão, North Alentejo
W150g F48% P148

Cabra Transmontano 🐐
Quinta dos Moinhos Novos, Vila Verde, north west Portugal
W200g F45% P148

Castelo Branco 🐑 🐐
Meimoa Co-operative, Beira Baixa Central
W1.5kg F48% P148

Évora 🐑
Small Dairies, Alandroal and Vila Vicosa, Alentejo
W120–200g F48% P148

Graziosa 🐄
Small Dairies on Island, Ilha Graciosa Azores
W10kg F40–45% P148

Nisa 🐑
Monforqueijo Co-operative, Alentejo
W300g F48% P148

Qunita dos Moinhos Novos Serrano 🐐
Quinta dos Moinhos Novos, Vila Verde, north west Portugal
W500g F48% P148

São Jorge 🐄
Cooperativa de Leitaria da Beira, Sao Jorge, Azores
W8–15kg F45% P148

Serpa 🐑
Small dairies, Beja, South Alentejo
W120–500g F50% P148

Serra d'Estrela 🐑
Mountain communities, Parque Natural da Serra Estrela, north Portugal
W500g–1.2kg F50% P147

Terrincho 🐑
Small farms and dairies, Trás-os-Montes, Upper Duoro Valley, north east Portugal
W800g–1.2kg F48% P147

THE REST OF EUROPE

THE NETHERLANDS

Edam 🐄
Co-operative, Edam-Volendam, North Holland
W500g–1kg F30–35%
A round ball shaped cheese with red wax-coated rind. Semi-hard with a mellow salty taste, becoming more intense with maturing.

Gouda 🐄
Small dairies, Gouda, South Holland
W20kg **F**45% **P**150

Leiden 🐄
Small dairies, Leiden
W3.6kg–9kg **F**20–40%
The original Cumin cheese:
look for the red rind farm cheese
with a cross-keys crest stamp.

Maasdam 🐄
Small dairies, all Holland
W15kg **F**45%
Like a Swiss-style Emmenthal
with large holes and a smooth
chewy texture.

Mimolette 🐄
Small dairies, North West Holland
W3kg **F**45%
Similar in flavour to the
French cheese.

Old Amsterdam 🐄
Small dairies, North Holland
W10kg **F**45%
A Gouda but made by larger
dairies than the Boerenkaas.

Smoked Cheese 🐄
Small dairies, all Holland
W250g–1kg **F**45%
Sausage-shaped cheese
eaten sliced into salads, in
sandwiches, or with sausages.

SWEDEN

Greve 🐄
Falbygden
W15kg **F**30–45% **P**153

Kryddost 🐄
Falbygden
W12kg **F**40% **P**153

Svecia 🐄
Falbygden
W12–15kg **F**28% **P**153

DENMARK

Havarti 🐄
Havarthigaard, Øverød, Copenhagen
W4.5kg **F**45% **P**153

POLAND

Bundz 🐑
Artisans, Podhale
W500g–1kg **F**40%
A creamy cottage cheese.

Golka & Oscypek 🐄 🐑
Artisans, Tatra Mountains
W500g–1kg **F**40%
Made with spindle and woven
basket moulds, salty with a
chewy texture.

Redykolka 🐑
Artisans, Tatra Mountains
W500g–1kg **F**40%
Artisan bird-shaped cheese.
Similar to Oscypek in flavour.

Ser Korycinski 'Swojski' 🐄
Agnieszka Gremza, Korycin
W2kg **F**40% **P**154

GREECE

Anthotiros 🐑 / 🐐
All Greece
W1–2kg **F**40–65%
Ewe or goat's milk cheese, or
mixed, mild and crumbly when
young becoming salty and drier
with age.

Feta 🐐 🐑
Mt Vikos,Thessalia
W50kg barrel **F**30% **P**154

Formaella of Parnassos 🐑 / 🐐
Parnassos
W2kg **P**33%
Ewe or Goat or mixed milks.
Rich and piquant semi-hard
cheese, good as a table cheese
or to fry.

Galotiri 🐑 🐐
Epirus/Thessalia
W2kg **F**14%
A ewe and goat's milk mixed
or just single milk cheese, with
a sharp, tangy taste, and soft
spreadable texture.

Graveira of Crete 🐑 🐐
Crete
W2kg **F**40%
Ewe and goat's milk or mixed,
aged for five months with a
sweetly earthy, robust taste.

Kalathaki of Limnos 🐑
Limnos Island
W2kg **F**25–30%
Ewe's milk or with a little goat's
milk added, and with a sour/
salty tangy taste.

Kasseri 🐑 🐐
Macedonia, Thessalia, Mitilini island
and Xanthi
W1–2kg **F**25%
Ewe and goat's milk or mixed
and rather like a Mozzarella
texture, which can be used for
topping pastry and melting, or
in a salad.

Manouri 🐑 🐐
Central and Western Macedonia/
Thessalia
W1–2kg **F**37%
Ewe or goat's milk or mixed,
rindless and with a smooth
texture and creamy rich taste.

GERMANY

Allgäuer Emmentaler 🐄
Bremenried Co-operartive, Weiler,
south west Bavaria
W80kg **F**45%
This cheese is usually sold at
around five to seven months,
but luckily a few are matured for

14 months, which opens out the
flavours to give a rich and nutty
layer of tastes.

Bachensteiner 🐄
Gunzesried Co-operative, Blachach
Valley, Bavaria
W200g **F**45% **P**154

Limburger 🐄
Zurwies Co-operative, Baden-
Württemberg
W200g **F**45% **P**154

Münster 🐄
Zurwies Co-operative, Wangen im
Allgäu, south east Baden-
Wüttemberg
W200g–500g **F**45% **P**154

BALKANS

Kashkaval 🐄
W500g–1kg **F**45%
Typical semi-hard ewe's milk
cheese, crumbly and salty.

HUNGARY

Liptaeur 🐄
Large production, all Hungary
W200g–1kg **F**30–40%
A salty, creamy cheese to spread.

ROMANIA

Aldermen 🐄
Romania
W1–2kg **F**45%
Buffalo Milk cheese with a
crumbly texture.

USA

Amablu 🐄
Faribault Dairy, Faribault, Minnesota
W2.7kg **F**45–48% **P**178

Avondale Truckle 🐄
Brunkow Cheese Co-op, Darlington,
Wisconsin
W9–10kg **F**45% **P**174

Battenkill Brebis 🐑
Three-Corner Field Farm,
Shushan, New York
W2.7kg **F**45% **P**200

Bayley Hazen Blue 🐄
Jasper Hill Farm, Greensboro,
Vermont
W3.4kg **F**48% **P**185

Big Eds 🐄
Saxon Homestead Creamery,
Cleveland, Wisconsin
W7kg **F**45% **P**176

Bijou 🐐
Vermont Butter & Cheese
Company, Websterville,
Washington
W55g **F**45% **P**190

Birch Hill Cakes 🐐
Hillman Farm, Colrain, Franklin
County, Massachusetts
W225g **F**45% **P**194

Bleu Mont Cloth Cheddar 🐄
Bleu Mont Dairy, Blue Mounds, Dane
County, Wisconsin
W5kg **F**45–48% **P**172

Bonne Bouche 🐐
Vermont Butter & Cheese Company,
Websterville, Washington
W115g **F**45% **P**190

Boucher Blue 🐄
Boucher Family Farm, Highgate
Center, Franklin County, Vermont
W1.5kg **F**48–50% **P**190

Bridgewater 🐐
Zingerman's Creamery, Ann Arbor,
Michigan
W200g **F**45% **P**182

Brigid's Abbey 🐄
Cato Corner Farm, Colchester,
Connecticut
W1.5kg **F**45% **P**198

Bûche 🐐
Juniper Grove, Redmond, Oregon
W150g **F**45% **P**168

Cabot Clothbound Cheddar 🐄
Cabot Creamery, Cabot, Vermont
W17kg **F**45–48% **P**187

Cadence 🐄 🐐
Andante Farm, Petaluma, California
W80g **F**45% **P**164

California Crottin 🐐
Redwood Hill Farm and Creamery,
Sonoma, California
W150g **F**45% **P**162

Camellia 🐐
Redwood Hill Farm and Creamery,
Sonoma, California
W200g **F**45% **P**162

Carmody 🐄
Bellwether Farms, California
W1.4kg **F**45–48% **P**161

Cavatina 🐐
Andante Farm, Petaluma, California
W100–200g **F**45% **P**164

City Goat 🐐
Zingerman's Creamery, Ann Arbor,
Michigan
W80g **F**45% **P**182

Classic Blue Log 🐐 or 🐄
Westfield Farm, Hubbardston,
Massachusetts
W125g **F**45% **P**195

Cloth-bound 18-month-Aged Cheddar 🐄
Fiscalini Farm, Stanislaus County,
California
W24kg **F**45–48% **P**160

Constant Bliss 🐄
Jasper Hill Farm, Greensboro, Vermont
W200g **F**45% **P**185

Coupole 🐐
Vermont Butter & Cheese Company, Websterville, Washington
W185g F45% P190

Dafne 🐐
Goat's Leap, Saint Helena, California
W200g F45% P162

Dante 🐑
Wisconsin Sheep Dairy Co-op, Spooner, Wisconsin
W3.6kg F45–48% P176

Detroit Street 🐐
Zingerman's Creamery, Ann Arbor, Michigan
W470g F45% P182

Dorset 🐑
Consider Bardwell Farm, Pawlett, Washington County, Vermont
W1.2kg F45% P192

Drunken Hooligan 🐄
Cato Corner Farm, Colchester, Connecticut
W600g F45% P198

Dry Jack Special Reserve 🐐
Vella Cheese Company and Mertens Farm, Sonoma, California
W3.5kg F48–48% P159

Dunbarton Blue 🐄
Roelli Cheese Haus, Shullsburg, Wisconsin
W3kg F45% P174

Dunmore 🐐
Blue Ledge Farm, Salisbury, Addison County, Vermont
W500g F45% P192

Eclipse 🐐
Goat's Leap, Saint Helena, California
W180–200g F45% P162

Edelweiss 🐄
Edelweiss Creamery, Monticello, Wisconsin
W85kg F45–48%
After pressing and hand-washing these huge cheeses are turned twice a week, with a salt-water rub to keep the rinds smooth. Excellent for fondue.

El Dorado Gold 🐐
Matos Cheese Factory, Santa Rosa, California
W1.4kg F45%
A tomme that has been brine- and whey-washed, then rubbed to form a smooth, thin rind with scattered white moulds and a chewy texture.

Elk Mountain 🐐
Pholia Farm, Rogue River, Oregon
W2.5–3kg F45% P168

Everona Piedmont 🐐
Everona Dairy, Rapidan, Virginia
W2kg F45% P202

Ewe's Blue 🐑
Old Chatham Sheepherding Company, Old Chatham, New York
W1.3kg F48% P198

Feta 🐐
Three-Corner Field Farm, Shushan, New York
W1kg F45% P200

Figaro 🐄 🐐
Andante Farm, Petaluma, California
W100g F45% P164

Flagship Reserve 🐄
Beecher's, Seattle, Washington
W7.5kg F45–48% P171

Fleuri Noir 🐐
Fantôme Farm, Ridgeway, Wisconsin
W180g F45% P174

Flora Pyramid 🐐
Hillman Farm, Colrain, Franklin County, Massachusetts
W175g F45% P194

Fresh Chevre 🐐
Redwood Hill Farm and Creamery, Sonoma, California
W150g F35% P162

Fresh Logs 🐐
Vermont Butter & Cheese Company, Websterville, Washington
W100g F45% P190

Garlic with Chives 🐐
Zingerman's Creamery, Ann Arbor, Michigan
W80g F45% P182

Grayson 🐄
Meadow Creek Dairy, Grayson, Galax, Virginia
W2kg F45% P202

Great Hill Blue 🐄
Great Hill Dairy, Marion, Plymouth County, Massachusetts
W2.7kg F45% P195

Great Lakes Cheshire 🐄
Zingerman's Creamery, Ann Arbor, Michigan
W2.2kg F45% P182

Harvest Cheese 🐐
Hillman Farm, Colrain, Franklin County, Massachusetts
W3.5kg F45% P194

Haystack Peak 🐐
Haystack Mountain Goat Dairy, Niwot, Colorado
W160g F45% P183

Hillis Peak 🐐
Pholia Farm, Rogue River, Oregon
W1kg F45% P168

Hooligan 🐄
Cato Corner Farm, Colchester, Connecticut
W600g F45% P198

Hopeful Tomme 🐄 🐐
Sweet Grass Dairy, Thomasville, Georgia
W2.25kg F45% P202

Humboldt Fog 🐐
Cypress Grove, McKinleyville, California
W470g–2.3kg F45% P166

Hyku 🐐
Goat's Leap, Saint Helena, California
W150–180g F45% P162

Hyku Noir 🐐
Goat's Leap, Saint Helena, California
W180g F45% P162

Julianna 🐐
Capriole Farmstead Goat Cheese, Greenville, Indiana
W350g F45% P181

Kiku 🐐
Goat's Leap, Saint Helena, California
W85–110g F45% P162

Krotovina 🐄 🐐
Prairie Fruits Farm, Champaign County, Illinois
W200g F45% P178

Kunik 🐐 🐄
Nettle Meadow Farm, Thurman, New York
W250–275g F45% P199

La Mancha 🐑
Locust Grove Farm, Knox County, East Tennessee
W3kg F48% P202

Lil Wil's Big Cheese 🐄
Bleu Mont Dairy, Blue Mounds, Dane County, Wisconsin
W1kg F45% P172

Lincoln Log 🐐
Zingerman's Creamery, Ann Arbor, Michigan
W900g F45% P182

Little Bloom 🐐
Prairie Fruits Farm, Champaign County, Illinois
W175g F45% P178

Little Darling 🐄
Brunkow Cheese Co-op, Darlington, Wisconsin
W1.5kg F45% P174

Little Napoleon 🐐
Zingerman's Creamery, Ann Arbor, Wisconsin
W80g F45% P182

Maggie's Round 🐄
Cricket Creek Farm, Williamstown, Berkshire County, Massachusetts
W500g F45% P195

Manchester 🐄
Consider Bardwell Farm, Pawlett, Washington County, Vermont
W1.2kg F45% P192

Manchester 🐐
Zingerman's Creamery, Ann Arbor, Michigan
W100g F45% P182

Marieke Foenegreek Gouda 🐄
Holland's Family Farm, Thorp, Wisconsin
W8kg F45% P176

Minuet 🐐 🐄
Andante Farm, Petaluma, California
W200g F45% P164

Mobay 🐐 🐑
Carr Valley Cheese Company, La Valle, Wisconsin
W2kg F45% P174

Mont St Francis 🐐
Capriole Farmstead Goat Cheese, Greenville, Indiana
W350g F45% P181

Moreso 🐐
Fantôme Farm, Ridgeway, Wisconsin
W150g F45% P174

Mount Tam 🐄
Cowgirl Creamery, Point Reyes Station, California
W250–300g F60% P161

Nancy's Camembert 🐑
Old Chatham Sheepherding Company, Old Chatham, New York
W900g F45% P199

O'Banon 🐐
Capriole Farmstead Goat Cheese, Greenville, Indiana
W175g F45% P181

Old Kentucky Tomme 🐐
Capriole Farmstead Goat Cheese, Greenville, Indiana
W1.3–2.25kg F45% P181

Old Liberty 🐄
Goat Lady Dairy, Climax, North Carolina
W1.5kg F45% P202

Pawlet 🐄
Consider Bardwell Farm, Pawlett, Washington County, Vermont
W4.5kg F45% P192

Petit Frère 🐄
Crave Brothers Farmstead Cheese, Waterloo, Wisconsin
W250g F45% P176

Piper's Pyramide 🐐
Capriole Farmstead Goat Cheese, Greenville, Indiana
W200g F45% P181

Pleasant Cow 🐄
Beaver Brook Farm, Lyme, Connecticut
W800g F45%
This cheese is matured for four to five months to give a mellow buttery, gently tangy taste. There is a toasty hazelnut edge with the more mature cheeses.

Pleasant Ridge Reserve 🐄
Uplands Cheese, Madison, Wisconsin
W4.5kg F45% P177

Point Reyes 'Original' Blue 🐄
Giacominis Farm, Point Reyes, California
W2.5kg F48% P160

Pondhopper 🐐
Tumalo Farms, Bend, Oregon
W4kg F45% P168

Prairie Breeze 🐄
Milton Creamery, Milton, Iowa
W9kg–18kg F45% P178

Pyramid 🐐
Juniper Grove, Redmond, Oregon
W150g F45% P168

Queso de Mano 🐐
Haystack Mountain Goat Dairy,
Niwot, Colorado
W1.8kg F45% P183

**Rawson Brook Fresh
Chevre** 🐐
Rawson Brook Farm, Monterey,
Massachusetts
W200g / 450g F35% P196

Red Hawk 🐄
Cowgirl Creamery, Point Reyes
Station, California
W250g F60% P160

Ridgeway Ghost 🐐
Fantôme Farm Ridgeway, Wisconsin
W150g F45% P174

Ripened Disc 🐐
Hillman Farm, Colrain, Franklin
County, Massachusetts
W140g F45% P194

Rita 🐄
Sprout Creek Farm, Poughkeepsie,
New York
W200g F45% P199

Rogue River Blue 🐄
Rogue Creamery, Central Point,
Orgeon
W2.3kg F45–48% P168

Roxanne 🐄
Prairie Farm, Champaign County,
Illinois
W180–200g F45% P178

Sally Jackson 🐄 🐐 🐑
Sally Jackson, Oroville, Washington
W300g–1kg F45% P171

San Andreas 🐑
Bellwether Farms, Petaluma, California
W1.4kg F45% P161

Sandy Creek 🐐
Goat Lady Dairy, Climax,
North Carolina
W120g F35% P202

San Joaquin Gold 🐄
Fiscalini Farm, Stanislaus County,
California
W12.27kg F45% P160

Sarabande 🐄
Dancing Cow Cheese, Bridport,
Addison County, Vermont
W225g F45% P187

Seastack 🐄
Mount Townsend Creamery, Port
Townsend, Washington
W150g F45% P171

Shenandoah 🐐
Everona Dairy, Rapidan, Virginia
W2kg F45% P202

Shushan Snow 🐄
Three-Corner Field, Shushan,
New York
W225–600g F45% P200

**Sierra Mountain
Tomme** 🐐
La Clarine Farm, Somerset, California
W1.2kg F45% P166

Small Plain Chevre 🐐
Fantôme Farm, Ridgeway, Wisconsin
W80–100g F45% P174

Smokey Blue 🐄
Rogue Creamery, Central Point,
Oregon
W2.3kg F48% P168

Snowdrop 🐐
Haystack Mountain Goat Dairy,
Niwot, Colorado
W175g F45% P183

Sofia 🐐
Capriole Farmstead Goat Cheese,
Greenville, Indiana
W250g F45% P181

Sophie 🐐
Sprout Creek Farm, Poughkeepsie,
New York
W200g F45% P199

St George 🐄
Matos Cheese Factory, Santa Rosa,
California
W5–10kg F45–48% P167

St Pete's Select 🐄
Faribault Dairy, Faribault, Minnesota
W2.7kg F45–48% P178

Sumi 🐐
Goat's Leap, Saint Helena, California
W200g F45% P162

Summer Snow 🐄
Woodstock Farm, Weston, Windsor
County, Vermont
W200g F45% P193

Summertomme 🐐
Willow Hill Farm, Milton, Chittenden
County, Vermont
W225g F45% P190

Ten-Year Aged Cheddar 🐄
Hook's Cheese Company, Mineral
Point, Wisconsin
W20kg F45% P174

Tarentaise 🐄
Thistle Hill Farm,
North Pomfret, Vermont
W9kg F45–48% P189

Thomasville Tomme 🐄
Sweet Grass Dairy, Thomasville,
Georgia
W2.5kg F45% P202

Three Sisters 🐄 🐐 🐑
Nettle Meadow Farm, Thurman, New
York
W115g F45% P199

Timberdoodle 🐄
Woodcock Farm, Weston, Windsor
County, Vermont
W800g F45% P193

Trade Lake Cedar 🐑
Lovetree Farmstead, Grantsburg,
Wisconsin
W2.7kg F45–48% P176

Truffle Tremor 🐐
Cypress Grove, McKinleyville,
California
W1.3kg F45% P166

Tumalo Tomme 🐐
Juniper Grove, Redmond, Oregon
W1.5kg F45% P168

Twig Farm Square 🐐
Twig Farm, Middlebury, West
Cornwall, Addison County, Vermont
W900g F45% P188

Twig Farm Tomme 🐐
Twig Farm, Middlebury, West
Cornwall, Addison County, Vermont
W1kg F45% P189

**Twig Farm Washed Rind
Wheel** 🐐
Twig Farm, Middlebury, West
Cornwall, Addison County, Vermont
W500g F45% P189

Two-Year Cheddar Block 🐄
Shelburne Farms, Shelburne, Vermont
W1kg F45% P190

Up In Smoke 🐐
River's Edge Chèvre, Three Ring Farm,
Logsden, Oregon
W150g F45% P168

Vermont Ayr 🐐
Crawford Family Farm, Whiting,
Addison County, Vermont
W1.8kg F48% P187

Vermont Shepherd 🐑
Vermont Shepherd Farm, Putney,
Westminster West, Windham
County, Vermont
W2.7–3.5kg F48% P189

Wabash Cannonball 🐐
Capriole Farmstead Goat Cheese,
Greenville, Indiana
W80g F45% P181

Weston Wheel 🐑
Woodcock Farm, Weston, Windsor
County, Vermont
W2.25kg F48% P193

Weybridge 🐄
Scholten Family Farm, Middlebury,
Addison County, Vermont
W225g F45% P187

Widmer 🐄
Widmer Cheese Cellar, Theresa,
Wisconsin
W450g–2kg F45%
Although this cheese may look
commercial, the flavours are
distinct, and the texture is
crumbly, due to the traditional
recipe and the commitment
to hand-crafting the cheese
throughout all the stages of
production. The flavours are
nutty and the crumble,
although a little moist, has
a good acidity level.

CANADA

**Avonlea Clothbound
Cheddar** 🐄
Cow's Creamery, near Charlottetown,
Prince Edward Island
W10kg F45% P205

Blue Bénédictin 🐄
Fromagerie de L'Abbaye St Benoît,
Saint-Benoît du Lac, Quebec
W1.5kg F48% P206

Blue Juliette 🐐
Salt Spring Island Cheese Company,
Ruckle Park, Salt Spring Island,
British Columbia
W200g F45% P207

Brebette 🐑
Ewenity Dairy Co-Op, Conn, Ontario
W250g F45% P206

**Cow's Creamery Extra Old
Block** 🐄
Cow's Creamery, Charlottetown,
Prince Edward Island
W200g–2.25kg F45% P205

Dragon's Breath Blue 🐄
That Dutchman's Farm, Upper
Economy, Nova Scotia
W300g F45% P205

Eweda Cru 🐑
Ewenity Dairy Co-Op, Conn, Ontario
W3kg F48% P206

Frère Jacques 🐄
Fromagerie de L'Abbaye St Benoît,
Saint-Benoît du Lac, Quebec
W1.5kg F45% P206

Gouda 🐄
That Dutchman's Farm, Upper
Economy, Nova Scotia
W6kg F45% P205

Le Moutier 🐄
Fromagerie de L'Abbaye St Benoît,
Saint-Benoît du Lac, Quebec
W1kg F45% P206

Marcella 🐐
Salt Spring Island Cheese Company,
Ruckle Park, Salt Spring Island,
British Columbia
W95g F45% P207

**Marinated Fresh Goat
Cheeses** 🐐
Salt Spring Island Cheese Company,
Ruckle Park, Salt Spring Island,
British Columbia
W140g F45% P207

Montaña 🐐
Salt Spring Island Cheese Company,
Ruckle Park, Salt Spring Island,
British Columbia
W4kg F48% P207

Mouton Rouge 🐑
Ewenity Dairy Co-op, Conn, Ontario
W1–3kg F48% P206

Old Growler
That Dutchman's Farm, Upper Economy, Nova Scotia
W 5.4kg F 48% P 205

Pied-de-Vent
Fromagerie Pied-de-Vent, Îles-de-la-Madeleine, Quebec
W 1.2kg F 45% P 205

Romelia
Salt Spring Island Cheese Company, Ruckle Park, Salt Spring Island, British Columbia
W 200g F 45% P 207

Sheep in the Meadow
Ewenity Dairy Co-op, Conn, Ontario
W 280g F 45% P 206

AUSTRALIA

Annwn
Ballycroft Cheeses, Greenock, Barossa Valley, South Australia
W 1kg F 45% P 210

Big B
Tongola Goat Dairy, Cygnet, Wattle Grove, Tasmania
W 800g F 45% P 210

Billy
Tongola Goat Dairy, Cygnet, Wattle Grove, Tasmania
W 150–250g F 45% P 210

Brinawa
Marrook Farm, North West of Taree, New South Wales
W 3kg F 45% P 209

Bulga
Marrook Farm, north west of Taree, New South Wales
W 10kg F 45% P 209

Capris
Tongola Goat Dairy, Cygnet, Wattle Grove, Tasmania
W 120g F 45% P 210

Cheddar
Pyengana Cheese Dairy:St. Helen's, Tasmania
W 1–14.5kg F 45% P 210

Curdly
Tongola Goat Dairy, Cygnet, Wattle Grove, Tasmania
W 250g F 45% P 210

Edith
Woodside Cheese Wrights, Adelaide Hills, South Australia
W 250g F 40% P 209

Etzy Ketzy
Woodside Cheese Wrights, Adelaid Hills, South Australia
W 125g F 25% P 209

Fromart
Fromart Cheeses, Eudlo, Queensland
W 4–8kg F 45–48% P 210

Gympie Chèvre
Gympie Farm Cheese, Gympie, Queensland
W 115g F 45% P 211

Ironstone
Piano Hill Farm, Gippsland, Victoria
W 5kg F 45% P 209

La Luna
Holy Goat, Sutton Grange Organic Farm, Central Victoria
W 150g F 45% P 209

Molton Gold
Gympie Farm Cheese, Gympie, Queensland
W 250g F 45%
Named after the Queensland gold rush in 1867, this cheese has a buttery, melting consistency with a bloomy thin rind.

NEW ZEALAND

Curio Bay Pecorino
Blue River Dairy, Blue River, Southland, South Island
W 3kg F 45% P 212

Galactic Gold
Over the Moon Dairy, South Wakato, North Island
W 240g F 45%
A slab of washed-rind cow's milk cheese that looks somewhat like Pont l'Eveque, but with a richer texture. This cheese accompanies a Riesling wine very well.

Gouda
Mercer Cheese, North Waikato, North Island
W 1kg–12kg F 40–45% P 212

Gruff Junction
Greenpark Farm, Christchurch, South Island
W 100g F 17–25%
These large Gouda cheeses can take on some wild and strong flavours, and like all goat's milk cheeses need taming, especially during the ripening and maturing stages.

Joie
Cloudy Mountain Cheese, Pirongia, Waikato Region, North Island
W 200g F 45% P 213

Kaipaki Gold
Cloudy Mountain Cheese, Pirongia, Waikato Region, North Island
W 300g F 45% P 213

Pirongia Blue
Cloudy Mountain Cheese, Pirongia, Waikato Region, North Island
W 300g F 45–48% P 213

Rich Plain & Cumin Gouda
Aroha Organic Goat Cheese, Te Aroha, North Island
W 450–900g F 38% P 212

Ricotta
Clevedon Valley Buffalo Company, North Island
W 200g F 35–40% P 213

THE REST OF WORLD

JAPAN

Selection of Farmhouse Cheeses
Kyodogakusha Shintoku Farm, Shintoku Town, Hokkaido.
W 250g–3kg F 35–45%
Cheesemaker Mr Nozomu Miyaiima produces five cheeses: Gouda with a light taste, Camembert, Blue Camembert, Mozzarella and a smoked cheese. The pure water from the Taisetsu mountains and the clean air create the perfect grazing and cheesemaking environment.

CHINA

Gouda
Yellow Valley Cheese Dairy, Taiyuan, Huangzhai Region
W 3kg F 30–40%
Dutch cheesemaker, Marc de Ruiter, makes superb cheeses, using milk from surrounding small family farms in the Huangzhai region. The cheeses follow a traditional recipe and are as good as anything you will find in Holland.

NEPAL

Chhena (Chhana)
Local dairies, Nepal, Bangladesh and neighbouring parts of India
W 300–500g F 30%
A fresh, unripened curd cheese that is similar to Italian ricotta. The soft, creamy cheese is used for making sweet desserts such as rasgulla, small balls of Chhena rolled in semolina and boiled in light sugar syrup.

Ragya Yak
Nomadic tribes, Nepal
W 500g F 25–35%
This cheese is not too strong with a dense, slightly gritty texture and a dark beige pate. There is a nutty, earthy aroma coming from the natural rind giving the cheese a hint of spice.

TIBET

Hand-made cheese, Yak's
Small isolated communities, Plateau Region
W 200g F 35%
The cheese curds are pressed into moulds and dried in open airy huts during production, to allow the wind and sun to filter through the cheeses. It has a very strong taste.

PHILIPPINES

Kesong Puti,
Small communities, Provinces of Laguna, Bulacan, Samar and Cebu
W 300g F 25–30%
Also known as Filipino cottage cheese, this simple style fresh cheese is made from the full fat milk of carabao, a domesticated species of Southeast Asian water buffalo. The curd cheese is soft, salty, and sometimes a bit sour.

INDIA

Bandel (Bandal),
Small dairies or Artisan, Bandel, East India
W 200g F 25–30%
This soft, salted, unripened cheese has a lovely aroma. During production, the cheese is shaped and drained in little baskets, then smoked. The cheeses are removed from the baskets, patted into flat circles and sold immediately after production.

Paneer (Panir),
Small Dairies or Artisan, All regions
W 100g F 25%
Probably the most well known of all Asian cheeses, Paneer is a traditional, semi-soft cheese used in many recipes in Indian cuisine. Ripening or setting is done with lemon juice and the finished cheese has a similar texture to tofu or a pressed ricotta.

AUTHOR'S ACKNOWLEDGEMENTS

As my publisher and friend would say, space is tight, so dear Jacqui Small, thank you. Just that. But there are also many other people to receive these two words from me. Kerenza Swift who, as Managing Editor, worked tirelessly and long into the night. I will miss the emails and the banter.

Lisa Linder's photography speaks for itself – simply beautiful. If you only knew the weather conditions we worked in – pelting rain, snow, wind, blazing sun – and all of this just outside my shop as we photographed in the doorway! Thank you, Lisa.

Lawrence Morton's design is not only precise but also chic and shows cheese in a whole different light. I think it is the most beautiful looking book on cheese.

It is always a bonus when free-hand drawings scatter a book, and many thanks to my daughter Kate for her talented contribution with the maps.

Wil Edwards, the photographer for the US cheeses handled the brief with charm and good humour and I am truly grateful for his work. Kate Arding my friend and US colleague helped gather together the cheeses for the photoshoot, and I thank her so much for her amazing skill and ingenuity in getting the U S and Canadian cheesemakers involved in the book.

I have good colleagues all over the world, and some close at hand too. Will Studd in Australia has been insightful but also generous with his time and knowledge. Laurie Gutteridge whose modern approach to artisan cheesemaking in Australia resulted in many interesting email 'discussions'. Sarah Aspinwall of Canterbury Cheesemakers in Christchurch, New Zealand gave me sound advice and opinions, as did Calum 'thecheesycurdnerd' – read his blog it's fascinating! Also many thanks to Adrian Lander who photographed the Australian cheeses.

Over the years I have met and become friends with many cheesemakers, producers of fine food and wine, and colleagues who help me gather and bring the merchandise to London; I have limited space but they know who they are and I couldn't run my business or have written my book without them. Their generosity in sharing their wealth of knowledge and supplying me with wonderful produce is the anchor of La Fromagerie. Long may it continue.

Finally, I love my family – everyone who knows me will understand the importance of my family. Both my beautiful daughters, Kate and Rose, have supported me through thick and thin, and Danny, my husband and business partner, has been there right from the start. My other family, my work colleagues, are also so important to my life. Without them La Fromagerie would not exist. My General Manager, Sarah Bilney, has strength to match the toughest challenge, and wit and wisdom to make each working day so enjoyable. From Cecile in accounts to my charming Cheese Managers and assistants, Shop Floor Managers and assistants, Chefs and Kitchen and Café crew, my continued thanks go out to you as you all work so hard to make La Fromagerie such a special place. Nothing sends shivers up my spine than someone I so admire saying something nice about me! Who could be less than impressed to know that Jamie Oliver would step up to write a foreword so heartfelt, and so many thanks to Nigella Lawson, Nicholas Lander, Sue Conley, Peggy Smith, Rose Gray and Ruthie Rogers for their kind quotes.